HOW TO PRAY

HOW TO PRAY

Tapping Into the Power *of* Divine Communication

HELENE CIARAVINO

SQUAREONE
PUBLISHERS

Cover Designer: Phaedra Mastrocola
In-House Editor: Joanne Abrams
Typesetter: Gary A. Rosenberg

Square One Publishers
Garden City Park, NY 11040
(516) 535-2010
www.squareonepublishers.com

Library of Congress Cataloging-in-Publication Data

Ciaravino, Helene.
    How to pray: tapping into the power of divine communication / Helene
Ciaravino.
    p. cm.
Includes bibliographical references and index.
    ISBN 0-7570-0012-6
    1. Prayer. I. Title.
    BL560.C495 2001
    291.4'3—dc21   00-012354

Printed in the United States of America

10   9   8   7   6   5   4   3   2   1

Contents

Acknowledgments

Many people have helped me in the creation of this book, from family members who encouraged me in the study of spirituality; to teachers, professors, and clergy who influenced me with their expertise; to friends who kindly shared their personal approaches to prayer; to congenial strangers in bookstores and cafés who engaged me in fascinating discussions. I am so impressed by how open and gracious people are to a quiet writer equipped with a messy pile of notes—not to mention a messy pile of curls—and an overflowing cup of coffee. To each and every person who contributed with either their stories or their studies, I express my deepest thanks. It is impossible to list all of the names—and I don't even know all of the names—but your faces and voices are in my mind, and your thoughts are in my book.

Now I'd like to express my appreciation to some people who have played extra-special roles during this project. In the professional arena, I have been blessed to work with a number of incredible people. Countless thanks to Rudy Shur, my publisher, who has given me so many opportunities and so much support; to Joanne Abrams, my invaluable editor and, truly, my co-writer at times, who has played such a crucial role in the development of this book; and to all the additional members of Square One Publishers who have helped make this book a reality, including Marie Caratozzolo, wonderful editor; Phaedra Mastrocola, gifted art director; Gary Rosenberg, talented typesetter; and Robert Love, caring business manager.

Also, I offer sincere thankfulness to the authors and editors of my research sources, who have allowed me to build upon such a strong foundation; to the members of the Theology and English Departments of Georgetown University, whose skillful teaching made me capable of writing books today; to Sally Campbell, generous neighbor and fellow writer, for her inspirational writing and helpful direction on Christianity; to Professor Eliot Wolfson of New York University, who answered my questions on Judaism; and to Hani Emari and the Muslim Sisters, for much needed help on Islam. And heartfelt thanks to Jane Sobie, fellow poet/writer and a beautiful soul, who has been a dear friend and a true inspiration during the writing of this book.

Of course, my family and closest friends influence everything I do, and have been of particular importance during the writing of this book. So to my parents, Dr. William and Helen Ciaravino, for the unconditional love, astonishing example, generous education, and a good bit of the rent money that I spent while freelance writing—I am so lucky to have you. To my younger sister and sure saint, Maureen Ciaravino—no words could capture how thankful I am for *exactly* who you are every day. To my older sister and stronghold, Francesca Brownsberger, and my brother-in-law and scholar, Professor William Brownsberger—the true theologians of the family—for everything from your extensive knowledge to the personal pep talks, immeasurable thanks and love. To my most precious nephew and godson, Joseph Brownsberger, for teaching me how to pray just by smiling at the moon—the thought of you makes *me* smile every day. And to Tom Affatigato, who has taken me on a tour of the universe, from mathematics to monasteries, from wormholes to warm hands, from the stars above to the sage within—because of you, I have seen so much more.

Finally, I must acknowledge two loved ones who are already complete in the Divine. To my childhood companion, the little angel who lived in my house for eighteen years and continues to live in my heart every day, thank you for sharing my soul. And to my Grandma, whom I thank for the *ceaseless* prayers—it may be true that it's hard to kill a bad thing, but it's also true that a good thing never dies.

Preface

It has been such a wonderful experience writing *How to Pray: Tapping Into the Power of Divine Communication*. I can think of nothing more fascinating than to dwell upon the various ways in which people call forth the Divine—within and without. And I remain humbled by the great knowledge and passion of the many spiritualists, writers, and scholars whose works have enriched my project and my life. I realize that in the process of writing *How to Pray*, I not only examined my own spiritual practices and beliefs, but also became hungrier for more. So this book has been a healthy and inspiring journey for me.

The information contained in *How to Pray* was obtained through several means: book and article research, Internet information, personal interviews, and my own prayer experiences. I observed and took part in a number of cultural traditions, and spoke at length with many wonderful people who enthusiastically guided me. I also had the benefit of prior study in theology. Even before my teen years were completed, I was profoundly drawn toward the ideals of Jesus Christ; had been a student of Judaism, Christianity, and Buddhism at the university level; and had participated in a number of spiritual retreats that fostered a strong interest in various prayer practices. In more recent years, I have become increasingly fascinated by the tenets and growth of Islam, as well as the undeniable connections between Eastern and Western spiritual thought. So *How to Pray* has been a natural extension of my studies and interests.

Furthermore, I am personally interested in discussing how prayer becomes more powerful with commitment and practice. Many people—including me at times—expect to experience ecstatic inspiration at the very start of their personal prayer lives. When prayer doesn't produce a magical swoon, they swing toward frustration, and maybe even despair. I feel there is a need to discuss the reality of prayer—its challenges, its progressive development, and of course, its beauty. We need to support one another and inspire one another to keep building our prayer lives. We will be more content as people, and more productive as a world, if we do so. This book is part of my contribution to that goal.

So, many thoughts in Parts One and Three of this book came from various writers' and spiritualists' experiences, and from my own experiences. But Part Two, which details world views of prayer, is more historical in its approach. It has been difficult to summarize the rich, complex traditions of some of the world's greatest religions. Every spiritual tradition is open to numerous explanations and interpretations. I cannot possibly represent the beliefs and techniques of every religious observer, or be arrogant enough to claim that I have captured the essence of the approaches discussed in this book. But I have tried my best to accurately depict the beliefs held by the majority of practitioners of each approach, and I certainly acknowledge that there are groups within each religion who will neither entirely agree with the descriptions, nor subscribe to the practices on which this book elaborates. In such cases, I defer to appropriate scholars, to clergy and spiritual masters, and to the practicing public itself.

Furthermore, I am aware that many practitioners and scholars of Buddhism take issue with labeling Buddhism as a *religion*. Some prefer to use the term *philosophy*, while others would select *lifestyle*. If, over the course of this book, the reader is disturbed by the inclusion of Buddhism under the general category of "religious approaches," I sincerely apologize. Please realize that no offense was intended and that, wherever possible, I did try to use responsible labels.

Out of concern for those readers who do not identify with the title *God* at the center of their spirituality, I have sometimes used terms such as the Divine, the Source, and the Absolute. Hopefully, this technique will open all readers to a more comprehensive examination of spirituality and prayer, and will demonstrate my desire to respect a wide range of views concerning what lies outside of the secular and organic world.

Finally, to avoid long and awkward phrasing within sentences, I have alternated the use of female and male pronouns according to chapter. When referring to the third-person prayer practitioner, odd-numbered chapters contain female pronouns, while even-numbered chapters use male pronouns.

Quite obviously, I have only scratched the surface of each prayer perspective described within the coming chapters. A far greater wealth of spiritual inspiration and prayer techniques is to be found in the reader's further study. This book simply strives to be an introduction to the four faiths discussed, and to serve as an encouraging guide for the person who wants to establish or revitalize a practice of prayer. I pray it serves you well.

Introduction

Have you ever noticed how, after spending several days eating chocolate chip cookies, salty chips, and greasy pizza, you wake up one morning and actually *crave* healthier food? All of a sudden you really want an apple, maybe some oatmeal, and a cup of hot tea—without the sugar. Even if you generally choose a cheeseburger over a green salad, you know the dissatisfying feeling of having a body chock-full of junk. Eventually, you want something better. Your body calls out for a change.

Or perhaps you've noticed how, when you are sick with an infection, your whole body begs for sleep. It knows that sleep will aid your recovery. If you heed your body's pleas for rest, you are likely to recover more fully and more quickly. You seem to inherently know how to heal yourself.

In the same way, the deepest and most fundamental *you* cries out for spiritual activity—for prayer—when it has gone long enough without. You know—or, at some level, you instinctively feel—that you need prayer to feel healthy, happy, and whole again. Otherwise, you would not have picked up this book.

Maybe you sense that there is something lacking in your life—that there is a void that is not being filled by the work, the play, the people, and the possessions that make up your current world—and you suspect that prayer is the missing element. Or perhaps you were raised with certain prayer techniques, but no longer find them suitable for your state of spirituality, and would like to investigate other effective forms of prayer. Maybe you need healing, you are in search of guidance, or you want to give praise in a new way. Or perhaps you simply want to discover the beauty of different prayer cultures—to learn how various religions and philosophies have made wonderful contributions to this age-old practice.

Whatever your reason for reading this book, here's the bottom line: Prayer helps. You won't always see how, nor will you always understand how, but prayer works to your benefit no matter which way you look at it. Countless people attest to this truth, from scientists, to members of religious orders, to lay people. Prayer is life enhancing and self-improving. Anything *that* positive is worth a try. And *How to Pray* will aid you in that effort, offering you both inspiration and solid guidance.

How to Pray does not attempt to argue the validity of one religious or philosophical approach over the other. Every religion and lifestyle discussed is of tremendous significance and value. Nor does this book set out to convince you of the existence of God. You already have a desire to turn to a higher union, a more vast power—God. That process of "turning to" is referred to as *prayer* in the following pages. The suggestions, techniques, and stories are presented simply to lend a helping hand as you begin to further develop your personal prayer life.

We will start by discussing general issues of prayer in Part One. This section includes definitions of prayer, information on the power of prayer, and an examination of the reasons why some of us don't pray.

Part Two studies several of the world's approaches to prayer. Within these chapters, you will learn about some of the history and prayer techniques used by four of the world's great traditions: Judaism, Christianity, Islam, and Buddhism.

Finally, in Part Three, we'll cover some basic principles involved in making the practice of prayer more effective. In addition, we'll look at several challenges encountered in prayer life—seemingly unanswered prayers, spiritual dry spells, and even the wonderful possibility of turning each day into a prayer.

How to Pray will support your natural power to communicate with God. Furthermore, it will help you develop that power more fully, just as you develop other natural talents through careful study and exercise. *How to Pray* confirms that you have so much to gain, from daily contentment to sublime fulfillment, through the practice of prayer.

PART ONE

Why Pray?

If you are interested in the study of religions and their philosophies, there is no lack of wonderful material on the subject. And it's all worthwhile—every source. Stop by a Christian Church in any given American town; delve into weekly Torah studies hosted by a local Jewish organization; investigate translations and commentaries of the Qu'ran at a public library; even log onto a website designed to explain the Buddha's teachings. There are countless ways to enrich your intellectual knowledge of spirituality and religion. But then comes the *practice* of spirituality. In a wide sense, that practice can be called *prayer.* Are you ready to apply yourself to the practice of prayer? If so, there are some issues that you should consider, and some teachings from which you can learn.

What preconceptions do you have about prayer as you start—or restart—on your journey? Which preconceptions are helpful, and which ones are destructive? Do you need to boost your confidence in the power of prayer? Are you frustrated by past experiences with prayer, by fears, or even by time constraints? These and other questions will be tackled over the course of the next three chapters. Part One of *How to Pray* will help you to define prayer, to understand its effectiveness, and even to rid yourself of some of the feelings that might be keeping you from the satisfying prayer life you desire—a prayer life that is well within your reach.

1

What Is Prayer?

There are countless phrases that could adequately define prayer, as the term means so many different things to so many different people. Nonetheless, this chapter discusses several carefully chosen definitions of prayer. Why bother, you may ask? It's worth exploring the various roles and elements of prayer because together, they foster a balanced understanding of prayer and its power. And a balanced understanding means a healthier attitude and a more effective practice.

While investigating what prayer is, it is equally helpful to acknowledge what prayer is *not*. So this chapter also identifies several incorrect, but commonly held, notions of prayer. Some people understand prayer in damaging ways. For example, they view prayer as the taming of a magical force or as a way to pass off responsibility. To hone your practice of prayer, you'll want to start off on the right foot by developing a wholesome understanding of prayer and its many life-enhancing capabilities.

HELPFUL DEFINITIONS OF PRAYER

Prayer is God's activity in our lives. Yet it is also our decided turning to God. Prayer is simple communication. In addition, it is profound self-examination. Prayer is carefully cultivated awareness, as well as spontaneous and "inexpressable groanings" (Romans 8:26). Some of the following definitions of prayer will be familiar, confirming what you have known as prayer all along. Others will challenge or extend your notions of prayer, hopefully sparking new insights. As you read the following definitions and quotations, you will see that they have been gathered from several religious and philosophical traditions. Each belief system adds another dimension to our discussion, allowing us to develop a more comprehensive answer to the question, "What is prayer?"

Prayer Is What God Does in Us and Through Us

In Christian Scripture, Jesus Christ tells his followers, "You do not choose me, but I chose you" (John 15: 16). These moving words instruct us to recognize God's activity in our lives. God actively manifests in us, and many spiritualists propose that God calls our attention to that presence by stimulating a deep longing within us. That longing creates the desire, even the instinct, to pray. Therefore, it follows that prayer is God working within us.

> *"We begin to pray believing that it is our own initiative that compels us to do so. Instead, we learn that it is always God's initiative within us. . . ."*
>
> From *Crossing the Threshold of Hope*, Pope John Paul II

Sister Briege McKenna, known internationally as a healer, has been traveling throughout the world for many years, providing comfort, calm, and healing to others. In addition, Sister Briege is the author of the book *Miracles Do Happen*. Prayer is the essence of her life, and she has many valuable things to say about it. When Sister Briege was interviewed by Father Jim Caffrey for a video titled "On Prayer," the Catholic nun discussed how prayer rises out of a hunger. This hunger, seemingly innate to human beings, is especially painful during times of crisis and stress. In our most vulnerable moments, we are naturally drawn toward a greater Source. We somehow know that there's a benevolent font of power and love that is accessible to us. In fact, Sister Briege herself began to develop her prayer life more fully when she was suffering with crippling arthritis. At this time, concentrating on the phenomenon of prayer, she realized, "Prayer isn't what I do, but what God does inside of us."

According to this viewpoint, God places the hunger in our souls; God triggers the prayer reaction. Thus, every prayer is something that God is working within us and expressing through us. We can choose to be receptive, but God takes action through prayer, bringing us into closer contact with the Absolute. So when we pray, we should feel confident that God is with us, sharing in the experience.

Prayer Is a Conversation With the Divine

The most basic definition of prayer is, simply, a conversation with God. We directly engage God in prayer, whether the mode of communication is language, silent meditation, dance, or any other form. Importantly, prayer is a dialogue, which means that listening is necessarily involved. For prayer to be truly effective, we must be willing to still ourselves and hear what God is trying to do in our lives. Unfortunately, many of us have a tendency to bubble over with requests and complaints. It is important to realize that conversation is a two-way street.

Prayer is not just an ordinary conversation. It is a special mode of communication, because it is reserved for and given wholly to God. Yes, God is always present. But through prayer, we place ourselves deep within that presence by turning our full attention to it. During the conversation of prayer, we surrender to the moment and rise above limited notions of time and space. Everything else takes a back seat to the very important discussion with God. As a result, a strong relationship is formed.

Think about your relationship with your best friend or your spouse. Conversation is a vital part of that relationship. This often involves spoken conversation, but can also take the form of unspoken thoughts communicated through body gestures, movements of the eyes, smiles, even emotional empathy. These conversations are powerful and liberating. They are the stuff that your relationship is made of. Likewise, your conversations with God—your prayers—are the blocks on which your spirituality is best built.

> *"Prayer is then not just a formula of words, or a series of desires springing up in the heart—it is the orientation of our whole body, mind and spirit to God in silence, attention, and adoration. All good meditative prayer is a conversion of our entire self to God."*
>
> From *Thoughts in Solitude,* Thomas Merton

In the preface to *The Power of Prayer,* edited by Dale Salwak, we learn that prayer "is a way to make contact with God to feel His presence even more surely." Therefore, it is a conversation that provides us with confidence, closeness, and comfort. By placing ourselves within the walls of this conversation, we remind ourselves that God is a real presence in our lives, not an intellectual concept or a distant myth.

Of course, this conversation can be made up of several elements. When we ask ourselves *why* we pray, we can loosely group the reasons into four categories: praise, thanksgiving, petition, and confession. For a further discussion of these elements of prayer, see "The Four Corners of the Prayer Square" beginning on page 9.

Prayer Is an Attitude of Eagerness and Love

As Lawrence Lovasik states in *The Basic Book of Catholic Prayer: How to Pray and Why*, prayer is "an active attitude of the soul" that involves "an eager longing for grace." Yes, more than words, prayer is an attitude. Unfortunately, the term *attitude* has developed a negative connotation: "He's got such an attitude!" When we think of attitude, we think of sassy kids on the playground. We think of a corporate cold-shoulder. Yet in a wider sense, attitude is the way we function and hold ourselves. And that's exactly what prayer is—the way we function and hold ourselves in God's presence.

When we approach God in prayer, we should aim to do so with sincerity, devotion, and humility. After all, God doesn't need our prayers; God's been doing just fine for the past couple of billion years. *We* need our prayers. Prayer is the way that we come to terms with our joys, wants, and desires. It is the way we answer our longing for communion and compassion, and the way we seek ultimate completion. Therefore, effective prayer is performed with zeal and eagerness, and carries a healthy affection for the creative force behind our world.

> "Without devotion and the consequent grace of God, man's endeavor is vain."
>
> Mahatma Gandhi

Prayer Is Remembrance

In his poem "Prayer (I)," George Herbert defines prayer, among other things, as "the soul in paraphrase." The word *paraphrase* is poignantly used, for it refers to re-expressing something that is already there. If

The Four Corners of the Prayer Square

Scholars and spiritualists often divide reasons for prayer into three or four categories. The first three categories are praise, thanksgiving, and petition. Other words that might be used for the same sentiments are adoration, grateful honor, and request, respectively. A fourth reason for prayer that some people acknowledge is confession—contrition or sorrow. This is especially common among people who practice religions that understand God not only as a loving Creator, but also as a Righteous Judge who decrees specific laws. Among such religions are Judaism, Christianity, and Islam.

Praise

Prayers of praise involve the general adoration of God, and are very important for putting us in the proper state of mind for effective prayer. We must firmly believe that prayer works—that God governs the universe through us and through prayer—in order for our prayers to effect change. The praising of God in prayer is a reminder of the glories of God. It confirms our trust that God is the All Good who can work through us to do amazing things.

Thanksgiving

In his famous work *The Prophet,* Kahlil Gibran wrote, "You pray in your distress and in your need; would that you might pray also in the fullness of your joy and in your days of abundance." Thanksgiving is repeatedly cited as the most important part of the practice of prayer. Being thankful during our prayers reminds us to see all the majesty, beauty, and dynamism in every occurrence of life. We learn to respect and enjoy all creatures and all things when we put ourselves in a thankful frame of mind. Most of all, we confirm God's influence on our lives, thus losing the obsession with self that is so attractive, but so detrimental.

Petition

Petition is what we most readily refer to as prayer. In fact, our word *prayer* comes from a Latin word meaning to entreat, to implore, to beg. One of the largest issues at hand in prayers of petition is healing—physical, mental, and spiritual. When we feel that things are out of our control, we often turn to God in the hope of reordering our personal universes. It is a natural inclination to pray for ourselves and for others, especially in times when fear is invading our lives.

Asking God for help is easy. Just open your heart and let the words, the tears, the emotions pour forth. However, it is also too easy to let this element of prayer become the overarching one. When this happens, prayer life becomes stunted and remains self-centered. There is nothing wrong with requesting guidance and aid from God, but always with the notion that "Thy will be done." God holds a greater plan than any which we can understand. What we ask for is not always the best thing in the long run.

Confession

Finally, some people practice confession prayers. They dwell on being heartily sorry for having offended God through sin—through actions, thoughts, and words that tear away at the relationship with God, instead of bolstering it. This is not to imply that we should be consumed by guilt, or that we should practice self-mortification. Confession prayer, or the expressing of sorrow, is healthy in that it calls our attention to our weaknesses. It encourages us to rethink any harm that we have caused, thus making us less likely to continue such behavior. Furthermore, it reminds us that we are connected to everything in the universe, and that every action of ours affects the world.

prayer is the re-expression of the soul, the redefining of ourselves in our universe and within God, then prayer is remembrance. We are turning back to something we inherently know. We remember our Source, and we go back home through prayer.

The idea of remembrance is brilliantly woven into the concepts of Buddhism. Meditating, in Buddhist practice, involves freeing oneself of the blindness caused by earthly life and the senses. We become attached to things and ideas during this lifetime, convincing ourselves that there is something permanent about status, ego, and action. But Buddhism teaches us that nothing is permanent, that desirous attachment is mis-leading, and that we essentially have to shed these delusions to rid our-selves of suffering. Only when we are freed from the suffering of igno-rance can we attain ultimate liberation, which is the loss of the self into the original, perfect state.

> *"All of us have the Buddha nature, or divine spark, in us. We do not have to search for Buddhahood outside because we are all originally Buddhas. In Christian terms, we do not have to search for God's kingdom outside because the Kingdom of God is within us. Similarly, in Islam the essence of human life is roh, which is the spirit of God. . . ."*
>
> From *The Complete Book of Zen*, Wong Kiew Kit

Buddhism does not include a concept of God, but shares something in common with Judaism, Christianity, and Islam when all of the latter define God as Perfect and All-encompassing Love. It is there that Buddhists can parallel their idea of the ultimate state—nirvana—with what Westerners have come to call God. When a practitioner of Buddhism attains nirvana, the occurrence is considered a reawakening. Similarly, prayer awakens us, again, to our more sacred and truer nature.

Prayer Is Medicine for the Human Spirit

This definition is derived from a phrase His Holiness the Dalai Lama used during a talk on spirituality at Gethsemani Monastery. In discussing the role of spirituality in our lives, the Dalai Lama referred to religion as medicine, stating that religions—all of them—"have a spiritual potential to help humanity by promoting human happiness and satisfaction." He explained that religion works toward curing human suffering.

Likewise, prayer serves as medicine for the human soul or spirit. Prayer has the power to heal our suffering, even if it doesn't take away every pain and discomfort. Through prayer, we learn to relinquish the pathological control that so many of us seek. We subdue the ego and find greater peace as part of a whole. Our bodies and minds grow healthier in response to the calm found in prayer.

> *"Prayer unites and mends the broken pieces of yourself into the one, beautiful wholeness. Prayer is cure."*
>
> From "Picture Prayer," Jeffrey Burton Russell

Prayer Is Taking Part in the World

In John Dalrymple's book *Simple Prayer*, the author states that prayer is partnership with God. It is offering ourselves in attention and service to God, and therefore accepting our role in making this world a better place. The energy and ideas that we gather through prayer can heal, comfort, renew, and create.

Viewing prayer as service—as the effort to share in creation of the world and bring all things closer to God—helps us avoid self-centered prayer. At a very shallow level, prayer is asking for things that will better our own lives, here and now. If we approach prayer in such a manner, it is nothing more than a means to get what we want. Like a spoiled child, we think that if we kick and scream enough, God will give in and magically produce the treats of life. Prayer is so much more than that.

Dalrymple suggests that we use the metaphor of a window to cultivate a healthy attitude about prayer as service. When we look at a window, we can do three things. First, we can look at the glass, perhaps noticing that it is dirty, broken, or even clean. When we do this, we miss the view outside, and the window is not used to its potential. Second, we can look at the window's reflection to see ourselves. The window then becomes an opportunity for vanity or self-preoccupation. Again, we lose the view. Finally, we can look through the window, allowing it to serve its greater purpose. Peering through the windowpane, to what is beyond, we come to learn so much more about our surroundings and our world in general.

Prayer is that window. It has the capacity to be used for great insight and contact—to be the means by which wonderful ideas can be created and great needs in the world can be identified. But we need to look *through* prayer to see God. We shouldn't stop at the window's glass, seeing only what is immediately in front of us—our immediate pains and the desires for instant gratification. We shouldn't use prayer simply to focus on ourselves, as that, in the end, is never fulfilling. We should use prayer to its fullest, to gain necessary insight and then spring into action in our world.

Prayer Is Introspection

According to Rabbi Irwin Katsof's book *How to Get Your Prayers Answered*, the Hebrew word for prayer is *li-heet-pallel*. The latter part of the word—*pallel*—means to inspect, examine, while the initial part—*li-heet*—makes the term reflexive. Therefore, prayer is self-inspection, self-examination. Through prayer, we learn about ourselves at deeper levels. And we come closer to God because we begin to understand how God can change us, not how we can change God.

Through the self-inspection conducted in prayer, we are honest, open, and sincere with ourselves. We tap into the divine expression inside of us, gathering energy and finding capabilities to which we might not normally gain access. Prayer is stepping away from the hustle and bustle of distractions. In this quiet place, we can see where we are weak and where we are strong. We can understand our role in the world. This leads to the next definition of prayer, which involves change. In order to change, first one must examine the self.

Prayer Is a Path to Transformation

While we have cautioned ourselves against using prayer solely as a means to concentrate on the self, it is healthy to use the insight gained in prayer to transform ourselves for the better. Through prayer, we cultivate a greater eye for the good and the bad, the healthy and the unhealthy. We see things for what they are, and attain the bigger picture of what's truly important. As a result, prayer spurs us on to personal change.

The Sufi movement of Islam teaches that the individual must transform the self, moving away from the ego, in order to achieve spiritual perfection. Lives of prayer bring us closer to perfection, and thus Perfection. The ego causes distortions in our vision; when we allow the ego to run our lives, it's as though we are putting on someone else's glasses. We can't see things correctly because we don't have the right prescription. Prayer can be likened to our own pair of glasses. It gives us clarity and helps us to mirror the attributes of God. And with improved vision, we see that each person is not a separate entity, but a part of a beautiful whole.

Through prayer, the individual becomes God-centered, not self-centered. It is at this point that transformation takes place. All of a sudden, the material world is less important; the happiness afforded by financial wealth, worldly status, and the like, proves to be quite unfulfilling. Sure, the luxuries might feel good, but in the face of a much greater happiness, they are not worth the damaging struggle.

The transformation may be unsettling at first; we may resist letting go of the sturdy selves that we have built up and decorated. Thomas Merton wrote, "Sometimes prayer, meditation, and contemplation are 'death'—a kind of descent into our own nothingness, a recognition of helplessness, frustration, infidelity, confusion, ignorance." But that's a good thing, albeit, an uncomfortable one. Loss of the self as an isolated "one" means celebration in a more fulfilling One. By seeing the insignificance of our own egos and their wants, we realize a better quality of life.

> *"You have held fast to 'I' and 'we,'*
> *And this dualism is your spiritual ruin."*
>
> From *Masnavi* 1: 3012, Jalal Al-Din Rumi

Prayer Is a Source of Protection

While addressing the definition of prayer, we cannot avoid the commonly held belief that prayer also serves as a force of good against certain forces of evil. This book is not a study of how prayer can combat the demonic, but it would be irresponsible not to make any mention of this aspect of prayer. Several religions, including Christianity and Islam, involve fervent beliefs in destructive spiritual forces. When there is such a belief in the demonic, prayer is a source of protection—physical and mental. It forms a shield around the practitioner, so to speak, of good intent and holy thought. It puts the practitioner under the favor of God, who is ultimately far more powerful than any "bad" force.

And prayer can strengthen the individual who prays against the vices and temptations within herself—lust, greed, envy, sloth, violent tendencies, anger, and other flaws that keep a person from being the best that she can be—just as it protects the individual who seeks protection from the harmful actions of tainted outsiders. Whether fighting an enemy without or within, many people view prayer as a source of enhanced immunity against what is not ultimately good.

Prayer Is a Dynamic Force

In the bestseller *The Power of Positive Thinking,* Norman Vincent Peale states that "prayer power is a manifestation of energy." This energy can heal the mind, revitalize the body despite aging, provide guidance, and increase your skills of discernment, just to name a few benefits. Prayer "releases and keeps power flowing freely." It is a dynamic force.

Peale understands prayer in terms of the sending out of vibrations— to others and to God. The human body emits magnetic forces. Peale proposes that prayer tunes up the many sending stations that give off magnetic power. As a result of the tune-up, striking power can pass through one being into another being and into the world, creating all sorts of effects. Prayer is a force, much like any other force, only its products are love, sympathy, support, and the like. Vibrations, triggered through prayer, spark many wonderful occurrences.

> *"Prayer is always an opus gloriae (a work, a labor, of glory)."*
>
> From *Crossing the Threshold of Hope,* Pope John Paul II

Prayer Is Giving Glory

In addition to the complex roles that prayer plays in our personal development and the development of our world, prayer is plain and simple adoration. Reveling in God, simply for the love of God, is the highest form of prayer. It is in giving glory that we find selfless happiness, because in doing so, we celebrate the source of unconditional and unending love.

Caught in a Prayer Loop

Can prayer catch you in an unending cycle? It sure can. Mother Teresa of Calcutta, a Catholic nun who spent her life caring for the starving and the dying poor, taught us that to pray better, you must pray more. As you pray more, prayer becomes easier. And as prayer becomes easier, you pray more.

Listen to any Christian hymn of praise to God. Watch the impassioned love displayed in the prayer gestures of the Muslim. Witness the reverent adoration of heads bowed during the recitation of a Hebrew prayer. Giving glory, or even the observation of giving glory, is healing and freeing. It is the ultimate purpose of prayer—to unite with Truth and find ecstasy in it. A surrender of the self leads to a sharing in a moment of glory, offered to God and enjoyed by the person who prays. We give glory during any kind of prayer—be it request, confession, adoration, or thanksgiving—because we come before God in recognition of God's love and knowledge.

DESTRUCTIVE DEFINITIONS OF PRAYER

We have considered many different aspects of prayer, and have found many ways to define it. But we can increase our understanding of prayer by thinking about what prayer is *not*. The power of prayer can be misunderstood and maligned, as evident in the following inaccurate definitions of prayer.

Prayer Is a Means to an End

Prayer to God is a healthy action in and of itself because, through it, we communicate with our Source and experience completion. Using it as a means to achieve an end—like some power tool that you could purchase at a hardware store—is destructive. If you view prayer merely as a way to get something, you reduce it to a one-dimensional, self-centered practice, and will surely be unfulfilled when your requests aren't answered in just the way you want. Prayer should be cherished for its benefit at the very moment it is experienced, not for what it can do in the future.

Prayer is not a stride toward the finish line. It is not a competition or a race: "If I say the right words, I'll win the prize! And the sooner the better!" That's no way to pray! Prayer is not your answer to God's exam or a bargaining device. It is simply a way to come into contact with your God in sincere and life-enhancing communication.

Prayer Is Passivity

It is certainly true that one of the benefits of prayer is an increase in tranquility. During prayer, we gain calm and insight, and therefore are often able to reduce the scattered thoughts in our harried minds. However, to view prayer as *passive* is to miss out on a large part of the prayer experience. Turning to God in prayer necessarily takes zeal and effort. That's why prayer is often referred to as the "exercise of the spirit." That does not mean that our muscles start moving, but our spirits certainly do! The power of prayer enlivens our spirits, awakening our creativity and stimulating our desire for change.

At the beginning of the chapter, we learned that God inspires prayer. Yet your response to God is *your* choice, not something that just happens to you. Thus, though prayer may be a relaxing practice in the way that it encourages physical and mental peace, it is nonetheless a practice—a chosen activity that includes your active participation. It involves remaining open and carefully listening. In fact, Thomas Merton spoke of the spiritual life as "a matter of keeping awake." And the greatest spiritualists would argue that, in prayer, you are most awake, being freed from the bonds of delusion.

> *"Prayer is not an old woman's idle amusement. Properly understood and applied, it is the most potent instrument of action."*
>
> Mahatma Gandhi

Prayer Is a Solution to All My Problems

We tire from responsibility. We grow fatigued from work and stress. Wouldn't it be nice to put everything in someone else's hands and say, "Here. Fix it." Some people approach prayer in this manner, and it is most unhealthy. When the desired solution does not reveal itself, such people blame God and live in anger.

Prayer is not a means of instant gratification. It is not a pill for all ailments. In fact, prayer involves cooperating and working with God to make changes in our lives and in the world. It often takes a lot of patience and perseverance. Prayer does not necessarily spell out or immediately trigger solutions to the troubles in our lives. Instead, through prayer, we gain insight and direction so that we can work productively toward a solution.

Prayer Is a Magical Formula

How easy it is to think of prayer as mysterious magic! We want to chant a few lines reverently, and then wait for the stars to start spinning in our favor. The truth is that prayer's power is not very mysterious. We know it comes from God and the expression of God in every being. We know it is effective when we pray with sincerity, confidence, and openness. There is no way that every prayer will be answered according to our will, but through prayer, we understand that God's will is best. This makes perfect sense.

Yes, the miraculous does happen through prayer, but that's because the Divine's nature, quite plainly, exceeds time, space, and the laws of physics. God is best not understood as a robed apothecary who mixes sparkling potions in his castle. And prayer is best not understood as a human's opportunity to exercise power over the universe's energy. Truthfully, if we need to attribute all sorts of unfamiliar and frightening qualities to prayer, then our spiritual lives must be very boring.

Some people use prayer as a source of entertainment, as if prayer were a mode of magic. They focus on the possibility of the paranormal, gearing their expectations toward visions and trance-like ecstasies. But prayer is not a drug, and is not about pleasing oneself or having idle fun. If a person turns to prayer in hopes of cultivating supernatural abilities, she is missing the point.

> *"Therefore let your visit to that temple invisible be for naught but ecstasy and sweet communion."*
>
> From *The Prophet*, Kahlil Gibran

CONCLUSION

Prayers come in all forms and all sizes. Yet we have the tendency to settle comfortably into one or two understandings of prayer, never really pushing ourselves to probe more deeply into the practice. Hopefully, this chapter has widened your perspective on prayer. Now let us consider some information on its effectiveness. In the next chapter, we'll study the relationship between prayer and science, and note how prayer is demanding recognition as a viable, life-enhancing practice.

2

How Effective Is Prayer?

It is easy to say that prayer can make us feel really good; that it opens the individual up to better understanding and therefore improves his life; that it can provide calm and contentment, thus improving health and happiness. But is there any proof that prayer actually works? Is it really worth our while? Can we evaluate prayer as we would evaluate any other "treatment" or "therapy" and prove its effectiveness? In very recent years, science has put forth good efforts to do just that. And there have been reputable studies that confirm prayer's power. But it is also important to realize that most of science's history is marred with a severe prejudice against prayer as a viable, respectable force for healing and well-being.

This chapter examines the relationship between prayer and science. It presents studies that not only confirm the power of prayer, but also provide some surprising insights into the process of prayer. Just as important, it optimistically suggests that increasing recognition of prayer's power is forthcoming. Science is beginning to see that the world doesn't work quite as our traditional high school textbooks led us to believe. And as a result, some great changes may be in store for us as science revaluates its old ideas about prayer.

SCIENCE TAKES THE PLUNGE INTO PRAYER

We live in a science-oriented culture. Evaluations are made according to *observation*—especially scientific and mathematical proof. The problem is that the power of prayer cannot be observed with the senses or recorded

---

on paper. We can report, for example, that a person's health improves, and that the person actively prayed prior to the improvement, but can we ever really link the prayers to the enhanced health without taking a leap of faith? After years of dismissing prayer as a "mind over matter" technique—a type of self-hypnosis—science is finally starting to probe deeply into this area.

In the 1960s, several studies were conducted on the effects of prayer, but they were too small to be considered convincing. For example, one looked at eighteen children who suffered from leukemia. Another involved forty-eight people with rheumatic illnesses. Both came up with positive feedback on the power of prayer. But while some people were encouraged by these studies, the strictly scientific community scoffed at their conclusions. In the opinion of these scientists, the research was simply not conducted in a manner that was convincing enough to put prayer into the medical journals. Researchers needed to prepare studies that would stand up against the scrutiny of science. Until then, studies wouldn't be of much value.

Fast-forward approximately two decades. Some say it was during the height of corporate obsession in the 1980s that a renewed interest in researching spirituality and prayer arose. Whatever the case, the New Age movement gained in popularity, promoting the benefits of prayer and meditation, relaxation, communion with nature, and a celebration of the metaphysical. All of a sudden, stores were selling prayer beads, crystals, zither recordings, and incense. Book publishers began turning out volume after volume on angel visitation and near-death experiences. Television shows on paranormal occurrences and miraculous events mesmerized audiences. It was obvious that the American public was spiritually hungry, and along with that hunger came a demand to know if prayer was truly effective.

It wasn't long before the benefits of prayer would be discussed not only around kitchen tables and in college classrooms, but also in medical research buildings and hospitals. The practice of praying for increased physical and mental health is more ancient than numbers can tell. But it was time to test the validity of such practice with well constructed scientific studies.

There were, and still are, many people who argued against the clinical study of prayer. The bottom line is this: Those who believe that prayer works have faith that surpasses numerical and material proof. They know how prayer operates in their lives from experience. In such light, putting God to the test seems ridiculous. And they have a strong point.

Why subject something immaterial and immeasurable to observation? The problem, as previously mentioned, is that we live in a science-oriented culture. Thus, it is thought that any scientific proof for or against prayer can provide us with the ultimate answer we are seeking. In plain English, if we can't prove something, it must be wrong. On the other hand, if something can survive scientific investigation and come out on top, it's considered valid. Consciously or unconsciously, many of us seek that type of confirmation.

So the following section looks at the most respected scientific studies conducted on prayer. But first, it should be noted that while many studies of prayer have yielded positive results, not *all* prayer studies have proven the physical efficacy of prayer. For those who believe in prayer, the failure of these studies means nothing. And even to those who have questionable or no faith in the power of prayer, it should be evident that scientific prayer studies can go only so far. It is impossible to absolutely "control" prayer in a study. Furthermore, answers to prayers are not always obvious, and not always given in ways that the scientific world would consider positive. For example, if a woman prays that her mother will receive help in her illness, the prayers might contribute to her mother's recovery from the sickness, or they might help the mother gain better coping skills to endure the illness. A clinical study on prayer's effectiveness would look only for the first outcome. Scientific studies measure the effects of prayer against only one desired result. So it is important to generally acknowledge the limits of studies on prayer—both those that are successful and those that are not.

SCIENCE STUDIES PRAYER AND HUMAN HEALTH

Scientists believe that the most accurate studies of prayer focus on *intercessory prayer*—that is, prayer offered by one person for the well-being of another person. This is due to the fact that the validity of prayer power on the individual who prays is easily argued; scientists can, and often do, attribute any health benefits to the placebo effect—that is, to the fact that the person *believed* prayer would work, and as a result, unconsciously willed the effect to take place. No one argues the power of the mind. It can certainly trigger physical events. But when it comes to intercessory prayer, we can't point to the individual's mind-over-body mechanism. The person being prayed for often does not even know that he is the beneficiary of another's prayers. As a result, the most widely respected studies on prayer have examined intercessory prayer.

Another point should be made before we look at the actual studies. In each study, the members of one group were assigned people to pray for them, while the members of another group were not. However, it was not known whether individuals in either group had family members, friends, religious-community members, or others praying for them. Thus, you can already see the complications involved in studying a subject such as prayer, even when the subject is limited to intercessory prayer. There is no way to truly control prayer. Having given this caution, let's consider the following two studies.

San Francisco General Hospital

In the late 1980s, Dr. Randolph Byrd was a practicing cardiologist at San Francisco General Hospital. He decided to conduct what has been called the first serious study of the medical effects of intercessory prayer. The controlled ten-month study—published in *The Southern Medical Journal* in 1988—was performed on 393 cardiac-care-unit patients. The general outcome gave reason to believe that patients for whom prayers are said fare better than other patients. In fact, some analyses of the study estimated a 10-percent difference between the groups.

The subjects of the study were randomly assigned, by computer, to one of two groups: 192 patients would be prayed for by a designated group of people, while 201 patients would not have prayers said for them. This was a double-blind study, meaning that the patients, the nurses, and the doctors were not aware of the group to which any patient belonged. Meanwhile, the individuals who prayed came from Roman Catholic and Protestant prayer groups, and were given the names of the patients and a small amount of data on their conditions. They were then asked to pray every day for the patients, but were not provided with any specific guidelines on how to conduct their prayers. The study was designed so that each patient in the "prayer group" had from five to seven people praying for him, and each person who prayed had a number of patients for whom he had to say prayers.

The results showed that the patients who were prayed for were five times less likely to need antibiotic treatments than those in the control group; only three patients in the prayed-for group needed antibiotics, as compared with sixteen patients in the control group. The prayed-for patients were also three times less likely to develop a condition called pulmonary edema; six patients in the prayed-for group suffered from pulmonary edema, while eighteen control-group patients did. None of the patients who were prayed for needed breathing assistance, whereas twelve of the control-group members required mechanical respiratory support.

This study not only shows the effectiveness of prayer, but also demonstrates that space and distance do not seem to affect the potency of prayer. There was no difference in effectiveness between the prayers of those who lived close by and the prayers of those who resided on the other side of the country. So the power from which prayer stems does not seem to be confined by our notions of time and space. Dr. Larry Dossey, author of *Recovering the Soul: A Scientific and Spiritual Search,* points out: "This suggests immediately that there is no 'energy' involved in prayer as we understand this term in modern science." Whether or not you believe that the power of prayer is translated into some form of physical energy, the bottom line is that prayer works.

Mid-America Heart Institute at St. Luke's Hospital

A 1998 scientific study conducted at St. Luke's Hospital, Kansas City, analyzed whether patients who are prayed for enjoy a speedier, less difficult recovery. This study, published in the well-respected *Archives of Internal Medicine,* declared the effectiveness of what is termed "remote intercessory prayer." More simply, it was found that the patients who unknowingly had people praying for them during the period of the study recovered more fully than those for whom designated people did not pray.

William Harris, who had accomplished his doctorate and specialized in research on heart disease, led the research team. The team also included medical doctors, including a cardiologist, as well as a psychologist, a statistician, a hospital chaplain, and a reverend. The study involved 990 patients, each of whom was admitted to the coronary care unit at St. Luke's Hospital. All suffered from serious, even life-threatening conditions, ranging from heart attack, to congestive heart failure, to severe coronary disease.

The patients in the St. Luke's study were split as follows: 466 patients were selected randomly and prayed for, every day, by five participating people; 524 were randomly placed in a control group for whom prayers were not said. A total of 75 people did the praying—all volunteers from the Kansas City region. They came from various denominations, and all believed not only in God's existence, but also in God's concern for each individual. And all volunteers believed in the healing power of prayer.

The volunteers were asked to pray "for a speedy recovery with no complications." Neither the patients nor the physicians of the patients were aware of the study. Prayers were not conducted in the hospital, but rather away from it. And the volunteers were not given any detailed information on those for whom they were praying. In fact, the only information they were given were the first names of those to whom they were assigned, and the fact that they were sick. The prayers were conducted for twenty-eight days, beginning one day after a given patient was admitted to St. Luke's coronary care unit.

What was the result? Dr. Harris firmly stated that the subjects for whom the volunteers prayed "just did better." He then explained what he and the researchers meant by "better." Thirty-five different health issues were studied to analyze the progress of the patients. For example, researchers looked at the numbers and types of medications that each patient required, how much time was spent on respirators, if a pacemaker was necessary, the length of the hospital stay, and the time in which either recovery or death occurred. The conclusion of the research team was that the patients who were prayed for ended up doing 11 percent better than those for whom prayers were not said. According to the rules of statistics, such an outcome is significant.

And the Research Continues

The studies examined above are just two—albeit the best known and most respected—of the *hundreds* of studies that have researched the topic of prayer's effect on health. An overwhelming majority of these studies have shown that prayer positively affects physical well-being. Moreover, David Myers, in his *Reformed Review* article "On Assessing Prayer, Faith, and Health," reports that interest in the link between spirituality and health is only increasing. More and more scientific attention is being directed at the power of prayer.

For example, Myers reminds us that Harvard Medical School runs an annual and very well-attended conference named "Spirituality and Healing in Medicine." There, the latest research on prayer is revealed. Furthermore, Duke University has formed a specific center to study how religion and spirituality affect health. And the number of medical schools that offer classes on spirituality and health has greatly increased, growing from three in 1994 to sixty-one in 1999. Clearly, scientific research into prayer is only in its infancy. In the coming years, we can look forward to further studies on the power of prayer and spirituality.

THE SPINDRIFT EXPERIMENTS

In addition to studies performed on the power of prayer in human healing, more general studies on prayer have been conducted. Take, for
example, the many studies performed by Spindrift, an organization
based in Salem, Oregon, that studies the effectiveness of different types
of prayer. Members of Spindrift conduct basic, simple experiments on
prayer in order to understand its power more fully. One of the philosophies that the Spindrift researchers assume is that every human being
possesses a certain divinity within, and that all divine aspects of our
selves come together to form a great Oneness. Interestingly, Spindrift
researchers don't limit themselves to human-to-human studies. Instead,
they try to get down to the very basics of prayer by considering how it
affects even something quite different from the prayer practitioners—
such as a batch of seedlings.

Prayers for Growth

Let's consider one experiment conducted on two groups of rye seeds, the
groups being of equal quantities of seeds. Both groups were placed within the same environment—a container filled with a soil-like substance
widely used in gardening. The researchers simply made two sections by
running a string down the center of the container, and then labeled one
side A and one side B. The study assigned people to pray for the seeds in
one group, and not the other. When the seeds had sprouted, the number
of rye shoots in each group was counted.

What were the results? Researchers found a significant difference
between the number of sprouts in the two groups. Specifically, the group
for which prayers were said contained more shoots than the control
group. The test was repeated many times, and involved new people each
time, but results remained consistent. It was concluded that prayers for
a specific group of organisms produce positive effects. These studies also
highlighted the power of the human consciousness over objects outside
of the body.

Prayers for Healing

Once the initial tests on the rye seeds were concluded, Spindrift researchers decided to take a new approach. Since we often apply prayer
to unhealthy individuals, researchers chose to apply it to unhealthy
seeds. But because it's impossible to pinpoint seeds that might be

Strength in Numbers

It is quite interesting to note that, in addition to studies on interces-sory prayer and personal prayer, quite a few studies have examined the benefits of practicing communal prayer. Time and again, people who are active in local religious communities—those who attend serv-ices at least once a week—fare better in terms of lifespan and health. Here's just a sampling of studies that have been published in various prestigious medical journals.

The *Journal of Gerontology* published the results of a study that followed 3,968 North Carolina seniors for six years. Within that time, it was found that 37 percent of those who did not regularly attend religious services died, while only 23 percent of those who attended weekly services died. Similarly, *Health Psychology* reported a study that collected data on 5,286 Californians over a period of twenty-eight years. After taking into consideration such factors as age, gen-der, ethnic background, and education, researchers found that those subjects who regularly attended religious services were 36 percent less likely to have passed away during the period of the study.

And there are many more studies of this type. For example, the *Journal of Chronic Disease* published a study of 91,909 people living in Maryland. The study group was tracked for a correlation between weekly attendance at religious services and occurrence of death. Researchers found that during the time frame of the study, those sub-jects who attended weekly religious gatherings were 53 percent less likely to die from coronary disease, 53 percent less likely to die from suicide, and 74 percent less likely to die from cirrhosis of the liver.

Of course, there are numerous factors to consider when review-ing these studies. For one, women tend to live longer, and also tend to be more spiritual. So if a study uses mostly women in the "atten-dees" group, it's likely that the group will enjoy greater longevity. (Note that at least one of the above studies *did* take gender into con-sideration when evaluating results.) In addition, people who are spiri-tually active tend to lead rather healthy lifestyles. Statistically, there is less substance abuse; more optimism, which leads to enhanced immunity; and stronger general concern for health among those who are religiously active. And people who are involved in their local religious communities are likely to receive support and help in times of need. This, too, can result in greater health.

The topic is an interesting one. It seems as though not only a well-developed personal prayer life, but also a healthy communal prayer life, are keys to greater physical and emotional well-being!

"unhealthy," the researchers added salt water to a container of seeds in an otherwise identical environment to the one previously described. Salt water puts stress on seeds, making it more difficult for them to grow in a healthy manner.

The results of this test proved even more dramatic than the results of those conducted on "healthy" seeds. This time, the number of shoots on the prayed-for side was higher than that on the unprayed-for side in an even greater ratio than found in the tests on unstressed seeds. This type of study was repeated several times as well, with a greater amount of salt added each time. And in each successive test, the number of shoots coming from the prayed-for group was larger in ratio to the control group, and larger in number than in the previous experiment. Therefore, researchers concluded that prayer works best when there are greater challenges or increased stress.

In order to back up the data on the salt-water-grown rye seeds, soybeans were used in a separate battery of tests. This time, though, stress was placed on the plants via temperature and humidity levels. The results were consistent with those that arose from the earlier rye seed experiments.

Is More Prayer, More Effective?

Now the researchers turned to another topic: Does the number of prayers matter? In order to investigate this question, Spindrift researchers set up four containers: a control container, the seeds of which would not be the subjects of prayers; container X; container Y; and container Z. The seeds in containers X and Y were prayed for as a unit; so were the seeds in containers Y and Z. Obviously, the seeds in container Y were to receive double the prayers. And guess what? When it came down to success in germination, the seeds in container Y did *twice* as well, leading to the conclusion that greater amounts of prayer have stronger effects.

How Much Should You Know
About the Subject of the Prayers?

Another conclusion noted through the Spindrift experiments was that the more a person knows about the subject of his prayers, the more effective the prayers will be. Tests showed that when a person didn't know anything about the nature of the seeds for which he was praying, the positive results of the prayers were a lot lower than when he did have some conceptualization of the seeds. This doesn't mean that he had to know exactly what outcome to pray for—that's often impossible, as we don't always fully understand illness or how it should best be handled. Besides, it's better not to impose our wills onto God or the universe. It means that the prayer practitioner was better off having a certain understanding or knowledge of his subjects, perhaps because it fostered an attachment and helped make the prayers more sincere.

Should Prayer Be Directed or Nondirected?

In studying prayer and its many forms, we come across two approaches: direct or directed prayer, and indirect or nondirected prayer. One objective of the Spindrift studies was to compare the two forms of prayer and see which is most effective.

Directed prayer occurs when a person prays for a very specific outcome, a very distinct result. In the Spindrift experiments, directed prayer was accomplished by praying for a quicker rate of germination. In *nondirected prayer,* no pinpointed goal is requested. For instance, to test the power of nondirected prayer, the Spindrift people prayed in an open-ended manner for the seeds rather than for a specific result. In all tests, results were consistent: While both forms of prayer were generally effective, nondirected prayer was *much more effective,* sometimes even doubling positive results. What author Larry Dossey refers to as the "Thy will be done" approach to the universe and God was determined to be the most powerful form of prayer.

As a result of their work, the Spindrift organization suggests that when praying for a subject, you keep an open mind and try not to form images and associations. Simply remain in a holy state of consciousness that *includes* the subject. In this way, you do not try to force your will upon the universe, but, instead, allow the universe (or God) to do what is more responsible and important in the larger perspective. Spindrift points out that, in fact, we often don't know what is "best" for the subject of our prayer—be it another person, a pet, or a plant. This is another reason that nondirected prayer is the better avenue. It simply leads the organism back to the most appropriate state.

These results do run contrary to the techniques of visualization that are encouraged in some schools of thought—and contrary to the preferences of many people who like to have a particular image or agenda in mind when they pray. But nondirected prayer worked best in the Spindrift experiments. If nothing else, this information reminds us to be leery of projecting too many of our own judgments and desires into prayers. We should attempt to remain open-minded and receptive to a divine plan that is a good deal larger than what we can immediately comprehend.

> *"Medical researchers, who have always preferred empirical evidence to the ephemeral, now 'appreciate that there are some unobservable processes,' says Kenneth Pargament, PhD. . . . 'We can't measure God directly, but we can measure the impact of belief. We can look at the footprints in the sand, the footprints left by faith.'"*
>
> From "Faith and Recovery," *Country Living's Healthy Living*

SCIENCE EXPLAINS BENEFITS TO THE PRAYER PRACTITIONER

Science has not limited its studies to the benefits of intercessory prayer for the person—or even the thing, in the case of a seed—for whom the prayers are said. A number of studies have also confirmed the positive effects of prayer on the practitioner himself. In fact, at an annual meeting of the American Association for the Advancement of Science, Georgetown University's Dr. Dale Matthews confirmed that people who regularly observe religious practices have been found to experience improvement of a number of severe health problems, including cancer, heart disease, high blood pressure, depression, alcoholism, and drug abuse.

Let's look at just a few studies to illustrate the type of confirmation that science has found concerning prayer's effectiveness on the prayer practitioner. One study, reported in the *American Heart Association Journal*, looked at mantra meditation, or word chanting, which is considered a form of Western prayer as well as an Eastern meditation practice. During this type of meditation, a prayer phrase, word, or sound is repeatedly recited at fixed tones and intervals. Remarkably, the study found that the blood pressure-lowering effects of mantra meditation were *comparable to* the benefits induced by medication, and *better than* the benefits gained from simply making lifestyle changes or performing progressive muscle relaxation.

And consider the following additional information. In 1995, a study conducted at New Hampshire's Dartmouth College tracked 250 open-heart surgery patients. The researchers concluded that those who included religion in their lives and had social support (which often "piggybacks" religious practice) were twelve times less likely to pass away. And at Duke University, 1,000 patients were assessed between 1987 and 1989 for the link between depression and hospitalization. During this study, researchers found that patients who made religion—including the practice of prayer—a part of their lives handled hospitalization much better than those who didn't.

Although science has not yet offered explanations for the effectiveness of intercessory prayer, it has attempted to explain benefits to the prayer practitioner. We'll consider these explanations shortly. But to understand the power of prayer for the practitioner himself, you first need to know a little about how and why stress occurs.

Modern culture bombards the individual with stress in the form of deadlines, traffic, financial worries, and more. While we may consciously know that these are intellectual or mental stresses, rather than physical threats, our bodies make no distinction between the two. Whether emotional or physical, actual or imagined, the body senses stress and sends stress hormones soaring as a protective measure. After millennia of being a species that, in order to survive, has reacted to any strange sounds, menacing predators, or sudden changes in weather, we are programmed to respond quickly and severely.

When it perceives a threat, the body makes a quick decision to stimulate the hypothalamus and begin the fight-or-flight response. This is the response that once enabled us to escape from that lion—and that now permits us to slam on the brakes before we hit the child on the bicycle. As part of the fight-or-flight syndrome, the nervous system releases hormones that act as messengers, alerting the body to heighten its defenses. As a result, there is a rise in metabolism, heart rate, blood pressure, breathing rate, and muscle tension. This is necessary in some circumstances, but when your body maintains a stress reaction over long periods of time, continually triggered by daily stressors, much physical damage occurs.

Fortunately, studies have found that prayer can help. Harvard Medical School's Dr. Herbert Benson found that as much as we can stimulate the hypothalamus into stressing the body, we can also relax the body to reduce the stress response. We can help ourselves achieve a restful state in different ways, but among the best techniques—arguably, *the* best techniques—are prayer and meditation. Medical researchers have postulated that prayer and ritual practices act as emotional triggers that set off biochemical reactions which actually diminish the levels of stress hormones in the body. Regular practice of this "relaxation response" leads to benefits that can last all day long. When stress levels are reduced, so are blood pressure, chronic pain, sleep disorders, anxiety symptoms, and many other health problems. Clearly, health—both mental and physical, not to mention spiritual—is enhanced as a result.

SCIENCE, PRAYER, AND THE PLACEBO EFFECT

From the viewpoint of a person who prays, prayer occurs on the spiritual level. It feeds the mind which, in turn, affects the body. But from a scientific point of view, the spiritual level is not applicable. And until recently, even the power of the mind over the body was not recognized as a valuable treatment mode by the scientific community.

It has always been standard research practice that, during studies to test the effectiveness of a medication, some study participants are administered the real treatment, while others are given *placebos*—fake pills or treatments—without their knowing it. If the treated individuals get better, and the ones on the placebos don't, the researchers can rather safely claim that the treatment is effective. But there is usually a glitch in the process. Most often, a certain percentage of the study participants who have been on the placebos actually improve in health.

For over fifty years, researchers dismissed such occurrences as statistical aberrations. Coining the term *placebo effect,* they didn't bother to investigate the reason why these people were getting better, and certainly didn't acknowledge that there was a powerful treatment method right before their eyes—the *body-mind connection.* It wasn't until the alternative health movement toward the end of the twentieth century that the body-mind connection was credited as a viable path to better health. Now we know that when people *believe* that they will get better, sometimes they do! And prayer certainly taps into this connection. As human beings, our minds partake in all of our activities, including prayer. So prayer affects the mind, and the mind influences the body.

The inflexibility behind the long-term refusal to recognize the mind-body connection is perhaps the same inflexibility that keeps many in the scientific community from touting the power of prayer today. It is easier, and more advantageous, for science to stick to physical, controllable solutions. Such methods work within the conventional model of science. But, as the next section reveals, the very principles of traditional science's approach to biology and physics—indeed, to the entire universe—are now being called into question through the study of quantum physics.

> *"We know that sensory experience and thoughts can affect neurochemistry and that the body's neurochemical system affects and is affected by other biochemical systems, including the hormonal and immune systems. Thus, there is probably a great deal of truth to the claim that a person's hopeful attitude and beliefs are very important to their physical well-being and recovery from injury or illness."*
>
> From "The Placebo Effect," in *The Skeptic's Dictionary*,
> Robert Todd Carroll

A QUANTUM LEAP

In general, the scientific principles on which we base our understanding of the universe is part of what is called Newtonian/Cartesian physics. This branch of science poses theories that help us comprehend how the physical world works. You are probably getting flashbacks to your high-school science teacher's blackboard drawings of atoms, complete with protons, neutrons, and electrons. But don't worry. There is no surprise quiz at the end of the chapter—just perhaps some surprising insights!

Newtonian/Cartesian physics bases its theories on observation and mathematical formulations. For many years, this system has predominated our way of understanding the universe. In fact, for quite some time, it seemed as though Newtonian/Cartesian physics was on the verge of uncovering the very secrets of the universe. After all, it was even able to figure out the structure of an atom! Everything seemed to have an inherent order; everything seemed explainable! However, a problem was developing—quantum physics.

Quantum physics goes one level deeper, into the *sub*atomic world. Yes, beyond the world of atoms there is a whole other story—one made up of bits of energy that *don't* follow an inherent order. With the advent of powerful computer imaging, this field has only blossomed. Researchers have found that the tiny, subatomic particles arise and dissolve unpredictably—without an observable pattern, from some unobservable background or matrix. At this level, the old scientific models don't work. Observation and mathematical formulations just can't apply to every system. That comes as no surprise to those who place credibility in prayer. To them, arguments that we can't *prove* prayer's effectiveness through observation, or record how prayer actually works, can easily be diffused by the fact that the power of prayer exists outside of the Newtonian/Cartesian model.

Within this world of subatomic matter, we can only define an unexplainable occurrence—for example, the disappearance of a particle at one energy level, and its reappearance at another—as a *quantum leap*. A quantum leap requires an acceptance that some things can never be fully explained by current scientific law. And that's not very different from the *leap of faith* that prayer requires. In the end, perhaps the practice of prayer effects a quantum leap of its own kind. It takes us, spontaneously and unexplainably, into the realm of spiritual energy.

> *"You and your environment are one. . . . In quantum terms . . . the distinction between 'solid' and 'empty' is insignificant. Every cubic centimeter of quantum space is filled with a nearly infinite amount of energy, and the tiniest vibration is part of vast fields of vibration spanning whole galaxies."*
>
> From *Ageless Body, Timeless Mind*, Deepak Chopra, MD

CONCLUSION

After reading this chapter, it is difficult to doubt that prayer is a healthy practice. It is also heartening to see that science and prayer are not as far apart as they once seemed. Prayer is being studied now more than ever.

However, it should also be considered that, at this point, science is not fully equipped to attain all the answers to all the questions, including how and why prayer is so effective. The fact that something cannot be explained by observation or computation does not signify that it is not valid. Prayer works, whether or not we know why it works.

If so much information confirms the benefits of prayer, why is it that so many people *don't* pray? Let's turn next to that interesting subject. Chapter 3 discusses several deep-seated reasons why an individual might find it difficult to turn to prayer, hopefully illuminating any stumbling blocks that might stop you from furthering your prayer life.

3

Why Don't We Pray?

If prayer has so many benefits, as discussed in Chapter 2, why doesn't everyone pray? Why is it such a struggle to pray at times? Why is it so easy to forget to pray, to make prayer a last priority, perhaps even to doubt prayer?

In identifying why people don't pray, we can trace most reasons back to fear. The remaining reasons have to do with the busy nature of our lives, the pride we face as people influenced by "rugged individualism," and plain old lack of faith. This chapter studies common reasons why people might not pray, and also suggests some viable solutions. You might find yourself saying, "Oh, yeah! I do that!" and "Hey, that could help!" If so, good for you! You are being honest with yourself and looking critically at your spiritual state. That's a necessary step in developing the prayer life that you desire.

FEAR

You might be surprised to discover how many hindrances to prayer life are firmly rooted in fear. For example, some people avoid prayer because they don't feel worthy of communicating with a perfect God. That translates into fear of inferiority in the face of an angry and unforgiving deity. Some people don't pray because they think it may be a waste of their time. That translates into fear that either they can't pray effectively, or that God doesn't care enough to listen. Some people don't pray because they are uncomfortable with the vulnerability that comes with opening themselves wholly up to God. That's a fear of intimacy. The good news is that people can overcome these fears. The following discussions look at the most common fears that prevent people from praying, and explain how you can redirect the energy lost on fear into a courageous and vibrant prayer practice.

> *"Fearlessness is indispensable for the growth of the other noble qualities. How can one seek Truth, or cherish Love, without fearlessness?"*
>
> Mahatma Gandhi

Fear of Inferiority

As human beings, we are as capable of shame, embarrassment, and low self-esteem as we are of pride, arrogance, and egotism. If you are like most people, there are times when you feel too ashamed to pray. Perhaps you feel that you haven't given sufficient attention to God to warrant His response in a time of need. Or perhaps you regret certain behaviors or events and, as a result, doubt your relationship with God. You may even go so far as to ask others to pray for you, but don't feel justified in asking for help yourself. You just can't find "the gall"—so you think—to ask for personal aid. How can you conquer these fears of inferiority?

Gaining a New Perspective

Throughout history, people have forged ahead through their feelings of inadequacy and self-disappointment by forming an image of God that helps them feel closer to Him. You may find some of these images helpful too. Two of the most common ways to feel greater closeness to God involve imagining Him as a loving parent, and visualizing Him as a spouse or intimate friend. You might call this process the *personification* of God—assigning to God the attributes of a human. Of course, God is not human, but picturing Him as a familiar person in a familiar scene may help you to understand God in *some* way, which is better than not understanding Him at all. And God, being All Things, does embody the qualities that would come with parenting and friendship, so it makes sense to use such images.

Many traditions, such as Judaism and Christianity, encourage the conceptualization of God as a loving parent. While God may act as judge, God is also a compassionate life-giver who seeks the betterment, not the harm, of His creatures. So let's build a story about a loving father and his child—a story that will help us examine the fear of being unworthy to pray.

Imagine a gentle father who simply adores his little girl. In fact, he recently spent quite some time and effort choosing a wonderful toy for that child, and gave it to her as a birthday gift. She has been enjoying it very much. However, the child does not realize her own strength, nor the fragility of the toy. One evening, while sitting on her porch, the little girl accidentally breaks a piece off the toy during play, and the toy no longer works properly.

The child understands that the toy was a gift from her dad, and a gift that he gave her so that she could have pleasure. She realizes that her dad is standing on the porch steps, watching her, and that he has witnessed her breaking of the toy. The little girl feels guilty and ashamed. Furthermore, she grows fearful that her father will yell at her, or that he will consider her a careless ingrate and never give her another toy.

Would that dad want the little girl to feel that way? Would he think such things of a child who simply did not know how to pace her actions and control her own strength? He'd probably be more inclined to share her disappointment and help her fix the toy. Meanwhile, the child learns to be gentler. Her failure to pace her actions was destructive to *her* life, not directly destructive to her father's life. The little girl is the one who suffers, and she is also the one who learns the lesson.

Place God in the parent's position, and place yourself in the girl's position. If you've broken something—a promise, a heart, a value, or anything else—you are the one who carries the disappointment and anger, not God. You are the one who is harmed by the ensuing events. God is calling you into communication, not pushing you away. You, in turn, must be receptive, just as the little girl simply has to be receptive to the parent's hugs and comfort after making a clumsy mistake.

We draw on a Hassidic Jewish concept—and also a Christian and Muslim mystical tradition—when we imagine God as a spouse or intimate friend. Again, let's use this image to examine the fear of being unworthy to pray. It is another way of visualizing God to make Him more familiar, and therefore more accessible in spite of our personal weaknesses.

Pretend that you are driving with an aging spouse. Your partner is anxious about a less-than-perfect health report just received from the doctor. He is completely preoccupied with this sign of aging and, in his agitation, he is not driving particularly well. He hits the curb and sends a hubcap flying off a wheel of the car—that is, the family's *new* car.

Because love brings calm and clarity, you understand that your partner didn't intentionally damage the car. He wasn't trying to upset *you.* He was so racked with anxiety that he did not perform his best at that moment. Let's assume that you are not hotheaded or obsessed with material objects—which, of course, is the case. Instead of railing at him for being an idiot, instead of heaping further insults on him about how aging has even affected his driving, you simply say that he has worked himself up into a terrible state. You tell him that he is all right, and that you will do your best to help him get through his worries—and to find the hubcap. When you truly love someone, any upset is a far second to the compassion you feel.

Now pretend that God is in the passenger seat and that you are the shaky spouse. So you've made a mess of a wheel; so you've gotten off track when it comes to certain things in life. God understands it all, because God is in you, experiencing what you are experiencing. There is no shame in mistakes; they are in the past. There is no excessive guilt in the face of perfect love, only repentance and forgiveness.

> *"A lover never seeks without being sought by his beloved.*
> *When the lightening bolt of love has pierced this heart,*
> *be assured that there is love in that heart.*
> *When the love of God grows in your heart, beyond any*
> *doubt God loves you."*
>
> From *Masnavi* III: 4393–4396, Jalal Al-Din Rumi

God is perfect and complete, not subject to destruction by human weaknesses or by offenses. You need not fear that God will react like an angry person; God is not an angry person, nor is He spiteful. In a perfect love, who or what could be spiteful? God exists in a bigger context than the mistakes we've made in our pasts, and encompasses more than the here and now. So do not hesitate to pray. *Whatever* has occurred in your life, you are worthy of turning to prayer.

Of course, imagining God as a compassionate person doesn't even begin to touch the entirety of God's nature. But it might give you the push you need to gain courage and pursue the practice of prayer. It is necessary to make the following point: Don't confine yourself to images of a masculine God if that doesn't work for you. Don't feel it is necessary to picture God primarily as a teacher if you have had bad experiences

Imagination Gone Amuck

While the act of imagining sometimes helps spark our spiritual energy, and can make God seem more accessible and loving, it is not helpful to continually rely on fantastical images and stories as the basis of your relationship with God. In *Thoughts in Solitude*, Thomas Merton reminds us, "If we depend too much on our imagination and emotions, we will not turn ourselves to God but will plunge into a riot of images and fabricate for ourselves our own home-grown religious experiences, and this too is perilous." So it is important to keep a state of clarity in your spiritual life. By all means, use you creative gifts to communicate with God in ways that you find effective. But also maintain a level-headed awareness of God. Avoid indulging in understandings of God that bend to your every desire. There will be no spiritual growth or challenge in a prayer life based solely on fantasy and fabrication.

with authority figures. At the outset of your prayer practices, choose images that are healthy for *you*. (For a further discussion of imaging God, see Chapter 8.)

Fear of Weakness and Failure

Perfectionism is pathological these days. So many of us have a paralyzing fear of making a mistake, of creating a mess. It's actually painful for some of us to ask for help. Do any of these questions sound familiar: If I turn to God, does that mean I'm too weak to handle things sufficiently? And if I do pray, but I don't do it right, am I only making things worse? If these questions strike a chord, the fear of weakness and failure may be hindering your spiritual growth.

Gaining a New Perspective

To overcome obstacles posed by the fear of seeming weak, it is vital to first realize that none of us is meant to be completely on our own. We are social creatures. The soul actively seeks completion through union with God and other beings. Therefore, it's not a sign of weakness and failure to turn to God in prayer. Quite the contrary, it's a step forward, for in doing so,

> *"Instead of worrying about the worthiness or orthodoxy of your prayer, instead of stewing over your failure to be perfect, think positively. Turn to a higher level of interaction with God. Believe in his presence and enjoy him."*
>
> From *Enjoy the Lord: A Path to Contemplation,* John Catoir

you lose some of the egotistical delusions of control that are so damaging to the body, mind, and spirit. In fact, praying to God is a sign of courage; it shows that you are open enough to rely on more than the sturdy self.

Second, it is a mistake to believe that there is a right way to pray and a wrong way to pray. Prayer does not have to be eloquent; it requires no fancy rhetoric and no advanced degrees. It is silence as much as words; movement as much as stillness. Furthermore, you don't have to get down on your knees to catch God's attention, nor do you have to say a set number of formulaic prayers to obtain favors. If you choose prayer techniques that involve these methods, that's fine. But you are not "messing up" if you don't mimic the prayer agenda of another person. The only way that your prayers will be effective for you is if they are truly *your* prayers. You inherently know how best to communicate with your God. Trust yourself. Realize that you can't fail at prayer. Any honest attempt at communication with God will be beautiful.

During a discussion at Gethsemani Monastery, the Dalai Lama suggested that anyone who fears he can't pray—who thinks "I can't do this," "I'm not skilled enough to do this," or the like—should reflect on ideas that encourage the soul. For example, he recommends that Buddhists ponder the notion that they contain *Buddha-nature.* This is somewhat akin to Judaism's concept of a divine spark in everything, as well as the Christian view that the Holy Spirit is alive in each one of us. Acknowledging Buddha-nature can embolden an individual, infusing her with confidence in her abilities to continue her spiritual journey. Another option the Dalai Lama suggested is that the Buddhist concentrate on the good situation at hand—that she has the time and the luxury to sit in meditation and work toward enlightenment. The simple fact that she exists in this lifetime, capable of growing closer to nirvana, is heartening. Similarly, every Jew, Christian, and Muslim can inspire herself with thoughts of God's constant presence and ever-flowing grace. Dwelling on such positive notions about her own capacities to tap into the Divine can help a person overcome fears of weakness and failure.

Mother Teresa once had a reporter run up to her and spurt out a rather awkward question: "Are you a saint?" Poking the man gently in the chest, she replied, "Yes, and so are you!" Mother Teresa's confidence in each person's spiritual strength teaches us that God does not discriminate. He doesn't keep report cards. What counts is not how much help you have to ask for, or how many words you say, but how much sincerity and love permeate your prayers. If you are already so precious and successful in God's eyes just by being you, how can you fail at prayer?

Fear of the Unknown

In his book *Recovering the Soul: A Scientific and Spiritual Search*, Larry Dossey, MD, coins the term *spiritual agoraphobia*. Much like psychological agoraphobia, which is a fear of open places, spiritual agoraphobia is the fear of the vast openness and selflessness of realizing "nonlocal mind." By *nonlocal mind*, Dossey means an aspect of ourselves that is beyond our earthly notions of time and space. Nonlocal mind, which we all possess, can access the Infinite and communicate on a higher level. Perhaps we can call it the soul. And it's the soul that takes action in prayer. Many people are afraid to pray because prayer calls us to enter into the vast and powerful space of the soul. In that space, we are not bound by the familiar laws of the physical world. As a result, some individuals anticipate feeling lost and vulnerable during prayer.

Gaining a New Perspective

To help quell fears of travelling the unknown in prayer, try to focus on prayer as remembrance, as described in Chapter 1. In that chapter, we discussed how prayer calls us to a re-awakening of something that we've always known—something of which we have always been a part, and is forever a part of us. So it makes sense to approach prayer as if it is a road home. Although it is not tangible or visible, the spiritual life *is* your home. Your intuition is calling you back to something fundamental and familiar. In developing this trust, and in entering prayer with this confidence, you are bound to chip away at notions of the spiritual realm as a large unknown.

To illustrate this solution, let's look at the story of Elizabeth, a teacher who leads a very routine-oriented life. Elizabeth is the type of person who does not like change or surprises; she desires the comfort of a set schedule and full knowledge of anything in which she gets involved. When Elizabeth became interested in strengthening her prayer life, one of the things that hindered her most was the fact that she hadn't previously been taught *how* to pray, nor could she know just where her prayers went, what they did, or how they worked. Essentially, she felt a loss of control, and it made her nervous enough to avoid praying.

Then Elizabeth went to a lecture on Zen Buddhism. During the discussion, she learned that in Zen teaching, enlightenment is considered a reawakening—a shedding of delusion, and the *recovery* of sight. She learned that the truth about ourselves and the world lies deep within us from the start, and that each of us inherently holds the power to access that truth. Hearing that she already had the capacity for the insight necessary to grow in her spirituality, Elizabeth felt less vulnerable in approaching prayer. She trusted that whether she was reciting fixed words or simply thinking about God's presence, she would be just fine.

In addition to viewing prayer as a road home, you can help yourself become more comfortable with the spiritual side of life by praying in ways that come easiest to you. While it is always helpful to have a mentor or to learn from others' examples, be true to yourself and enter into prayer in ways that *you* find particularly appealing. For example, if you like nature and feel close to the Divine when in natural settings, dedicate some time to God by walking through a forest or strolling on the beach. Simply become aware of the Divine Presence in that familiar setting. You don't have to imagine your prayers going up to a distant, unfamiliar realm; Heaven or Paradise is as much here and now as it is in the future or beyond the universe. You don't need to pressure yourself to delve into the mysteries of existence; just enjoy the moment at hand, for it, too, is infused with spiritual energy. By allowing yourself to see God in what is most beautiful and familiar, you may be able to conquer your fear of entering the space of the soul.

Think about how a child often hates to go to sleep at night. A toddler will struggle to stay awake because she fears what will happen when she closes her eyes and drifts away. She's afraid that Mommy will disappear, or that something will harm her. Even the expression "to *fall* asleep" communicates a certain vulnerability or instability. But as the child grows, she realizes that sleep is a natural part of the day, and that sleep feels great! The benefits of sleep are unmatched, and it becomes as vital as breathing and eating. On a metaphorical level, isn't prayer like sleep? At first, you may feel afraid to go into it on your own. Will your regular life disappear? Will you have to change? Will you find out things that you don't want to know? With time, you will realize that prayer is a natural part of your day, and that prayer feels great! The benefits of prayer become unmatched, and it will become central to your spiritual health.

Furthermore, there is no need to place heavy demands on yourself, such as long prayer sessions or expectations of the paranormal. Start small, conducting brief prayer sessions in which you talk to God as though you were talking to another human. Work on letting go of super-stitions. Visions and fitful ecstasies are not the norm. God doesn't want to scare you; He won't surprise you with flying objects or allow you to drown in some immaterial dimension. God has always been with you and in you, and you have always had access to the soul's space. Prayer doesn't lead you into anything brand-new. Instead, it allows you to turn your full attention back to a part of you that you've always held inside.

Fear of Being Disappointed

Perhaps you have tried prayer—you have sincerely and devotedly asked God for help—and you found the answer unsatisfying, or you received no answer at all. After a disappointment in life, it is natural to shy away from reliance on the source of that disappointment. In order to avoid repeating that awful letdown, you might very well hesitate to be hopeful again. So if your past prayers weren't answered in the ways you expect-ed, you may fear that, at best, prayer really won't do much good, and, at worst, prayer will end up hurting and disappointing you.

And maybe the fear of disappointment doesn't even come from a past prayer experience. Perhaps someone you trusted ended up disappointing or betraying you. Now you are supersensitive when it comes to relin-quishing control and putting yourself in another's care—even in God's care. What can you do to relieve this hesitancy?

Gaining a New Perspective

To dissolve the fear of being disappointed, consider two steps. First, realize that God is not human. Therefore, He is not fickle or subject to emotional whims. He is not selfish and therefore prone to betrayal. The relationship that is fostered through prayer is not vulnerable to changes in loyalty. God's presence is unwavering and the love of God is unconditional, but you must allow yourself to be receptive to it. If you have one set notion of how God should reveal an answer, you are working at a disadvantage. You are trying to control God and to script your future. That brings us to the second step.

Remind yourself that prayer doesn't change the world to suit the individual's needs. It changes the person who prays, widening her perspective and developing the insight necessary to change things for the better. Don't set yourself up for disappointment by viewing prayer as a magic formula that will produce the white rabbit if you wave the wand just so. Certainly have confidence that God will hear you and help you, but avoid thinking that your immediate desires are definitely what should be heeded. God is goodness and love. He will provide what is necessary for the continued creation of your world and the entire universe, if you ask. But that doesn't mean that you will immediately see, hear, or understand God's answers. Be patient, and trust that God is working within you, tending to the problems and the wonders at hand.

> *"Everything we need for growing into a full, rich relationship with God is already available in our lives. We just need to pray, stay open, and not become discouraged."*
>
> From *Jewish Spiritual Guidance: Finding Our Way to God*,
> Carol Ochs and Kerry M. Olitzky

If you think about it, were every prayer of every prayer practitioner to yield the requested outcome, the world would be a mess. Utter chaos and contradiction would arise from the indulgence of everyone's desires. We have to trust that there's a bigger, better plan unfolding, of which we are a part. As a force of love and goodness, God is tending to both your heart and the universe all at once. That's why you are bound to face times when things don't turn out the way you think or feel they should at that moment. But if you enter into prayer with a receptive and open mind—with an attitude of "Thy will be done" instead of "My will be done"—you won't be so disappointed. With this approach, instead of demanding a specific outcome, you will pray, "I sincerely want this to happen, but I also accept that I cannot see the entirety of what is unfolding, and I trust that You, God, will yield what is best." For more discussion on seemingly unanswered prayers, see Chapter 9. And for a little more encouragement, see "You Are Not Alone," on page 47.

Fear of Intimacy

Many people experience a fear of getting too close to God through prayer. Prayer might work too well, making God a vibrant presence in daily life! For some, it feels a little like Big Brother is watching. Are you a bit frightened to let God in? Intimacy often means responsibility, and that can be scary. And an all-knowing, ever-present God is definitely intimate with you. He is there at every fight, every gossip session, every embrace. What happens if you don't feel ready for this Presence?

Gaining a New Perspective

Fear of intimacy with God should be handled like any other fear of intimacy. Don't overwhelm yourself with demands; start slowly and learn trust in God. Begin by imagining God as a friendly, caring Force that will help you make good decisions and find peace. If you believe that God is within you and acting through you, it won't feel like you are performing in front of a hidden camera. Rather, it will feel as though you are listening to, and being true to, the deepest part of yourself.

If you are just beginning your prayer journey, give yourself some slack. Pray in a place where you don't feel too alone. You might consider praying with a group at first, and then gradually working into a personal prayer practice. You might start by making an effort to bless people in passing and to thank God at random times throughout the day, and then eventually work up to sessions in which you sit in silence and become more introspective. Perhaps you want to consider using prayer aids—soft music and calming incense—to keep tension at a minimum. Keep reminding yourself that God has been with you and in you at all times, and that prayer time is just a full turning of your attention to that aspect of your life. And rest assured that as you continue to practice prayer, you will become more familiar with your God. He will turn out to be like an old friend, a close confidant, with whom it is pleasing to dwell. You are likely to make changes in your life as a result of prayer, but those changes will be a natural result of better insight and desire, not of fear and pressure.

Fear of Silence and Stillness

Our fast-paced world does everything in its power to cheapen silence and stillness. We become restless at lulls in conversation. We dismiss amusement rides that don't plummet at top speeds. We turn on the television or CD player the moment we enter the house. So it's pretty easy to feel a little nervous about personal prayer. It often involves quiet—maybe even silence—and stillness. Do you anticipate boredom? Are you afraid of coming face to face with emptiness? Are you nervous that upsetting or even frightening thoughts will flood your mind? If so, you're not alone. Yet there are many ways to initially to diminish that silence and, over time, to learn to revel in the stillness and peace of prayer.

Gaining a New Perspective

The truth is that many of us are more comfortable making noise, because external sound masks the inner cries that we want to avoid. It's time to be honest and face those cries. Silence and stillness can take some getting used to. However, through them, we learn how to heal ourselves and our world, as well as to truly enjoy life. We have to familiarize ourselves with silence and stillness, just as we have to familiarize ourselves with the layout of a new house or the movements of a new dance. Always keep in mind, though, that God never leaves us empty, and prayer is always done in God.

Comfort with the quiet and stillness of prayer comes with practice and time. But it's worth it. Subtleties of experience arise in silence and stillness, which are both therapeutic and spiritually energizing. In moments of quiet and calm, our bodies, minds, and spirits recharge, reorder, and remember. You may find that your creativity blossoms, that you come up with wonderful ideas. You will return to daily life refreshed and invigorated. To help you achieve that comfort, here are a few ideas.

If stark silence is too much to start with, consider diminishing the severity of the silence with quiet background music. As you begin your prayer session, click on a pleasant, calming CD or cassette. Some effective types of music are quiet chants, religious hymns, or even some classical or New Age music that you find meditative. Another option is to pray outdoors, where there are sounds of nature. You might like to hear the lapping of the ocean or a lake, or the rustle of wind in the trees. This will reduce any nerve-wracking notions of isolation. Of course, if you reside in a crowded urban center, this may not be a possibility. In such a case, a recording of nature sounds might put you in a pleasant state of mind.

If feelings of restlessness keep you from enjoying stillness, you may want to practice forms of prayer that involve bodily movements. Perhaps prayer gestures, like bowing and prostrations, would help you feel less tense during prayer. Or perhaps dance would help you express certain feelings and frustrations. Even a slight swaying and the quiet singing of your prayers might make prayer time a little easier.

Lastly, if the silence of prayer troubles you, consider starting with fixed prayers—prayers that have already been written and with which you may already be familiar. Whether you read the prayers out of a book

You Are Not Alone

In her videotaped interview with Father Jim Caffrey, "On Prayer," Sister Briege McKenna tells a beautiful story of trust and faith. It reminds us not to mistake *feeling* alone with *being* alone. God is always there; He will not abandon or disappoint us. In turn, we should make efforts to be trusting, patient, and brave.

A young Native American came of age and now faced an initiation ceremony. The rite of passage would induct him into the tribe as a man. The test was to go deep into the forest as night approached, and to sit on the ground, remaining still, until the sun came up. The boy was not allowed to bring a companion or weapons, but had to survive on his own. It was a test of courage and will. As night continued and the boy sat still in the pitch black of the forest, he endured the presence of wild animals, the strange smells, the unknown sounds. He was terrified, but he remained.

With the first wisps of dawn, the young man's vision was restored. And there, in front of him, was his father. In fact, his father had been there throughout the night, waiting and watching. All that time, the boy had thought he was alone, but there behind the veil of darkness was a loving and protecting parent.

God is like that parent. As we endure this earthly life, we can't see or touch God in the ways that we sometimes desire. It's so easy to feel alone and disappointed in the emptiness that seems to surround us. But God is there, behind the veil. And if you open yourself up to His aid, He will help in times of need.

or recite them from memory, the readiness of words may make the quiet less intimidating.

Fear That Personal Requests Are Too Insignificant

Considering that so many people in the world have overwhelming problems—problems like starvation, illness, and poverty—do you feel a little petty asking God to help you do well in a new job, or to guide you in patching things up with a friend? If so, you share in a common assumption that your personal problems are too small to even be considered by a "big" God. Perhaps you are afraid that asking for help will demonstrate selfish audacity. Maybe you even fear that the requests will be dismissed—that God will give you the cold shoulder because you were self-centered enough to ask for his assistance. Does this sound familiar?

> *"God is Infinite. He has the capacity to have an ongoing individual relationship with every human being on the planet."*
>
> Aish HaTorah (Fire of the Torah)

Gaining a New Perspective

Remind yourself that God is not human. God doesn't turn His attention away from you to hear another's prayers. He is not characterized by an attention span that can be short or long, depending on mood and subject matter. The reason that God is so sublime is that He is everywhere at once, permeating everything at all times. He is a personal God—existing inside you, solely for you—as well as a transcendent God.

Think of how the sun shines down from the sky. If you go out on a Saturday morning and bask in the sun, does that diminish the sun? Is that a selfish act? Not at all! You are taking appreciative advantage of a wonderful source of warmth and light. That's why it's there! Are you too insignificant for the sun to reach? Not at all! You can feel its healing power right away. Are the millions of people on earth ranked in importance, with some warranting more sunlight than others? Not at all! Every person has her own experience of or relationship with the sun.

Well, God is like the sun, and practicing prayer is like laying out in the sun. Prayer doesn't drain a limited source of mercy; God is unlimited. And if God is shining in your spiritual sky, why would you refuse to accept the gift? It won't take away from anyone else's experience of God. God is shining in their personal universes just as powerfully and completely as in yours. You have your very own relationship with Him that exists independently of others' relationships with Him. God's love and mercy is not allotted or rationed out. It is always overflowing with plenty.

OTHER REASONS WHY PEOPLE DON'T PRAY

As discussed above, fear—fear of inferiority, of intimacy, of silence, of any number of things—is one of the chief reasons that people don't pray.

But there are other reasons why people avoid, postpone, or reject the practice of prayer. Fortunately, like fear, these roadblocks can usually be overcome, freeing you to enjoy a rewarding spiritual life.

Lack of Time

Do you cringe at the thought of fitting yet another commitment into your daily schedule? Are you already sleep-deprived and continually harried? If so, you may not pray for the simple reason that you don't have a solid hour of "self" time available to reserve for prayer each day. You may not even have thirty minutes! And your schedule is so unpredictable that you can't possibly "pencil in" prayer sessions during the week.

Unfortunately, some people deprive themselves of prayer's benefits because of an all-or-nothing philosophy: "If I'm going to pray, then I'm going to do it right—long, quiet, uninterrupted sessions with flawless focus. If I can't make that commitment, it's just not worth it." And there are always occurrences that prevent such a stringent commitment. There are sick parents to tend to, children to feed, overtime to put in, bills to pay, friends to counsel, and much, much more. So where does that leave prayer?

Gaining a New Perspective

First, it is very important to shed the notion that prayer has to claim an extensive period of time, or even that there is a right way and a wrong way to pray. Sure, you will find that some prayer techniques are more effective than others. And you may find that prayer is best when you are able to enjoy an extended period of quiet and stillness. But just because you cannot arrange a daily, hour-long, solitary session doesn't mean that you should give up the entire practice. It's okay to fit prayer into your day at any time, in any place, in any way, for any duration. Once you adopt this perspective, you'll find that there are countless prayer opportunities. You may start praying more than you ever thought you would!

For example, think about all the time that you spend alone in the car, driving to work, to the supermarket, to the library, to campus—whatever applies to you. These moments can be used to say a few beautiful fixed prayers, or just to converse with God as you would with a friendly passenger. Perhaps you'd even like to play a few hymns and sing along. Or maybe you'd like to observe some of the people in the cars around you and bless them, finding a connection with the divine spark in each of them. These are all forms of prayer—and perfect forms, at that!

How about practicing awareness of God, and maybe even articulating some of your personal thoughts and needs to Him, during your morning jog? How about taking a few minutes to thank God for the good food as you prepare dinner, and to say a couple of blessings for the food animals and the crop harvesters that took part in providing it? Such activities keep you in conscious communication with God, and *that* is prayer. Prayer does not have to take a long time to perform. Prayer can be spontaneous, improvised, and brief.

You may also want to reconsider your life schedule, and then attempt to give prayer a higher priority. As you read through this book, you will realize the amazing power of prayer. It has the ability to make you a happier, healthier person. Once you begin to practice prayer regularly, you may even find that prayer brings with it a calm and clarity that make you more effective as you go about your daily activities. So shifting things around to reserve a prayer space several times during the week—or even once a week—is definitely worth the effort.

PRIDE

Many people, especially those raised on the American ideal of self-sufficiency, tend to take the maxim "Physician, heal thyself" a little too seriously. Our culture glamorizes the notion of personal independence. A hero is a stalwart man who doesn't cry and never asks for help. The woman who redeems her gender is the one who succeeds on her own, and outdoes the person sitting next to her, as well. And so we are convinced that if we are really worth anything, we'll be able to manage things without the aid of others. Therefore, we sometimes force ourselves to go it alone. That's an ideal that is destructive to every part of life, including spirituality. It fosters the belief that we shouldn't need God, and certainly shouldn't need prayer.

Gaining a New Perspective

To overcome pride that keeps you from a more active prayer life, take a critical look at severe self-sufficiency. The "rugged individualism" that has been cited as the pathway to the American dream can actually do harm. When the individual assumes that she is in this life by herself and for herself, she places limits on her growth. Such extreme pride diminishes the human experience. Much enrichment is gained from establishing and enhancing relationships. This is true not only of relationships with other people, but also of relationships with God.

Through the relationship with God that is created in prayer, you will reap countless benefits. Prayer has an unmatched ability to fill you with good, wholesome energy. It brings possibility, hope, insight, and knowledge. Your work will be more productive. Your outlook on life will be more optimistic. You will notice more beauty and experience more fulfillment. Egocentric pride can deprive you of these gifts.

If you find yourself too proud to pray, think about your inextricable link to the many people and creatures of this world. Think about how almost everything you do involves something that someone else has contributed. At work, do you use a computer or other machinery? Someone designed that machinery, and someone fixes it when it breaks. Do you keep in touch with friends through the mail? Someone makes the paper that you write on, and someone delivers that mail. You can think of endless examples. Just give yourself a minute or two, and notice how the efforts of others flood into your mind. No matter how independent we think we are, we depend on the earth and its creatures, on mutual respect, on natural law, and on a benevolent creative force.

The truth is that we need God. We need the way God accepts us through a child's smile. We need the way God holds us in a mother's hug. We need the way God nourishes us through the fruits and vegetables of the land. We need the way God speaks to us in the beauty of music and the breath of the wind. Acknowledging God and dependence on His creations does not diminish the power of the individual. It enhances the individual by making her a key part of a brilliant project—an irreplaceable, precious member of a divine family.

LACK OF FAITH

If you chose to pick this book up and to become involved in its subject matter, then you probably don't suffer from a complete lack of faith. Something has attracted you to God, and you have invested some sort of confidence in prayer. But some people have no faith. They possess no belief in a God with whom they can develop a relationship. In fact, some possess no belief in any kind of God at all. So understandably, they don't pray. What would be the use?

Gaining a New Perspective

Arguments for the existence of God are beyond the scope of this book. But even assuming that a person lacks faith, there are quite a few reasons to pray. Prayer can be viewed as a turning to the highest level of the self—the most profound and creative part of the self. During prayer time, when attention resides in awareness of the most powerful aspects of the individual, the person who prays can find inspiration for better ideas and attain fuller understandings of herself and her world.

The practice of prayer can also be calming, and everyone can use a little more calm in their lives. Achieving a state of personal quiet and stillness, allowing the burdens of the ego to drift away, the person who prays can move closer to clarity, health, and the enjoyment of life. Prayer affords the practitioner a time, space, and fuel to reorder her personal world and renew her personal energy.

Then there is the simple truth that prayer is beautiful. As a form of art, as an avenue for the creative drive found deep within, prayer is lovely. It is like playing the piano. Each word, image, or moment of contemplation is like the striking of a key that produces a pure, wholesome sound, satisfying the heart and the senses. So the practice of prayer can be worthwhile even for the person who lacks faith in God and prayer's effectiveness. No matter which way you look at it, prayer enhances the quality of life.

CONCLUSION

Prayer is much more effective when you pray with confidence and positivity. By letting fear, too many obligations, or pride permeate your prayer life, you allow negativity to spoil your spiritual actions. But once you've shown a light on the dark reasons that keep you from praying, and once you've implemented some solutions, you wipe away the negativity. That's when you are ready to begin a balanced prayer life—and when Parts Two and Three of *How to Pray* become particularly helpful. They offer guidance and support by providing information on various types of prayer, effective prayer attitudes, and even prayer aids.

PART TWO

World Approaches

Much can be gained by studying the world's religions. Every religion has its own view of the world and of the Absolute, and its own understanding of how human beings can communicate with the Divine. Thus, each is a rich source of insight into and instruction on the practice of prayer.

There are too many spiritual approaches to allow us to tackle all of them within this book. However, Part Two discusses four of the world's major religions: Judaism, Christianity, Islam, and Buddhism. An exploration of Judaism serves as a fascinating opening to this section, as Judaism is considered the parent of Western religion and the first culture to turn wholeheartedly—in prayer and in lifestyle—to the recognition of one supreme God. Then the key elements of Christianity are considered, including the belief in a God so loving and so close that He came in human form to redeem people from sin and to teach forgiveness. The chapter on Islam studies a vibrant religion that offers expressive prayer practices that demonstrate service and devotion to its God, a Righteous Master. Finally, Part Two takes a look at the ancient tradition of Buddhism—its emphasis on liberation from suffering and ignorance largely through the discipline of mind and body.

Within each of the chapters in Part Two, you will find a summary of general beliefs about God or the Absolute, information on how prayer is viewed within the religion, and descriptions of several of the tradition's prayer techniques. Of course, this book can only scratch the surface of these ancient, complex religions. However, its purpose is not to delve into these systems of belief on a scholarly or even historical level, but to examine ideas and practices that may enhance your prayer life.

For accuracy's sake, it should be stated that Buddhism is not truly a *religion*, as there is no supreme deity under its perspective. Some scholars refer to Buddhism as a philosophy, while others call it a lifestyle. Nonetheless, Buddhism is included in this book because of its wonderful capacity to foster expansion of perspective, loss of ego, and union with the Truth or Absolute. Like Judaism, Christianity, and Islam, it strives toward the final goal of attaining True Knowledge and All-Consuming Love.

4

Judaism

Judaism is considered the parent of Western religion as we know it today. In fact, Jewish history dates back thousands of years before the Common Era, when the fathers of Judaism dwelled in the lands of today's Middle East and began entering into covenants with their one supreme God. The Jewish people were the first to declare belief in *monotheism*—that is, a belief in only one God. In reward for their insight, their God named them His Chosen People. He communicated specific laws by which they should abide, and, in return, promised His loyalty and protection, as well as a future homeland. From those biblical times to the present, Judaism has formed one of the most devout and developed notions of God's presence, and one of the richest prayer traditions.

A BRIEF HISTORY

Jewish tradition teaches that in biblical times, long before any written accounts of history, God spoke to Abraham, the first of the Hebrew patriarchs. God promised Abraham the land of Canaan and a long line of descendants who would be God's Chosen People. In turn, Abraham had to follow God's guidance and directions, be loyal to Him only, and have every male child circumcised. Abraham obediently followed God's instructions and came upon a safe land for his people. He was confident that God would protect the Jewish people and make them His, always.

The family history continued, with journeys toward more fertile lands, struggles for power, and internal fighting, as well as prosperity.

Abraham's lineage prospered in number and continued the covenant with God. Over hundreds of years, famine made survival difficult in the lands where Abraham's descendants—the Jewish people—resided. As a result, they ended up in Egypt and were eventually enslaved. Slavery was cruel, and the people prayed that their God, who many years before had promised them prosperity in a land of their own, would hear their cries and answer their prayers.

Finally, God spoke to Moses, a Jewish man who had fled punishment in Egypt. God asked Moses to lead the Jewish people out of slavery, and gave Moses His assurance that miraculous signs would take place to allow this event to occur. Through a series of God-ordained occurrences, the Jewish people escaped slavery and moved into the desert, where they traveled for many years in pursuit of the Promised Land. But they also had to keep to a binding set of God's commandments and a more extensive covenant. Social and personal lifestyle rules were set in stone—some believe they were *literally* set in stone, inscribed by God on large stone tablets during communication with Moses. Eventually, the Chosen People would reach their land and enjoy its fruits for a time. Due to political strife and competition, however, the land would be taken away from the Jewish people more than once. To this day, many members of the Jewish community struggle to maintain recognition of the Promised Land—which is now the country of Israel—as the Jews' inherited homeland. They also await a promised Messiah, who is destined to restore world peace for all.

Over the centuries, as an oral tradition became a written tradition, and as religious ritual became fixed, many extensions of the covenants of God and His commandments were etched out. It is important to note that there are basically four schools of Judaism in America today: Orthodoxy, which includes the mysticism-rooted Hassidic community, mentioned several times in this chapter; Conservative; Reform; and Reconstructionist. Orthodox Judaism is the most traditional, while Reconstructionist Judaism is the most liberal and altered from strict traditional observances. This chapter attempts to discuss the beliefs and practices of Judaism in general. It does not delve into the differences between the Jewish communities, but addresses what is relatively common to and accepted by the vast majority of observers of Judaism. The culture, as a whole, enjoys numerous traditions that are geared toward offering praise and thanksgiving to God. Before touching on the prayer traditions that have developed, let's look at the notion of God that arose among the earliest Jews, and is still held today.

THE CONCEPT OF GOD

At the basis of Jewish thought and culture is the oneness of God. When Judaism was born among a group of agrarian tribes, the surrounding cultures were *polytheists*—believers in many gods. The early Jewish people came to rely on their God as the Supreme and Absolute, the God who is responsible for every creation and redemption. They also understood Him as the one who acts as judge and who requires specific conduct and ethics.

The concept of God as one is inarguable in Judaism. God cannot be divided into expressions, or parts, even in mystical terms. Yet this understanding of God also makes it difficult to conceptualize Him, let alone to communicate with Him. So over the course of Jewish history, certain human attributes have commonly been assigned to God.

Lawrence Hoffman, author of *The Way Into Jewish Prayer,* describes the Jewish perspective on God wonderfully when he states that the reality of God is beyond personification. No matter what adjectives are assigned, the words cannot possibly capture the experience and the reality of Ha-Shem, the Jewish God. (Please see the inset "Naming God," found on page 58, for more information on God's various titles.) Therefore, there is no strict depiction of God in Judaism. However, different communities, prayers, and books refer to God in different ways, from Creator, to King, to Lord, to Lover, to Father, to Mothering Presence, to Redeemer, and much more. God is personified as a shepherd by some, as a warrior by others, and as both at different times. This ability to form so many different images of God demonstrates the richness of Jewish culture.

In Jewish Scriptures, God is often personified as a male parent and as a ruler over the Chosen People. However, feminine qualities are also assigned to God. The loving presence of God is actually referred to in the feminine—*Shechinah,* or sometimes, *Shekhinah.* For the Jewish people, it is important to recognize that these are human constructions of God, created in an attempt to grasp the ungraspable.

Furthermore, in Scriptures, the Jewish God shares in human emotions and in the daily lives of His people. He seems capable of love, anger, care, offense, and other qualities that we attribute to humanity. Judaism believes that God is both near and far, inherently in each of us, but also transcendent. God is infinite and always, rising above our notions of time and space, but also very involved in the history of the world and its people. So along with the singularity and sublimity that Jews attribute to their God comes a firm understanding that God hears the individual's prayers. Prayer becomes a conversation between Ha-

Naming God

Within Jewish tradition, sacred writing, prayer, and discussion, we find many different titles for God. George Robinson's *Essential Judaism: A Complete Guide to Beliefs, Customs, and Rituals* presents a comprehensive list of such terms. Here, we will review just a couple of the most commonly used names for God.

The most sacred reference to God is *YHVH,* or Yud-Hay-Vav-Hay. This holy name is never spoken aloud due to the amount of reverence it demands. When a reader comes across this name and needs to pronounce it, he substitutes the name *Adonai,* which translates into "Lord." Other titles for God used often in prayer include *Elohim,* translated simply as "God," and *El Shaddai,* meaning "God Almighty." Yet another common name is *Ha-Shem,* or *Hashem,* which translates into "The Name." Widely employed in literature and speech, Ha-Shem is considered the most acceptable title of God for use in written texts.

In general, observant Jews do not vocalize God's sacred names outside of prayer and sacred contexts. This is done to grant utmost respect to their Creator, Lord, and Judge.

Shem and His people, communally and personally. Each person has the ability to partake in dialogue with God, and is encouraged to talk to God about even the smallest of matters. That is why traditional Jews constantly bless God upon the performance of everyday activities—prior to eating, when seeing a beautiful view, upon the birth of a baby, before reading Scriptures, even after using the restroom!

The Jewish God is far more powerful than any evil force that may threaten creation. In fact, God is viewed as the only force capable of creation, and therefore is responsible for both joyous and tragic events. When an individual offends God, he must seek atonement, being personally responsible for redeeming himself. God accepts prayer as a measure of atonement. Formal prayer obligations originally replaced animal sacrifice, which once was viewed as an act of penance. Yet atonement is not the only reason the Jewish people pray to their God. They also pray to Him in sheer praise, sincere thanksgiving, and passionate petition.

Finally, the Jewish people trust that God will continue to care for their community and the world. Observant Jews believe that God will send a Messiah at some unknown time, as promised in the Scriptures. This Messiah will restore peace and justice not only to Israel—the Chosen People and their land—but also to the entire world, which is presently in disarray.

In Jewish thought, God communicates with the part of the human that is often referred to as the "soul." The parallel Hebrew term is *nashamah,* meaning breath. The soul is the part of each person that God will take at death, and perhaps return to a body in the afterlife. It is the part that possesses God's divine energy. There are no strict beliefs spelled out on what happens after death. Of course, certain communities favor certain beliefs. But as a people, Jews do not hold one fixed picture of the life to come, and many do not believe in any afterlife at all. What the general Jewish community does confirm is God's presence among and within His people, and the power to communicate with and appeal to that presence through righteous living and through prayer.

THE CONCEPT OF PRAYER

There is an important statement to make at the outset of our discussion on Jewish prayer. Judaism is community oriented at its core. All prayers used in service and all sacred texts are geared toward the preservation, hope, faith, and love of the Jewish people, biblically referred to as the Israelites. Therefore, Jewish writers and leaders carefully highlight the idea that prayer has a strong communal purpose, and that each Jew should take part in community prayers and services. The reference to "our God," instead of "my God," in so much of Jewish prayer, communicates this constant awareness of the individual's position as a part of a whole. It also diminishes the sense of aloneness that is so destructive to the human spirit and so pervasive in today's culture.

That being said, Judaism does promote a personal relationship with God. As explained previously, the Jewish tradition supports that God hears and tends to each individual. However, even when a Jewish person prays for private intentions or in an informal manner, he is to be aware that he is part of a larger group, and that his intentions reflect on the group, as well as change the group. When we study this concept of prayer, we realize that the community is essential, but that each individual's private prayers to God are also essential. Due to this emphasis on the power of prayer, prayer is an obligation as well as a gift for the observant Jew.

Where Did the Prayer Tradition Begin?

Early in Jewish history, during biblical times, prayer was spontaneous. God was petitioned and thanked whenever a person felt moved to do so. Thus, there are Bible stories that tell how the fathers of Judaism simply called out to God and asked for help. No strict prayer regimens were established; prayer was neither fixed nor guided. This continued even through the time of the First Temple in Jerusalem, which dates back several hundred years before the Common Era. Here's a little more history to fill in the gaps.

History tells us that the Jewish tribes escaped from slavery in Egypt through the favor of God. For many years they traveled the desert, until finally settling in their holy city of Jerusalem. Later, during King Solomon's reign, the First Temple was established in 957 BCE. Prayer continued to be spontaneous and personal for the average person. During particularly tough times, when a person wanted to make extra effort in prayer, he could go to the Temple and pray in its holy space. Meanwhile, the Levites—members of the tribe of Levi chosen to assist the Temple's High Priests—performed formal prayers in the form of psalms. In addition, the Temple's High Priests performed acts of sacrifice and other ritual on behalf of the Jewish people at large. But the common man performed personal prayer in an informal manner.

Although the Jews had made their home in Jerusalem, defeat of the territory led to their banishment and the destruction of the First Temple in 586 BCE. The new rulers of the territory allowed the Jews to continue to practice their faith, but dispersed them in order to weaken their strength as a community and thereby avoid organized uprisings. The Jews therefore gathered in various locations and created new centers of worship. Scholars theorize that this is when the places of Jewish study and prayer known to us as *synagogues* first started forming, although not under that particular name.

A large number of the Jewish people eventually returned to Jerusalem to take back the Promised Land. In 20 BCE, they began construction of their Second Temple, and reestablished their community life. Yet in 70 CE, the Second Temple was destroyed and a wide scattering of the community again occurred.

It was largely when the Jewish people had to conduct their worship outside of the First and Second Temples that the prayer practices that exist today began to take shape. A large part of Jewish worship in the Temple was the sacrifice of animals and food. The priests would conduct such offerings on behalf of the people, and therefore, God was *formally* worshipped through the High Priests. But when the Temples were destroyed, there was no role for the special priest class. And without the priests, the people communicated directly with God to perform their own atonement and to seek favor for the community. Formal prayer in daily and weekly life became obligatory for the preservation of the Jews, who believed that they were chosen as a group by God to bear His truths and adhere to the conduct He wishes for all humanity. Even today, while rabbis lead services and cantors lead song within synagogues, it is the power of the community—not special rites lead by clergy—that is thought to make Jewish prayer effective.

How Important Is Prayer in the Jewish Tradition?

It is a commandment from God—a *mitzvah*—for the Jewish person to conduct prayers every day. Certainly, observant Jews follow very strict prayer regimens. There are specific prayers recited a specific number of times each day. And special additional prayers are recited on holy days and during festivals. Throughout the course of history, scholars have had many disagreements regarding these obligations. For example, during the Middle Ages, Moses Maimonides (1135–1204), recognized as one of the greatest philosophers and scholars of the Jewish people, taught that the Torah—the sacred Scriptures of the Jews—requires prayer only once a day. That prayer, claimed Maimonides, should contain elements of praise, supplication, and thanksgiving, at minimum. But others have argued that set prayers are necessary during morning, afternoon, and evening, to coincide with the times that animal sacrifice was originally performed at the Temple.

As you will learn in the discussion that follows, today, observant Jews do pray three times a day by religious obligation, and enact blessings throughout the day and night according to their own spiritual observances, as well. In addition, Jewish prayer can also include informal prayer and meditation.

How Is Prayer Practiced?

The Jewish people practice both fixed and spontaneous prayer. Furthermore, some choose to pursue personal meditation practices. Whether planned or impromptu, in words or in silence, Jewish prayer is infused with respect for a loving and righteous Father.

Certain fixed prayers are assigned directly to the Chosen People under commandments given in the Torah and under Jewish law, as detailed in the Talmud. Others are selected by the individual throughout the day, in the form of blessings. Much of the cultural uniqueness of Jewish prayer life is found in the fixed prayers. These prayers necessarily take the form of words, and words are essential to the Jewish faith. They carry the history and the vibrant sense of community that is so important. Whether said aloud in a synagogue or silently "spoken," the fixed prayers that developed in Judaism remind the individual prayer practitioner of his place in a larger community. They also provide him with the comfort and support of ancient family ties and a shared spiritual energy. In addition, the fact that fixed prayers are often said in Hebrew brings a reverence to Jewish life, as Hebrew is the language of God's revelation. (For more about the importance of words, see the inset on page 63.)

The fixed prayers for daily and Sabbath use are found in the Jewish prayer book or *siddur*. Any Jewish specialty store is sure to carry a variety of prayer books. Various rabbis in various regions have compiled their own siddurs throughout history. However, there is a general consistency among all of them. Included in every siddur are the obligatory Shema and Amidah, both of which are discussed in detail later.

Observant Jews recognize three daily prayer services, which are conducted in the synagogue but also performed by some Jews at home, according to their own chosen type of observance. These include a morning service, called the *shacharit* or *shakharit;* an afternoon service, termed the *minchah* or *minkhah;* and an evening service, titled the *ma'ariv* or *ma'riv.* (Spellings vary according to dialect and source, but are usually very similar.) The shacharit is the longest service. And it is not uncommon to join the afternoon and evening services, saying them right before and right after sunset, at the same sitting.

In addition to the more formal fixed prayers, a vast array of fixed blessings is practiced by the observant Jew. There is a blessing for almost every activity that is performed throughout the day. A section on blessings is also found later in this chapter.

Because the Jewish God is not only a communal God, but also a personal God, faithful Jews practice spontaneous prayer, as well. Much as a believer of any other faith would "talk to God" for various reasons—in joy, contentment, fear, anxiety, need—a religious Jew may engage in conversational prayer with his God.

Finally, some members of the Jewish community practice meditations that have risen out of Jewish mysticism, or Kabbalah. (For a brief

The Importance of the Word

The selection and recitation of the correct words is very important to Jewish prayer. The rabbis who created the prayers made great efforts to choose the best words, avoiding superfluous praise and maintaining reverence. Many Jewish writers, leaders, and scholars clearly explain that Judaism is a "hearing" religion. It relies on hearing the word of God through Scriptures, and on interpreting the laws of God's covenant with the Jewish people through commentaries and analyses in the Talmud, the book of Jewish laws and commentaries; and the Midrash, a verse-by-verse interpretation of the Scriptures. The Talmud instructs the reader to "come and hear." Therefore, there is much emphasis placed on the power of words for people of the Jewish faith.

In *Jewish Prayer: The Adult View,* author Lisa Aiken explains that reciting the words of prayers is an important part of Jewish worship because pronouncing the words forces God and our relationship with Him to become more of a reality. To approach God in a relationship, we must strive to communicate fully and effectively. Articulating our thoughts makes us really think about what we are feeling.

The traditional language of Jewish prayer is Hebrew. It is this language that is believed to carry the most weight in prayer, as it is the language in which God revealed Himself to His Chosen People. Therefore, Jewish prayers are taught and preserved in Hebrew. That way, distortions cannot occur to the subtleties of the prayers. Even the shape of the letters and their arrangements carry significant meaning. However, in America today, many people who choose to observe Jewish prayer traditions do not speak Hebrew. Thus, numerous translations of traditional prayers and sacred books are available. In addition, the Hebrew version of prayers is often accompanied by a *transliteration*—the representation of Hebrew in the Latin alphabet—so that the words can be pronounced by people who cannot read the Hebrew language.

discussion of Kabbalah, see the inset on page 65.) Jewish meditation practices often involve listening and imaging. In *Jewish Spiritual Guidance: Finding Our Way to God*, Carol Ochs and Kerry Olitzky explain that true prayer actually brings the practitioner toward, and eventually into, silence. In fact, according to these authors, prayer's ultimate aim is the "indwelling presence of God, *Shekhinah.*" Sometimes, during this immersion, a person is moved to dance, sway, or bow. But meditative prayer is most often done in stillness. (See page 77 for more information.) Jewish meditation techniques are crucial to mystical branches of Judaism, but are not commonly practiced by the general Jewish community.

What Are the General Intentions of Prayer?

In the Jewish tradition, the general intentions of prayer are praise, termed *shevach;* petition, termed *bakasha(h)*, which includes intercession for both the practitioner and others; thanksgiving, termed *hodaya;* and confession, termed *vidui.* It is important to note that confession prayers, or prayers of atonement, are said to admit weaknesses and errors *not* for the sake of avoiding future punishment, but for personal and communal healing.

But can prayer change God's will? The Jewish faith recognizes that God's will is supreme. We cannot coerce God through bargaining or trickery. However, through proper conduct and observant living—which includes an active prayer life—a person can be spared some trouble in the world and, for those who believe in one, attain happiness in the afterlife.

Therefore, while prayer does not have the capacity to change what has already happened, nor to override the natural order of the universe, the Jewish faith generally holds that a person can petition God for guidance and aid—and receive it, if the intentions are wholly good. In *Entering Jewish Prayer,* author Reuven Hammer aptly explains this concept. According to Hammer, the Jewish God can be implored, but not compelled. If a person receives an answer to a prayer—in a direct or indirect way—it is not that he has changed God's will. Instead, his faith and prayer practices have made him capable of further interacting with God, of better handling situations, of being more receptive to God's gifts.

"Prayer is our humble answer to the inconceivable surprise of living."

From *Man's Quest for God*, Abraham Joshua Heschel

Finding Answers in Kabbalah

At various times throughout our lives—and more often for some people than others—we find ourselves exploring the "big questions." Why do I exist? Where did I come from? Where am I going? Why do beings suffer? Can I attain total peace and fulfillment in this world? These and other related explorations are addressed in Kabbalah study. Kabbalah—sometimes written as Kabbala or Cabala—is the Jewish mystical movement that arose in twelfth century Europe. This branch of Jewish thought provides a method by which the human being can grasp his position in the universe. It not only requires familiarity with the Torah and Talmud, but also prescribes numerous meditation and prayer techniques that enable the practitioner to gain greater insight into the spiritual realm.

Through Kabbalah, the practitioner seeks to understand the spiritual forces that permeate everything in the universe—how they work, and why they are occurring as they are. Language and symbolism are extremely precise in Kabbalah study, and therefore must be used very carefully. Every word, letter, number, and accent of the Scriptures is studied for the mysteries it is believed to contain. Kabbalists use material terms to describe the spiritual realm. It is important to understand that the mental images called forth by these terms do not actually exist in the spiritual realm, but are only symbols. The person who is not well studied in Kabbalah may mistake the symbols and labels for reality. That would be incorrect.

There are generally two systems of Kabbalah. The first is The Order of the Creation of the Worlds and Spirit. It studies the spiritual forces that stem from the Creator, and pass through a number of worlds before they reach our own. The second system is Comprehension or the Steps of Prophecy and Spirit. This system is concerned with the spiritual forces that are born in our world, and travel back up to the Source or Creator. The forces of the second system are reliant upon the laws of the first system, and these laws are learned during Kabbalah studies. Once the laws are understood, a person can act accordingly to fulfill his purpose in this world, which is to attain the highest understanding of all creation.

Once the practitioner achieves the knowledge of the spiritual forces—instead of merely the material forces—in everything, he can watch the visible world occurring as though he were an observer. He is said to understand suffering and even achieve perfection in this world. The Kabbalist is then able to control his own life, and is not influenced by the limits of time and space that are so anxiety-provoking for humanity. Tranquility and joy result.

While Kabbalah studies were at one point highly secretive and—due to the difficulties and intensities of the methods—taught only to very learned Jewish men after the age of forty, the practices have now been opened up and even popularized. The best known Kabbalah text is the *Zohar,* a mystical commentary on the Torah. Written by Moses de Leon in the thirteenth century, the *Zohar* is a foundational text, and is a primary source of information for those interested in learning more about Kabbalah.

While the Jewish religion generally teaches that prayer is heard by God, in some form or way, and also answered in some way, it is important to note that several of Judaism's greatest thinkers have disputed this request-and-answer role. Moses Maimonides considered prayer chiefly a meditative act that restores communion with God and enhances His relationship with His Chosen People. Maimonides was directly opposed to wordy, lengthy prayers that attempt to compel God into action with flattery. He was also opposed to prayer for the sake of request—for changing the natural order of things as laid out by God's hand. In his book *The Way Into Jewish Prayer,* Lawrence Hoffman states, "He [Maimonides] went so far . . . as to say that in principle, the only really apt prayer that describes God is pure silence."

Similarly, the founder of Hassidism, the Baal Shem Tov (1700–1760), taught that prayer can be used to communicate further with God, but that we shouldn't expect physical, earthly responses that change the natural events of time and daily living. Still, many traditional Jews feel that through prayer, some guidance and favor can be gained.

Does Jewish Prayer Involve Angels and Saints?

According to Jewish Scriptures, God has messengers who carry out specific tasks for Him. These messengers, referred to as *malakh,* might be human—such as the prophets—or might be nonhuman. As the original Scriptures were translated into Greek and then Latin, the term *malakh* was translated into "angels," and the messengers were then understood to be solely nonhuman. So the idea evolved that God does have helpers

Some Common Blessings

Blessings, or benedictions, are a large part of Jewish prayer life. They can be formal and planned, or spontaneous. It is helpful to categorize blessings into three groups: benedictions said before enjoying something material; benedictions said before performing a mitzvah, or commandment; and benedictions said at a special time or occurrence, good or bad. Below are some examples to illustrate these various types of blessings.

A blessing said before a meal would fall into the first category. An example is, "Blessed are You, O Lord, our God, who brings forth bread from the earth." A sample blessing before performing a commandment, such as the lighting of candles during a holiday or simply washing your hands is, "Blessed are You, O Lord, Our God, Who sanctified us with his commandments and commands us to _____." (Fill in the blank with the activity.) And blessings are appropriate even when bad things happen. The Jewish faith teaches that God has a hand in tragedy, as well. So a blessing upon an upsetting event might be, "Blessed are You, O Lord, Our God, the true Judge."

Author Reuven Hammer offers us some beautiful examples in *Entering Jewish Prayer.* His blessing upon waking is, "Blessed are You, O Lord our God, king of the universe, who removes sleep from my eyes and slumber from my eyelids." And he offers a wonderful blessing upon the passage of time and an era of change: "Blessed are You, O Lord, Our God, who has kept us in life, sustained us, and brought us to this season." These further illustrate how the Jewish practice of blessings calls the individual to appreciate every gift from God—to recognize God's hand in every item and every occurrence.

who relay messages to the human race, and that these helpers are super-human. Furthermore, these "angels" are divided into groups, such as the cherubim, who praised God in His desert dwelling during biblical times.

As centuries passed, it was understood that angels were most often beings of praise, and therefore were more than willing to be involved in the relaying of human prayers, as well. They could block the transmission of these prayers, or they could hurry the messages to God. This development in the belief of angel aid was heavily influenced by Christian beliefs. No set opinion of intercessory roles of angels or even helper souls is expressed in Jewish sacred literature. Therefore, it is up to the individual to decide if he believes in angels and other messengers.

Does the Jewish community pray to saints and ancestor souls? Some people who practice the Jewish faith do go to gravesites of loved ones who have passed on. There, they pray with those loved ones in mind, and some believe that they can ask the loved ones, who are perhaps in the next world, to seek favor for them. The same goes for admirable, righteous souls who have died, such as famous rabbis. Communities often are drawn to a given rabbi's works and teachings, and always make it a point to bless the soul of the rabbi when his name arises in conversation. However, there are no saints in the Jewish tradition. Jews do not pray in adoration to any souls, and definitely don't pray in front of depictions of saints. In fact, they don't even pray in front of depictions of God. No statues or icons are used, as doing so would violate the strict commandment from God that His Chosen People worship neither other gods nor images.

PRAYER TECHNIQUES

Now that we have explored the Jewish understanding of God, as well as prayer's role in a person's relationship with God, it's time to look at some techniques of and approaches to Jewish prayer. Interspersed throughout the following section are a few prayers and excerpts from prayers that you might like to add to your own practice.

Blessings or Benedictions

The largest component of Jewish prayer is the recitation of blessings—in Hebrew, b'rakhot. At home and elsewhere throughout the day, blessings such as prayers said before meals, after using the toilet facilities, or upon seeing a beautiful landscape, foster potent awareness of the gifts we are given, even though many of the blessings are just one-line prayers.

During services, many longer, paragraph-form blessings are recited. Jewish tradition teaches that a person should perform one hundred blessings per day, which seems quite overwhelming. Yet an observant Jew who recites the Amidah (see page 74) three times daily is already accomplishing fifty-seven blessings. Only forty-three to go!

It is common for a Jewish blessing, short or long, to start with *"Barukh atah Adonai,"* translated as "Blessed are you, Lord." An example of a blessing is the one said upon seeing a beautiful landscape or horizon: "Blessed are you, O Lord our God, who created the universe." Obviously, this short prayer offers recognition and thankfulness to God. The blessings used in traditional Jewish prayer are pre-composed, and Orthodox and Conservative Jews follow the law that forbids people from adding new blessings to the original list, which was finalized in the tenth century, Common Era.

The Torah leads us to believe that blessings are a part of Jewish life, performed to thank and praise God. The Talmud confirms it, stating that if man wants to enjoy this world, he is obligated to procure God's permission, as the world is God's. Without blessing the things we enjoy and experience, we violate the sanctity of creation and life. We don't acknowledge God's hand in everything, and therefore don't attain proper permission to benefit from the earth.

> *"The surest way to suppress our ability to understand the meaning of God, and the importance of worship, is to take things for granted."*
>
> Abraham Joshua Heschel

And blessings have another purpose, as well. In his essay "Feeding the Universe," Rabbi Pinchas Winston, basing his statements on the teachings of the Kabbalah, explains that the Hebrew word for blessing starts with *bait*, the letter *b*. This letter signifies the number two, which refers to increasing something. Therefore, when we bless God or something that He grants us, we ask Him to increase His Presence in our lives.

By blessing the objects, people, and events around you, you can practice prayer at any time. The Jewish tradition has encouraged this technique of increased awareness and good will by fixing blessings and making them obligatory. But many people look upon the practice not as an obligation but as a joyful endeavor. They recite the blessings simply from the gratitude in their hearts.

Sacred Reading

Judaism places great value on sacred text, especially the books of the Bible. It is believed that God talks to his people through the Bible. The words are actually the voice of God. It is not surprising, therefore, to hear that many observant Jews find both comfort and meditative wholeness through Scriptural reading as a form of prayer. It gives them a chance to simply listen to God. And listening is as much a part of prayer as speaking. The chief sources of sacred readings include the books of the Torah and the Book of Psalms.

The Torah

The term Torah is often used to refer to the entire body of text commonly called the Old Testament, and sometimes even refers to Jewish sacred literature in general. But the truest, most accurate definition of the term is the collection of the five books of the Pentateuch: Genesis, Exodus, Leviticus, Numbers, and Deuteronomy. These books are also referred to as the Five Books of Moses.

Study has always been a form of prayer for the Jewish community, and reading from the Torah is considered prayer because the material is continually studied for revelation. God gave the Torah to the forefathers of the Jewish community as a gift, to reveal their covenant with God—the rights and privileges He wished to bestow on them, and the acts He wanted them to perform in return. If they held to the covenant, they would enjoy God's promises. Learned sages and rabbis have been gifted with interpreting and expanding on the ideas contained within the Torah, and every person is encouraged to study it, as well. In this way, the Jewish people continue their conversation with God, always enhancing it or understanding it more fully.

The Torah tells a story, ultimately preparing the reader for entrance into a promised land. This is something the human being innately desires—admittance into a land blessed and bestowed by God. The Torah ends before the Jewish people reach the Promised Land, which teaches us that we are on a continual journey. It is important to at least briefly review the themes of this very crucial collection of text, which is such a vibrant part of Jewish prayer life.

Genesis discusses creation and the early Jewish people who eventually moved into Egypt from their homeland, due to famine. After hundreds of years in Egyptian enslavement, Moses begins to lead the group out of Egypt, toward a land that has been promised to them by God. The books of Exodus, Leviticus, Numbers, and Deuteronomy chronicle the experiences of the Chosen People as they move across the desert, wandering toward the Promised Land. The conclusion of the fifth book leaves off with the Israelites, or Chosen People, standing at the foot of their Israel.

The Bible continues with other books, including the Book of Joshua, which tells of the conquering of the Promised Land. But it is important to recognize that the Torah itself is about journey, suffering, and hope. It is about search and development, and teaches us patience and coping.

The Book of Psalms

It would be remiss not to mention the importance of the Book of Psalms to Jewish devotion. Because of the way it addresses so many human conditions—fear, love, joy, battle, spiritual dryness, the journey, and more—this biblical book is recognized for its timeless applicability to every human being. The Psalms are believed to have originally been written as poems to be sung in community. But as part of the Bible, and as a strikingly beautiful part at that, the Psalms have become regular pieces of study. Readers often find that when in need, their instinct is to open to a psalm that holds special meaning for them. There is always a message to be gained, a lesson to be learned, and comfort to be found. (See page 72 for the text of several psalms.)

Liturgical Prayers

The communal liturgy—the synagogue prayer service—is the center of Jewish prayer. And at the heart of the communal liturgy are two prayers, the Shema and the Amidah. These prayers, which are the main constituents of worship, can also be recited at home if a person opts for private prayer.

The Shema

This prayer is the creed or declaration of the Jewish faith. It is so important that Jewish tradition encourages a brief meditation time before the recitation of the Shema, even if just for a few seconds. In order to shut out distractions and prepare himself for this testament of faith, the Jewish prayer practitioner is encouraged to close his eyes, or to cover them with his hand, and then to dwell on the Oneness of God. At this time, he should also make himself aware of his obligations and his thankfulness to God.

From the Book of Psalms

The following excerpts will give you an idea of how diverse and how
beautiful the Bible's Book of Psalms is. It is said that there is at least
one psalm applicable to every human pain and joy. Even the limited
selection below demonstrates why these verses have universal, timeless appeal.

"How long, O Lord? Will you utterly forget me? How long will you
hide your face from me? How long shall I harbor sorrow in my soul,
grief in my heart day after day? How long will my enemy triumph
over me? Look, answer me, O Lord, my God!"

Psalms 13: 1–4

"The Lord is my shepherd; I shall not want. In verdant pastures he
gives me repose; Beside restful waters he leads me; he refreshes my
soul. He guides me in right paths for his name's sake. Even though
I walk in the dark valley I fear no evil; for you are at my side with
your rod and your staff that give me courage."

Psalms 23: 1–4

"Have mercy upon me, O God, in your goodness; in the greatness
of your compassion wipe out my offense. Thoroughly wash me from
my guilt and of my sin cleanse me."

Psalms 51: 1–4

"Praise the Lord in his sanctuary, praise him in the firmament of his
strength. Praise him for his mighty deeds, praise him for his sovereign
majesty. Praise him with the blast of the trumpet, praise him with lyre
and harp. Praise him with timbrel and dance, praise him with strings
and pipe. Praise him with sounding cymbals, praise him with clanging
cymbals. Let every thing that has breath praise the Lord. Alleluia!"

Psalms 150: 1–6

The Shema

The Shema, a prayer that is traditionally recited three times a day by observant Jews—in the morning, evening, and just prior to bedtime—is the creed of the Jewish faith. It opens with a statement of firm belief in the oneness of God, and follows with an articulation of commands that God asks of His Chosen People. The formal Shema service involves three biblical passages—Deuteronomy 6: 4–9; Deuteronomy 11: 13–21; and Numbers 15: 37–41—as well as accompanying benedictions. However, the individual prayer referred to as the Shema is simply Deuteronomy 6:4–9, and is commonly referred to as the *Shema Yisrael*.

———————◄O►———————

Hear, O Israel, the Lord is our God,
The Lord is One.

Blessed is the name of His glorious kingdom
Forever and ever.

And you shall love the Lord your God,
With all your heart, with all your soul,
and with all your possessions.
And these words which I command you
This day shall be upon your heart.

And you shall teach them to your children
And speak of them when you sit in your home,
When you walk up the way,
When you lie down and when you rise up.

And you shall bind them for a sign upon your hand
And they shall be Tefillin between your eyes.
And you shall write them
On the doorposts of your homes
And upon your gates.

The Shema is then proclaimed. It is traditionally said three times daily—in the morning, in the evening, and immediately before sleep. The full Shema service opens with the basic confession or tenets of Judaism: "Hear, O Israel, the Lord our God is One. Blessed be the name of God's glorious kingdom forever." Then it includes three paragraphs from the Torah: Deuteronomy 6: 4–9, Deuteronomy 11: 13–21, and Numbers 15: 37–41. These passages revolve around Jewish ritual, including the obligation to recite the Shema at specific times during the day. Within these passages are also the commandments—or mitzvahs—to wear prayer pieces called *tefillin* (discussed on page 87); and to erect on each doorpost a small object called a *mezuzah*, which contains Torah passages. See the inset on page 73 for a translation of the version of the Shema most commonly used during private prayer. It includes the text of the first passage taken from Deuteronomy.

During a prayer service, the Shema continues with additional text that discusses issues of reward and punishment. This section of the liturgy ends with words concerning how God led the Israelites out of slavery in Egypt, offering them a redemption to freedom. It is then appropriate that the next full prayer, the Amidah, begins with blessings that address how God will redeem His People in the future.

The Amidah

In *The Way Into Jewish Prayer*, Lawrence Hoffman informs us that while the Shema is *about* God, the Amidah is said *to* God. It is a conversation with Him about the needs of His people. The Amidah, which is literally translated as "standing"—and also known as the Shemoneh Esreh or Esrei (the "eighteen benedictions") or the Tefilah (the "Prayer")—originally consisted of eighteen blessings, and now holds nineteen. The Men of the Great Assembly composed the Amidah's eighteen blessings around 260 BCE. The nineteenth was added sometime around the second century, in response to heretics and informants that were negatively affecting the sense of Jewish community.

When performed in the synagogue, the Amidah is read in parts, silently at first, and then aloud by the leader. The faithful stand during this prayer to offer themselves as servants before their King, making their requests known to Him and seeking His favor. Furthermore, the standing position is supposed to mimic the angels, who are biblically reported to have one centrally positioned foot upon which they stand during praise to God. The times designated to say the Amidah were originally chosen to coincide with sacrificial ceremonies in the Temple. Now the prayer is

From the Amidah

As explained on page 74, the Amidah—one of the key prayers of Jewish liturgy—is composed of nineteen separate blessings. Below, you will find two excerpts from the Amidah. They are suggested even as individual prayers in Elias Kopciowski's *Praying With the Jewish Tradition*. The first blessing discusses God's protective presence. The second discusses the trust that the Jewish religion places in God, and the recognition that God's presence is constantly with the people of Israel.

◄○►

You, my God,
are eternal and all powerful:
through you and in your time
the dew comes down,
the wind blows
and the rain falls.
You feed the living.
You uphold those who waver,
those torn apart by doubt,
those in anguish
and those, indeed, who risk
　falling into sin.
You restore the sick
and set the prisoners free;
you bring the dead back
　to life
according to the promise
　that you gave
to those who lie in darkness
in the earth.

◄○►

O Lord our God
and God of our fathers,
we trust in you
for our lives
which we commit into
　your holy hands,
for the soul dwelling
　within us
which you preserve,
and for the wonders
that you perform daily in
　the world
from morning to night.
Eternally holy God,
whose mercy is constantly
　renewed,
our hope is ever in you;
you have never betrayed us
or abandoned us,
nor hid yourself from us.

regularly recited three times a day at synagogue services—in the morning, afternoon, and evening—customarily while facing Jerusalem. An example of a blessing in the Amidah is this one for knowledge: "You give man knowledge, and you teach people ideas, understanding, and comprehension. Blessed are You, Who gives knowledge."

During the opening blessing, observant Jews bend at the knees when coming to the word, *Barukh* or *Blessed;* then bow at *atah* or "are you"; and finally return to a straight-standing position upon the arrival of the word *Adonai,* "Lord." This sequence of movements is repeated at the end of the first blessing, and near the end of the entire prayer, too. The gestures are aimed at increasing concentration, which is of key importance as the powerful words of request reach God and ask kindness of Him.

There are three opening blessings of the Amidah, and they cover the following: praise of the early fathers of the Jewish faith; praise of God's power, manifest in everything up to the resurrection of the dead; and the worshipping of God's holiness. Then there are twelve request blessings, which range from individual to worldwide petitions. As explained in *The Essential Talmud* by Adin Steinsaltz, these blessings include requests for knowledge, repentance, forgiveness, redemption, healing, agricultural success, return of exiles, just judgment, punishment of the evil, reward for the righteous and prayerful, restoration of Jerusalem, return of the rule of the House of David, and a petition that all these requests be fulfilled. The final three blessings tie everything up, first requesting that worship and God's spirit be restored in the Temple, then expressing thanks for life and all its goodness, and finally imploring God to bring peace. Some excerpts from the Amidah, which is too long to reprint in its entirety here, can be found in the inset on page 75. These prayers are appropriate for private use as well as communal worship.

In *Jewish Wisdom,* Rabbi Joseph Telushkin explains that the concluding paragraph—the nineteenth blessing—was added to the Amidah service over the course of history. This final blessing—which is both comforting and inspirational—is suitable for *any* prayer practitioner: "My God, keep my tongue from evil, and my lips from speaking deceitfully. Help me ignore those who curse me, and let me be humble before all. . . . Frustrate the designs of those who plot evil against me, and make nothing of their schemes. . . . May the words of my mouth and the meditations of my heart be acceptable in Your sight, my Rock and my Redeemer." After the recitation of the Amidah, it is traditional to make your own requests and praises, informally, to God.

Adon Olam

Composed during the Middle Ages, the following is a morning prayer, although some also recite it at bedtime. The Adon Olam highlights the timelessness, the transcendence, and yet the nearness of God to our souls and our bodies.

————————————◄o►————————————

Master of the World who was king, before any form was created.
At the time when He made all through His will, then His name was
    called 'King.'
And after all is gone, He, the Awesome One, will reign alone.
And He was, and He is, and He will be in splendor.
And He is one, and there is no second, to compare to Him or be His equal.
Without beginning, without end, to Him is the power and rulership.
And He is my God and my living Redeemer, and the Rock of my fate in
    times of distress.
He is my banner and He is a refuge for me, my portion on the day I cry out,
In His hand I entrust my spirit, when I sleep and when I wake.
And my soul shall remain with my body, HaShem is with me and
    I am not afraid.

Meditation

As discussed earlier in the chapter, while community is central to Jewish prayer, a personal relationship with God is important for spiritual health, and meditation practices help us to attain this private closeness to the Divine. *Hitbodedut* is the Hebrew word that comes closest to our term *meditation*. It literally translates to "aloneness," and refers to those times when we remove ourselves from the distractions and rush of the world. Fixed prayer is not recited, and in this period of silence and stillness, the soul finds communion with God.

In biblical stories that date back millennia, we find examples of Isaac and Jacob—two of the fathers of Judaism—temporarily removing themselves from the daily community to isolate themselves in prayer with God. The attachment to God accomplished during meditation is called *devekut* in Hebrew.

Praying With Nature

In his book *The History and Varieties of Jewish Meditation,* Mark Verman dedicates an entire chapter to the link between nature and Jewish prayer. He explains that the original Jewish community was largely agrarian, living off the land. But in the sixth century, the Jewish people experienced the Diaspora—an exile from Israel during which the community was scattered, their land taken away, and their lifestyles inevitably changed. Thus, says Verman, "Judaism became an indoor religion." Keep in mind that the Jews of the Diaspora were often forced to practice their faith in isolated communities. It is thus quite understandable that the original connection with the land—the celebration of nature and its closeness to God—is not as apparent in Jewish worship today. But, in fact, nature meditation has been promoted since biblical times, and has played a large role in the lives of many highly respected Jews.

For example, Mark Verman studies the religious practices of Rabbi Nachman of Bratzlav (1772–1810), considered a Hassidic master. Rabbi Nachman found that meditating in a nature setting—field or forest—

Generally, the highly developed meditation practices that exist in the Jewish culture have come to us through the Kabbalah—a collection of mystical traditions that arose around the twelfth century, and were often based on interpretations of the Hebrew Scriptures. Some of these practices involve intricate visualizations that can be accomplished only after years of study, while others require specific movements to coincide with Hebrew consonants and vowels in various sacred words. Still other meditation techniques are simpler prayer forms, such as breathing techniques or the repetition of a word.

Meditation should be practiced in a quiet enclosure, be it a room in your house or a synagogue—unless, of course, you are praying in a nature setting. (See the inset beginning on page 78.) It is also thought that the feeling of being draped can help to remove the meditator from the distractions of daily life. Thus, some great teachers have recommended the use of the prayer shawl over the entire head and shoulders during opened his eyes so that he could see and be newly moved by the world each day. Thus he was able to escape the mundane and cocreate the sacred in daily life. In Rabbi Nachman's homilies and conversations, he used to speak of how nature helps a person to pray, how the plants join in the activity of prayer and give that person greater strength. He spoke of how the grasses simply sing praise to God, without any distraction or the expectation of anything in return, and confirmed that we can learn from such devotion. Therefore, Rabbi Nachman encouraged two hours of outdoor meditation each day. The first hour should be spent in silent concentration, during which the heart becomes prepared. The second should be spent speaking to God.

In his book, Verman also cites a beautiful quote from N. Glatzer's *The Judaic Tradition*. According to Glatzer, every element of nature, including plant, bush, sand, and soil, desires and reaches toward its celestial source. Humankind absorbs these longings and is influenced by them, so that each person, too, craves to locate the holiness that he feels swelling inside. Glatzer explains, "It is during prayer that all these pent-up desires and yearnings are released. Through his prayer, man unites in himself all being, and lifts all creation up to the fountainhead of blessing and life."

meditation. (See page 86.) Or, as in the story of King David in the Bible, one can simply go under the covers at night and pray!

Jewish teachings also explain that a life of temperance promotes better meditation. Therefore, the avoidance of carefree indulgences in food, wine, and sex is likely to enhance the power of your meditation. So is maintaining proper hygiene and a good attitude. All of these elements affect balance in the body and mind.

"Meditation inhibits the constant flow of ordinary thoughts by replacing random, mundane musings with focused contemplation of the Infinite. Through meditation, we can become attentive to the Divine imprint upon our lives."

From *The History and Varieties of Jewish Meditation*, Mark Verman

As mentioned earlier, some of the meditation techniques used in Jewish culture are highly complex and require years of practice. A few of the more accessible techniques are described below.

Breathing Exercises

The most prominent prayer in Jewish worship is the Shema, discussed earlier, on page 71. The Shema begins with the command, "Hear, O Israel. . . ." Many Jewish scholars and writers point out that Judaism is predominantly a hearing culture when it comes to prayer. The Jewish people are therefore instructed to *listen* to God through Scriptures, through teachings of the sages and rabbis, and through communication with one another. Breathing exercises can be used prior to prayer to enhance this listening. They can also be practiced on their own as a form of meditation. Slowing down the mind and body, they open the individual up to hearing and feeling God's presence.

According to Carol Ochs and Kerry M. Olitzky in *Jewish Spiritual Guidance: Finding Our Way to God*, we hear our breath when we focus on it. That makes us sensitive to the act of listening—not that we physically hear God, but we are drawn into ourselves, away from the material world. In addition, some of the greatest Jewish scholars have taught that when Moses received God's commandments for the People of Israel, those standing at the base of Mount Sinai heard only a low murmur of inarticulate sounds, as God's voice was too holy for the general human ear. That murmur was like the sound of breath before the first letter of God's name, *Adonai*, is pronounced. Thus, when we listen to our own breath, it is as though we are again listening to that transcendent voice heard at Mount Sinai. What a beautiful way to view the power of breathing exercises!

The creation story for the Jewish community tells that God breathed into man, thus creating humanity. Therefore, breath is also associated with the soul. The Hebrew word for soul is *neshamah*, while the word for breath is *neshimah*. The relationship is obvious. Breathing is viewed as an activity that allows movement between the internal and external spheres; between the soul's chambers and the gift of the world. As humans and as God's children, we are asked to exist in both spheres, and the movement of breath symbolically and physically allows that.

A simple breathing meditation, developed by an anonymous Hassidic master, demonstrates the way breath can be tied into worship. According to commentary written by Rabbi Hirsh of Zydaczow and discussed in Mark Verman's *The History and Varieties of Jewish Meditation*, on every inhale, the master would focus on the name *Elohim*, and on every exhale, he would think of the name *Ha-Shem*. Both of these terms are traditional Jewish titles for God. From such practices we learn about God-centered breathing. Every breath is an opportunity for reflection upon the Creator.

Another breathing technique involves awareness of breath as a gift from God, and the active decision to return every breath to its source. On the inhale, the practitioner concentrates on ingesting God's essence. On the exhale, the practitioner returns the energy and power to God, then waits momentarily to be filled again. This cycle reminds us of our dependence on God, as well as our active participation with Him. The relationship with God then becomes visceral and life enhancing.

Word Meditation

Both those trained in Kabbalah and everyday prayer practitioners use single word meditations. With this practice, a single word is chosen and repeated for up to fifteen minutes. Such a word might, for example, be *shalom*, meaning "peace," or one of the names of God.

The repetitive nature of word meditations allows the practitioner to become rhythmically entranced. We could simply call this activity *chanting*. In the history of Kabbalah, music was added to provide interludes during word meditations. Thus, music became an important part of preparing for and maintaining the practice of meditation.

Today, when we think of chanting and music, the Hassidim practice of niggunim may spring to mind. Niggunim is actually the humming of a set melody—no words are employed. Rhythmic humming is very powerful. It provides an atmosphere of reverence and a break from the limiting use of language. (For a little more information on the role of music in Jewish prayer life, see the inset on page 82.)

Candle-Gazing

The meditation technique of focusing on a candle's flame is intended to develop concentration and to change the meditator's perspective. Such a silent, still activity helps the practitioner break away from the mundane, and become more sensitive to the moment. In fixating on the flame, the practitioner loses self-centered tendencies and finds a calm within which he is open to communication with God.

According to Mark Verman in *The History and Varieties of Jewish Meditation*, mystical Jewish tradition offers two ways to practice candle-gazing meditation. The first is to fixate on the flame as an avenue of concentration. The flame holds a unity and a mystery. The practitioner

Music On the Mind

Those who have attended Sabbath services at Jewish synagogues are not likely to forget the enchanting, reverence-inspiring songs that are sung—and sometimes hummed. The Jewish people take great pride in the music that accompanies their worship. They find the melodies very effective for calming the mind and stimulating the heart. Therefore, it is not surprising that various Jewish spiritualists suggest that a person sing his *personal* prayers in his mind, as well. Some Jewish prayer books also include this suggestion.

The thought of—and even a subtle swaying to—a melody inside one's mind while thanking, blessing, and imploring God is an effective way to concentrate even further on the significance of the words in prayer, as it prevents rote recitation. To attain a true awareness of God, prayer must be passionate. Bringing music to your personal prayers is one way to accomplish greater passion and to trigger sincerity of heart.

dwells on how the flame cannot reach higher unless it is connected to the "coarse matter" of the candle below. Such concentration not only pulls the practitioner away from secular stresses, but also reminds him of how he can perform holy service through the use of his entire body—the "coarse matter" of his existence. Ironically, a greater perspective on the self's relationship to God can be achieved by losing the self in meditation.

The second candle-gazing technique involves merging oneself—mentally!—with the flame. The practitioner either imagines himself moving into the flame, or imagines the flame entering into him. Either way, the visualization of oneness encourages a feeling of illumination and unity, symbolically merging the soul with God.

Letter Meditation

Yet another form of traditional Jewish meditation is fixed concentration on each letter of the Unique Name: YHVH. The practitioner pictures each letter in his mind, as though he was looking at each one with perfect vision. Each letter is immeasurably large and bold. Dwelling on the infinite scale of these letters, he allows his heart—the seat of Jewish meditation—to be taken over by awareness of the immeasurable nature of God. Although this technique sounds simple, it is not easy to do. In fact, it takes a long period of practice to make effective strides in this technique.

Even this relatively brief exploration of Jewish prayer techniques demonstrates the spiritual richness of Judaism. From liturgical prayers to spontaneous blessings, there is so much to learn about Judaism's search to move closer to God. And this search involves not only the prayers themselves, but also the many ways that have been developed to enhance the practice of prayer.

ENHANCING THE PRACTICE OF PRAYER

In *The Way Into Jewish Prayer*, author Lawrence Hoffman reminds us that while we may have natural tendencies to pray, the Jewish faith sees prayer as a discipline and an art that must be studied, worked at, and developed. Over time, many approaches have been found to help the practitioner more readily develop this art. By adopting the right state of mind, assuming an appropriate prayer posture, and perhaps using prayer accessories, the practitioner can imbue each prayer with greater meaning and reverence.

Adopting the Right State of Mind

Jewish teachings emphasize the importance of the prayer practitioner's state of mind. The following discussions may help you think more deeply about your approach to prayer, and therefore aid you in achieving better concentration and balance during your prayer sessions.

Pray With Kavanah

It is critical to prevent prayer from becoming a routine and meaningless activity. Especially since so much of Jewish prayer stems from fixed, traditional discourse, Jewish spiritual teachers emphasize the importance of approaching every prayer session with new intention. The Hebrew word *kavanah* refers to that newness of intention—the passion of the moment—that a person brings to heartfelt prayer. Kavanah keeps a person from simply running off words by rote. It involves more than concentration; it means feeling the prayers, listening to the words, creating a vibrant experience. Jewish prayer aims to attain a balance between kavanah, which allows new meaning and feeling, and *keva*, or fixity.

Even though many observers of the Jewish faith pray in Hebrew and might not understand every word they speak, kavanah is still possible. It rises out of the feeling of oneness with the community and with God through what have become sacred words, sounds, and sentiments. Kavanah is what causes some people—especially members of Orthodox communities—to become so enraptured in prayer that they bow and sway. When you enter into prayer this deeply, it is essentially manifesting its energy in your body through movement. Then you know that you are practicing kavanah.

Work Toward Hitlahavut

Hitlahavut is Hebrew for the ecstasy that can be found in God's presence. It can be experienced on occasion, when in very effective and deep states of prayer. Hitlahavut is mostly associated with meditation and contemplation, and especially with mysticism. But any person who practices prayer can strive toward this ecstatic state. It is a joy in the loss of self, and therefore the ceasing of personal pain and burden, that is attained when a person enters into union with God.

Practice Tikkun Olam

Mystical Judaism encourages a tradition known as *Tikkun Olam.* Meaning "repair of the world," Tikkun Olam reminds us that we are called to a more extensive relationship with God than simply that of the father and child. We are asked to be God's friends and partners, and thus to cocreate the world with God. This means taking part in an adult relationship with God, and taking action in the world.

The Jewish religion seeks to inspire the person who prays to keep the intention of Tikkun Olam alive in prayer life, both during prayer sessions and in the wider sense of prayer, as a person moves through the day. This awareness of the individual's role in the world around him maintains a sense of zeal and purpose, and fosters a much more visceral notion of prayer. Every prayer and every action can be used as a step toward restoring goodness and peace in the world.

Prayer Postures

Because, as human beings, we were born into the body, the body is a necessary part of our communication with the Divine. Through different prayer postures, we can maintain our focus on prayer, can show our reverence for God, or can express the joy we feel when we are in God's presence.

In Judaism, the most common prayer position by far is simple sitting. This comfortable posture prevents fatigue and allows the practitioner to focus on the prayers themselves. In addition, during formal, fixed prayer in the synagogue, many prayers are said standing up. This demonstrates the practitioner's reverence and awareness.

Kneeling is considered a sign of respect before God, who is conceptualized as a master. In the days of powerful rulers, when a subject went before a king to make a request, kneeling was considered the proper protocol. Because this carried over into some forms of Jewish worship, some people still choose to kneel during their personal prayer times.

It is not uncommon for members of intense prayer groups, such as the Hassidic Jews, to gesture during individual meditation and even communal prayer. Observant Jews may sway, shake, or even dance as they pray. Some schools of thought liken swaying and shaking to sexual ecstasies. In fact, there are some people who even consider prayer an act of "making love to the Divine." So gesturing is a further manifestation of the joyous union with God in prayer.

Bowing is also practiced during certain prayer rituals. For example, during the recitation of the Amidah (see page 74), some prayer practitioners bow at the word *baruch*, which is part of every blessing. The traditional eighteen blessings were supposed to coincide with eighteen vertebrae, and a bow during each one would thus loosen the spine and enhance the health of the body, as well as the spirit. Within the Jewish tradition, bowing is performed in a very specific way. First, the knees are bent. As the knees are straightened, the practitioner bows at the waist, and then returns to a standing position.

Some individuals also practice prostration as a means of demonstrating humility and respect. The morning synagogue service used to include a time of prostration, when the congregants would lie down and put their faces to the floor. This occurred after the recitation of the Amidah. The Hebrew term for prostration, *nefillat appayim*, literally means "falling on one's face."

Prayer Accessories

Some observers of the Jewish faith use traditional prayer accessories at specific prayer times. For instance, when about to perform the morning service, some worshippers put on prayer shawls. The Torah actually assigns the wearing of such garments, so that traditional Jews consider the practice to be obligatory. Orthodox Judaism reserves the use of these prayer accessories to men. However, some women in Reform and Reconstructionist communities choose to use them, as well. Tefillin and yarmulkes, too, were once used only by men, but now are also worn by some women.

The Tallit

As mentioned above, the Torah commands the Jews to wear the prayer shawl, called the *tallit*, for morning prayer. Note, though, that there are actually two types of prayer shawls. Even prior to donning the large prayer shawl, male Orthodox Jews put on a *tallit katan*, or small prayer shawl, which is a type of four-cornered undershirt with fringes, called *tzitzit*, hanging from each corner. While dressing in this garment, a specific blessing is recited: "Blessed are You, Adonai our God, Ruler of the Universe, Who has sanctified us and commanded us concerning the tzitzit." This undergarment is worn all day.

The larger *tallit*, also equipped with tzitzit, is placed over the shoulders only for the morning prayers. Again, before actually putting the tallit on, a blessing is recited, sometimes with the tallit draped over the head: "Blessed are You, Adonai our God, Ruler of the Universe, Who sanctified us with His commandments, and commanded us to wrap ourselves in tallit."

Generally, if you are to wear the tallit for only a short time, you do not need to recite the blessing. But if you are attending a full morning service at the synagogue, it is protocol to perform the blessing. The fringes on the tallit are symbolically arranged, being of particular number and tied in certain knots to carry very specific symbolism. Once on, the tallit should fall over the shoulders, with the fringes lying in the four corners around the body.

Many observers of Judaism confirm that the prayer shawl heightens the wearer's sense of the seriousness and sacredness of prayer. It involves a ritual that is specifically Jewish and specifically associated with prayer time. Furthermore, the shawl acts as a cover, warding off distractions and actually forming a sacred space around the wearer.

The Tefillin

In addition to wearing the prayer shawl, Orthodox men, as well as other men and women who have made it part of their prayer service, don the *tefillin* or *phylacteries*. The tefillin are two tiny wooden boxes, each holding small scrolls that contain four passages from the Torah (Exodus 13: 1–10 and 11–16, and Deuteronomy 6: 4–9 and 13–21). Leather straps that pass through openings at the tops of the boxes allow the practitioner to tie the tefillin on. One box is worn on the head, while the other is placed on the arm, as described below. Again, according to the person's community prayer book, he or she will recite corresponding blessings and readings as the tefillin are fastened on.

Placement of the tefillin on the body seems quite complex to the newcomer. However, the routine becomes second nature after a while. The armbox goes on the left forearm muscle, facing the heart. Left-handers place it on their right arm. A blessing concerning God's commandment to don the tefillin is recited. The corresponding strap is then tightened and wound seven times, counterclockwise, around the forearm. Hassidic Jews and Sephardic Jews—those who descend from the Jews who lived in Spain and Portugal—place the knot facing away from them and wind the strap clockwise. For both protocols, the remainder of the strap is wound around the palm, and another similar blessing is said.

Now for the headpiece! The piece is placed so that the box lies above the hairline and is centered between the eyes. The knot of the headpiece should be located at the base of the skull. The straps fall over the shoulders and down the chest. "Blessed is God's majesty for ever and ever," is declared. Finally, with the ritual almost complete, the armpiece strap originally wound around the palm is undone and then wrapped three times around the middle finger. The remainder of the strap is wrapped around the ring finger and palm, while a particular blessing is said concerning betrothal to Ha-Shem.

Historically, this prayer accessory was supposed to inflict some discomfort on the body. The purpose was not only to offer a sacrifice to God, but also to keep the person awake and aware during prayer. Today, many religious observers do not believe in voluntary pain. However, they do mention that by adjusting the tefillin so that there is an awareness of its presence, they also increase their awareness of the prayer process. Furthermore, this religious article adds a certain element of tradition and sacredness to prayer time.

The Yarmulke

The *yarmulke* (pronounced *yar'•mull•kah*) is simply a little skullcap—a small head covering. Many people incorrectly pronounce this Yiddish term as *yammica*. In Hebrew, the little cap is called a *kippah*. Many Jewish men don the yarmulke during prayer as a sign of respect for God and humility before Him. Others wear the yarmulke all of the time—not only when in the synagogue or during prayer.

The practice of wearing the yarmulke probably stems from traditions in the East, where, historically, covering the head was considered a sign of respect. Also, in ancient Rome, servants had to cover their heads. So head coverings have long been a symbol of obedience and acceptance of one's place in society.

Neither the Torah nor that Talmud instructs the Jewish community on the wearing of yarmulkes. This prayer accessory is worn solely according to a custom that developed over time. But today, it serves as a reminder that a person should act in respect and obedience before God.

The tefillin and tallit are not used on the Sabbath. It would be considered a transgression to employ them on the Sabbath and also at night, with the exception of the Yom Kippur holiday. They are used only in the morning. However, the yarmulke can be worn at all times.

CONCLUSION

Judaism has developed a high art of prayer over its centuries of practice. Traditionally, it insists upon a daily, fixed prayer routine. Yet it also promotes newness of intention and simplicity of thought in prayer. After all, prayer is recognized as the "service of the heart" according to Jewish text, and the heart is much more than language and law. One thing is clear: In Judaism, prayer is inextricably tied both to history and to the present. It grows out of experience and expands into the moment, elevating the soul and restoring the world. The Jewish approach to prayer confirms that prayer is as much a beautiful and exciting gift as it is a religious obligation.

5

Christianity

 Christianity was born from the Jewish tradition, and therefore shares its early systems of belief, prayer, and even Scriptures with the Jewish community. However, in the person of Jesus Christ, the Christians found the long-awaited Messiah. Considering Jesus Christ not only a Savior but also a God-Man, Christians believe that God expressed Himself on earth as a human being. Jesus forged a new covenant, asking humanity to place love of God and neighbor above all other law, and offered that, in return, forgiveness of sins and everlasting spiritual life would be given through His saving acts.

The belief in a God-Man inspired the Christian community—the Church—to revise its notion of God. Within several hundred years, the Church developed a perspective that includes one God who consists of three divine persons—the Father, the Son, and the Holy Spirit. And this perspective necessarily affected prayer life, adding new techniques and approaches to the Judeo-rooted traditions.

A BRIEF HISTORY

Our present history lesson picks up where the chapter on Judaism left off. In the previous chapter, we learned that the Jewish community waits for a prophesied Messiah who will restore peace and fulfill God's covenant with the Israelites. Christians believe that Christ—also commonly referred to as Jesus and Jesus Christ throughout the following pages—*is* the Messiah. But the peace that Christ bestows is not a political or economic peace; it is a personal peace.

Jesus' Life

Jesus was born to a humble Jewish family in Nazareth. According to Christian belief, God placed His divine essence in the body of a young virgin, Mary—also called the Blessed Mother. Christians proclaim that Christ was conceived by a miracle of the Holy Spirit, not by natural human means. His ministry didn't start until He was about thirty years of age, yet according to accounts, Jesus was a prodigious teacher of sacred text and law even as a young boy.

Jesus was a carpenter by profession, but a dynamic social and religious reformer as well. He encouraged people to love God above all things, and to love one's neighbor as oneself, promoting two principles that were already established in Jewish Scriptures. Jesus extended the covenants made between God and the Jewish people to place greater emphasis on these principles. He was highly concerned with placing the spirit of compassion and social justice over blind obedience to the law. But He also claimed to hold the way to God's kingdom, and many fellow Jews, in addition to political leaders, were infuriated by this declaration. They feared that the allegiance Jesus asked for was a transgression against the Jewish God.

To His critics, Jesus was irreverent and too liberal. His comrades were often the poor, the sick, and the outcast. Because He talked in metaphor, many people found His words threatening. He was not without His share of enemies. Yet to the people who were mesmerized by Jesus, this God-Man possessed miraculous gifts and enlightened knowledge. Jesus gained a reputation for being a performer of miracles—a healer—and as a result, great crowds followed and gathered around Him. He became known as a compassionate, learned, and just man.

At thirty-three years of age, under the reign of the Roman ruler Pontius Pilate, Jesus Christ suffered capital punishment. Before He was sentenced to death, He endured a number of tortures. He died by crucifixion—that is, He was nailed to a cross while still conscious. The death was extremely painful and humiliating. Christians look to the fact that God offered Himself, in the person of Jesus Christ, in such a humble way. This proves His selfless love to them, and also makes Christians confident that in the afterlife, a person will not be judged by secular status or wealth, but by spiritual integrity.

Three days after Jesus Christ's death, Christians believe that He rose from the dead. Friends and family going to annoint His body found Jesus' tomb empty. He apparently visited with His circle of friends, explaining how they should continue the new way of life in which He had instructed them. He asked them to tell all the world about Him—about how He had conquered death, and would now bring forgiveness and eternal life to all who believed in Him.

Christian history also teaches that Jesus ascended into the afterlife, body and soul. But during His final visit before His ascension, Jesus endowed the apostles—His twelve chosen followers—with the Holy Spirit, the third person of God, to grant them the knowledge, courage, and inspiration necessary to do the work of Jesus Christ on earth.

The Spread of Christianity

The religion that developed as a result of Jesus' life and teaching is called Christianity. Upon the request of Jesus, and in zealous love for Him, Jesus' closest followers spread out into the surrounding regions and began teaching Christ's message of love and salvation. After several hundred years of persecution—but nonetheless, successful evangelization—Christianity became the official religion of the Roman Empire, and began to spread throughout the world. And under Roman rule, the calendar was recreated to begin modern time with the birth of Christ. Therefore, what we refer to as the Common Era begins at the approximate date when Jesus Christ was born.

Over two millennia, Christianity developed and grew. Dogma and doctrine were established, a patriarchy was put into effect, and many writings on Jesus' life were collected and compiled. During this history, the Christian Church, originally called the Catholic Church, split into denominations. First, in 1054, came a great break between the Roman Church and the Eastern (Byzantine) Church. Eastern Orthodoxy developed in Eastern Europe, while Western Europe remained Roman Catholic. Then, in the sixteenth century, the Christian Church went through a Reformation during which various Protestant sects formed due to disagreements with some of the policies of the Roman Catholic Church. A German clergyman, Martin Luther, is noted as the man who started the Protestant movement.

Christianity Today

Today, there are numerous Christian denominations. Greek Orthodox, Russian Orthodox, Roman Catholic, Anglican, Lutheran, Episcopalian, Methodist, and Baptist are just a few of the Christian churches. Despite disagreements regarding certain doctrines, all Christians share the same basic understanding of God, and also center their faith on Jesus Christ—His coming, His life, and the salvation offered to those who follow Him. They believe that complete union with God is enjoyed in the afterlife if a person lives in accordance with Jesus' teachings. And they are confident that their God is always with them, lovingly guiding them back to righteousness if they are receptive to His call.

Many of today's Christian leaders take part in *ecumenism*. This is a movement that works to unite Christians by fostering respect for and understanding of fellow denominations. It endeavors to reestablish the sense of community among *all* Christians that was enjoyed in the early Church, thus healing divisions.

THE CONCEPT OF GOD

The Christian God is considered one supreme power, but that power manifests itself in three expressions: the Father, the Son, and the Holy Spirit. Obviously, Christianity promotes a familial understanding of God in the first two persons of this Holy Trinity. God the Father is the authoritative, all-powerful, creator side of God. God the Son, who is Jesus Christ—also called the Sacred Heart and the Lord—is the brother and the savior of humanity. Finally, the Holy Spirit is the energy of inspiration and knowledge that is God; it is God's continual presence in the world and in every human's consciousness.

Many Christians find the notion of a three-part God rather helpful. Because different people are drawn to different concepts of God, it is advantageous to have several images from which to choose. By considering images of God as father, brother, and inspirational spirit, the Christian is bound to find one visualization of God that is personally productive.

Two of the three images of God offered in traditional Christianity are, obviously, male. Since it is believed that God did express Himself to humanity as a man in Jesus Christ, it is easy to understand why the perception of God as male is commonly accepted among Christians. Plus, Jesus Christ, Himself, instructed followers to pray to God as *Abba*, or father. So Christianity began as a patriarchal religion. The Church fathers were always male; only men were allowed to be clergy. Today, several Christian denominations accept female ministers, but the images of God are still largely male. Yet Christians fundamentally accept the fact that God is larger than gender—that our human images are simply aids to communication with God.

To understand the Christian concept of God, it is necessary to understand the Christian concept of sin. For Christians, sin is a harmful activity that causes the human soul to move away from God, rather than toward God. Human beings, it is believed, have sinful tendencies—that is, tendencies to do things that cause hurt, division, and anxiety—and therefore remove themselves from the total love and peace found in God. God came to earth in the form of Jesus Christ to offer forgiveness for the destruction caused by these tendencies. He gave Himself in sacrifice, allowing Himself to be put to death, so that He could take on all the sins that ever were and ever will be committed, suffer punishment for them, and therefore cleanse the human race by proxy.

As long as humanity observes the lifestyle that Jesus taught, humans can be assured of happiness in the afterlife with God. In the Gospel of John, we read, "For God so loved the world that He gave His only begotten Son, that everyone who believes in Him may not die, but have eternal life. For God did not send His son into the world to condemn the world, but that the world may be saved through Him" (John 3:16–17). Because Jesus is *of* God, Christians believe that He wasn't *made*, but always has been in existence. Christ is coeternal with God the Father and the Holy Spirit.

People who convert to Christianity often say that they were drawn to the religion's concept of a loving God who has tenderness for the weak and sinful. While God is considered Supreme Judge, His personification in Jesus Christ brought Him into the people's daily lives. Jesus was known for His ministry to the poor, sick, sinful, and outcast. He welcomed them into His community with open arms, defying the social and religious prohibitions of His times to do so.

While Christianity focuses on love of God and fellowship among humanity, it also teaches the belief that there are dark forces—demonic, evil, or destructive elements—at work within the world. God is the Supreme Creator, yet He grants His beings free will. This means that "bad" things continue to happen in a "good" world. That's exactly what happened with Satan.

Some Christians accept that a personified evil force, called the Devil or Satan, traverses the universe. According to the story, Satan was at one time a very powerful angel. Out of greed, pride, and malevolence, he and his companions battled God for power. And they lost. Because God allows free will, He did not obliterate Satan for his actions. Satan therefore continues his underworld reign, and human beings, as God's most cherished creations, are his main target for revenge. In a constant battle to uproot God's good presence in the universe and to plant malice and harm in its place, Satan and his followers maintain a never-ending mission to lead God's people into sin.

In modernity, some Christians think of Satan as a concept created by humans to explain why bad things happen in the world, and why people are weak and malicious at times. They understand Satan as a symbolic personification of the bad side in all of us. Whether a Christian literally or figuratively believes in the demonic, Christianity asserts that God is more powerful than all other forces and can overcome evil on any level. Prayer is a means to increase God's activity in our lives, and fight off harm. That leads into our discussion of the concept of prayer in the Christian tradition.

THE CONCEPT OF PRAYER

Christian prayer aims at developing and intensifying a personal relationship with the Trinity. Contrary to some mistaken views of Christianity, a clergy member is not necessary in order to "access" God. It is believed, in some Christian denominations, that clergy hold a special privilege to consecrate the Eucharist, which means to mystically bring Jesus' presence into bread and wine, which the community then shares. And clergy members are often revered for their long-term study of sacred Scriptures and doctrines. But the individual is thought to have her own power to communicate with God.

The Christian is encouraged to take part in both group and private prayer. Prayer is a gift and a privilege. It is for the world at large and for each person. And as Christ came to spread a message of personal salvation, emphasis is placed on the Christian's daily and private relationship with God. Private communication with God is capable of being enjoyed at any time, anywhere.

Where Did the Prayer Tradition Begin?

Just as the Christian religion has its roots in Judaism, so does Christian prayer share the same roots as Jewish prayer. Pages 60 to 61 present information on the process through which personal and communal prayer approaches came into play for these two religions. However, the traditions that are uniquely Christian began, of course, as a result of Jesus' instructions on prayer.

Jesus offered His followers detailed guidance on the subject of prayer. He recited a specific prayer, the Lord's Prayer, discussed later in this chap-

Touch forehead.

Chest.

One shoulder.

Other shoulder.

Hands together.

The Sign of the Cross

Many Christians "bless themselves" or "make the sign of the cross" on their bodies at the beginning and close of a prayer session. This involves simply tracing the shape of the cross on the body, through certain gestures. First, the Christian states, "In the name of the Father" while touching his forehead (see photo 1). Then he declares, "and the Son," and touches the center of his chest, in the area of the heart (see 2). Finally, he recites, "and the Holy Spirit. Amen." When articulating "Holy Spirit," he touches each of his shoulders (see 3 and 4). Catholics touch the left shoulder first, while Protestants touch the right first. And when reciting "Amen," he brings his hands together, either palm-to-palm or in an inter-locking manner (see 5).

Each gesture links the worshipper with a certain aspect of the Christian God. Touching the forehead in reference to God the Father reminds the Christian that God is the Mind, the Intuit of the universe. In touching the heart when reciting Christ's name, the Christian remembers that Christ came to earth to teach love and compassion. Finally, the Holy Spirit provides in-spiration and therefore guidance to the Christian. It makes sense that the shoulders are touched upon reciting the name of this member of the Trinity. It is the shoulders upon which someone can place his hands and guide you with steadiness and strength. So "making the sign of the cross" helps Christians to recall the three-fold concept of God that has proven effective throughout two millennia of worship.

ter. He taught His believers to address God as Father. Furthermore, Jesus warned people against the profuse use of words in prayer, as well as hypocritical public displays of prayer. Jesus actually instructed His believers not to heap word upon word, as though the right number of words would convince God to respond accordingly. Therefore, Christianity places more emphasis on the heart during prayer, and less on the words. That being said, there is a large tradition of fixed prayer, within liturgy and outside of liturgy, in Christianity. And Jesus encouraged His followers to speak with God privately, removed from rush and noise, as well as to gather in His name and to share Holy Communion.

How Important Is Prayer in the Christian Tradition?

Prayer is central to Christian life. Like Judaism, Christianity promotes both the transcendence and the nearness of God. And prayer is the Christian's bridge to this God, in all His unfathomable glory and all His natural presence in our souls.

Christianity has been defined as a lifestyle as much as a religion. When practiced faithfully, that lifestyle necessarily involves prayer. Prayer is the time given specifically to awareness of God, and that awareness is at the foundation of what it means to be a Christian.

> *"Christian prayer is response to God the Father, through Jesus Christ, in the power of the Holy Spirit."*
>
> From *The Book of Common Prayer*

Also, for some of the longer-established Christian denominations, like Roman Catholicism and Greek Orthodoxy, prayer is so necessary to the individual's spiritual health that weekly and holiday services—or Masses—are obligatory. It is considered a transgression against God *not* to take part in this form of communal prayer. Therefore, the degree of significance that is placed on prayer is quite clear.

How Is Prayer Practiced?

Christianity teaches that private prayer is necessary for the soul's strength and virtue. Christians use a variety of prayer techniques, including fixed prayers, spontaneous prayers, meditation methods, and contemplation methods. But before we delve into a further discussion of these practices, let's take a brief look at prayer services offered in community, as group prayer services are also a mode of worship for the Christian.

For certain Christian denominations, such as Roman Catholic and Greek Orthodox communities, the Mass is the highest form of prayer and is obligatory, once a week, to fulfill Christian obligation. And for those who choose, the liturgy of the Mass is also available every day. For these communities, the Mass is the opportunity to receive the Body and Blood of Christ. Jesus actually offers Himself in sacrifice, mystically, once again, and performs the changing of the bread and wine into the substances of His flesh and blood through the priest. This ritual is called the Liturgy of the Eucharist, or Holy Communion.

Protestant worship tends to be more liberal. Obligations to attend prayer services are not as strict, and the Liturgy of the Eucharist—the sharing of bread and wine (or, often today, juice)—is understood largely as a commemorative act. Most Christian denominations offer daily and weekly prayer services for those who choose to attend. However, while some also provide daily or weekly communion services, others share communion only once a month—or even once every three months. Due to the many differences in services between denominations, it is impossible to present a standard ritual of observance. Some involve a good deal of singing and a long sermon; others involve three Scripture readings and a shorter sermon, as well as a communion service. Whatever the circumstance, communal prayer is viewed as personally enhancing and as world enhancing. It is Christ-centered, and it inspires the individual so that she will perform more prayerful, Christ-like acts in her private life. Now, let's consider the importance of personal prayer.

> *"And I say unto you, ask and it shall be given you; seek, and ye shall find; knock, and it shall be opened unto you."*
>
> Luke 11: 9

Christian prayer can be voiced, or it can be silent and mental. It can involve words, images, or simple dwelling with God. In vocal prayer—which can be said aloud or in the mind, but in either case is reliant on language—the words are much less important than the intention behind them. But words do help the person who prays to channel intentions. According to *The Basic Book of Catholic Prayer: How to Pray and Why,* by John Lovasik, certain word prayers have the power to stimulate devotions and changes in a person because they so aptly explain and confirm beliefs. That is the benefit of fixed prayer. Several fixed prayers are offered in insets throughout this chapter. A Christian fixed prayer may be addressed to any of the three members of the Holy Trinity, and for some denominations, to saints and angels who will aid the prayer practitioner with intercession.

Although fixed prayer is an important part of Christian worship, Jesus made it clear that His teachings apply to more than formal prayer time. This means that prayer should permeate the whole day, and conversation with God should occur as frequently as possible. After all, the Christian God is an ever-present and personal God who is continually accessible. So spontaneous prayer is encouraged in the practice of

Come, Holy Spirit

Christians traditionally recite and sing prayers to the Holy Spirit—the third person of God. Such prayers, like the one below, often involve a request for guidance and faith. By the way, the term *Pentecost,* used in the following prayer, refers to the event during which the risen Christ, present in body, granted God's presence in the form of the Holy Spirit to the twelve men whom He had chosen to lead His church. It is believed that at that moment, a tongue of flame descended over each man's head, symbolizing that the knowledge and courage of God would now be with them continually.

―――――――――◄○►――――――――

Come, Holy Spirit, fill the hearts of your faithful, and kindle in them the fire of your love. Send forth your spirit, and they shall be created and you shall renew the face of the earth. O God, on the first Pentecost, you instructed the hearts of those who believed in you by the light of the Holy Spirit; under the inspiration of that same spirit, give us a taste for what is right and true, and a continuing sense of his presence and power; through Jesus Christ our Lord. Amen.

Christianity. From short adorations like the Jesus Prayer (see page 109) to simple everyday conversation, the Christian makes herself further aware of God's presence in her life by performing unplanned prayers. These could be as simple as a "Thank you!" upon seeing a beautiful tree, or a "Please help me!" during a tense family disagreement. Whatever the situation, nothing is too small for God.

In nonvocal prayer, the activity is not based on using language skills to articulate communication with God. Instead, there is a great focus on silent dwelling either on God or in God. Nonvocal prayer is involved in certain *meditation* practices and all *contemplation*.

As alluded to, Christian meditation can be vocal or nonvocal. Because meditation is intended to bring the practitioner into deep focus on God through quiet concentration skills, it is essential that this type of prayer be individual. Techniques range from dwelling on the personal pertinence of Scriptural passages to concentration on breathing. Several aspects of Christian meditation are explored later in this chapter. (See page 111.)

Finally, there's contemplation, which is always individually and silently performed. Many Christian teachers confirm that the more prayer is geared toward sheer enjoyment and praise of God, and the less it is geared toward self, the more intimate one's prayer life becomes. That's what contemplation entails—just dwelling with God. See page 113 for a discussion of this mode of prayer.

What Are the General Intentions of Prayer?

Christ told His followers, "Ask and it shall be given you" (Luke 11: 9). Thus, Christians often turn to God for help. Prayers of petition or supplication are a large part of Christian prayer. But it should also be clear that Christian prayer blooms far beyond that. It is an act of praise, an expression of contrition for sin, and a way to thank God for His generosity. Therefore, the general intentions of Christian prayer are identical to those of Jewish prayer: praise, thanksgiving, petition, and confession. Importantly, confession prayers are meant to help cleanse the Christian from the sins that now mar her spirit. She prays not only with the intention of realizing the weight of her wrongs and thus remedying or avoiding them in the future, but also with the intention of healing her relationship with God, who has been offended by her acts.

Moreover, Christianity places a large emphasis on ministry or service to humanity. Jesus Christ made this aspect of Christianity clear through His own concern for the sick, the poor, and the outcast. Thus, there are many prayers that demonstrate a concern for others and for the environment. (For an example of this type of prayer, see "Prayer for the Poor and Neglected," below.)

In the Christian viewpoint, are prayers of request intended to change God's will? Can humans convince God to change the flow of things? Christians, in general, believe that by showing faith in and commitment to God, an individual can receive certain favors from Him. That doesn't necessarily mean physical favors; it often refers to spiritual graces. God may decide to manifest Himself more clearly because of a person's devotion and attention. So the intention of prayer is not to change God's will, but to invite God to reveal Himself in the individual's life and work, helping her create a more desirable, beautiful, or tolerable situation. The inset on page 101 offers a prayer for guidance, while the prayer on page 102 asks Jesus to fill every moment of the day with His presence.

Christians do believe in free will, as well as a shared responsibility that God gives humanity to take part in further creating the world with Him. That means that humanity holds the God-given right to make conscious decisions, and thus take part in the great plan of creation and existence. Prayer may be viewed as an avenue of involvement in this process. When a person prays to become pregnant, or prays for healing, for

Prayer for the Poor and Neglected

The following prayer, found in the Episcopalian Church's *The Book of Common Prayer*, emphasizes the Christian concern for the unfortunate, the poor, the needy. Christ asked that His followers love their neighbors as themselves. Therefore, the true Christian concerns herself with praying even for those whom she doesn't personally know.

◄○►

Almighty and most merciful God, we remember before you all poor and neglected persons whom it would be easy for us to forget: the homeless and the destitute, the old and the sick, and all who have none to care for them. Help us to heal those who are broken in body or spirit, and to turn their sorrow into joy. Grant this, Father, for the love of your Son, who for our sake became poor, Jesus Christ our Lord. Amen.

A Prayer for Guidance

The following prayer is a traditional request for aid from God. It is taken from *The Book of Common Prayer*, according to the use of the Episcopalian Church. Note the emphasis placed on the constant awareness of God's presence, and the belief that God individually aids those who implore His help. Also observe that all three persons of the Trinity are mentioned.

―◄○►―

O heavenly Father, in whom we live and move and have our being:
We humbly pray thee so to guide and govern us by thy Holy Spirit,
that in all the cares and occupations of our life we may not forget thee,
but may remember that we are ever walking in thy sight; through
Jesus Christ our Lord. Amen.

instance, she is asking to take part in designing the unfolding plan. God makes room for this, leaving certain things open for possibility.

Usually, the intention of petition is to gain in understanding or to contribute to forming a better situation in the future, not to skew the natural course of things. But when God does alter what seemed like a set course of events as a result of prayer—or out of sheer compassion—such an event is called a "miracle." A miracle is a change that God effects supernaturally rather than through another human being. Miracles are how Christians explain things like spontaneous remissions, sudden changes in natural weather crises, and the like.

Does Christian Prayer Involve Angels and Saints?

From its early days, the Christian Church held fast to a belief that some of God's angels—His supernatural helpers—tend to humanity, while others offer continual praise and service to God Himself. In this belief system, certain angels who tend to humanity serve as messengers, delivering God's words to those whom He chooses as prophets. Others serve as guardians, and bring comfort and healing to humans.

Some Christians believe that by praying to angels, they can obtain further guidance and protection. Alongside this understanding is the con-

Prayer for Jesus' Presence

The following prayer is attributed to Saint Patrick. It asks Jesus Christ to fill every moment and every action with His loving presence.

————————————◄○►————————————

Christ, as a light, illumine and guide me.
Christ, as a shield, overshadow and cover me.
Christ, be under me. Christ, be over me.
Christ, be beside me, on the left hand and right.
Christ, this day, be within and without me.
Christ, the lowly and meek, Christ the all-powerful,
be in the heart of each to whom I speak—
in the mouth of each who speaks to me—
in all who draw near to me, or see me, or hear me.

cept that angels can also be asked to intercede for humans—to ask God to respond to people's needs and desires, possibly with better results than might be achieved by human entreaty alone. Thus, among some Christians, you will find the recitation of prayers such as, "Saint Michael, the Archangel, protect us."

Traditionally, some forms of Christianity, such as Roman Catholicism and Greek Orthodoxy, also practice prayer to *saints*—particularly pious people who have passed away, and have since been canonized by the Church. These souls, who now reside in union with God, can intercede on an individual's behalf, asking God to grant her prayers. So some Christians pray to saints hoping that, through their intercession, God might look favorably upon their requests. Miracles and conversions have been attributed to the action of saints in peoples' lives.

Specific types of prayer are linked with communication with saints. For instance, when praying to saints, it is not uncommon for Roman Catholics to say *novenas,* which are fixed prayers said for a certain number of days, with specific intentions in mind. Nor is it uncommon for Roman Catholics to meditate upon depictions of saints. Special devotion is given to the Blessed Mother, or Virgin Mary, who was Jesus' earthly mother. Numerous prayers are composed for this significant figure, including the most recognized "Hail Mary." (For the text of this prayer, see the inset below.)

It is important to note that most Protestant denominations do not believe in the veneration of saints, including the Blessed Mother. Members of these communities fear that such worship shifts the focus of praise from God, and places it on the memory of a human being. Such Christians argue that the focus of prayer should be Christ-centered, and that anything else is too close to idol worship. Quite differently, Christians who do observe prayer practices that involve saints and angels believe that they are simply praying within a larger communion of souls, with one helping the other in times of need.

PRAYER TECHNIQUES

Christianity is so varied in its denominations, and therefore in its specific practices, that it is impossible to come up with a list of prayer techniques that applies to all members of this religion. But today, several

The Hail Mary

For many Christians, Jesus' earthly mother serves as an exemplary model of peace, acceptance of God's will, and strength in times of trouble. For those Christians who do believe in praying through the intercession of saints, and who wish to model their lives after significant religious figures, devotion to Mary, the Mother of Christ, is very effective. The following prayer is just one of many fixed devotions to this important biblical and spiritual figure. It blesses Mary's strength of character and holiness of life, while imploring her intercession.

———————◄○►———————

Hail Mary, full of grace,
the Lord is with you.
Blessed are you among women,
and blessed is the fruit of your womb, Jesus.
Holy Mary, Mother of God,
pray for us sinners,
now and at the hour of our death. Amen.

forms of Christian prayer do commonly play roles in various Christian lives. Some of the techniques discussed below cover general practices, such as Scripture readings and meditation. Others refer to specific prayers that were composed hundreds of years ago, and have proven helpful in the lives of countless individuals. Perhaps you will find one or two to which you are personally drawn.

Sacred Reading

You may recall the discussion on sacred reading in the chapter on Judaism. The Jewish faith makes no real distinction between the study of sacred writings and prayer itself. After all, reading Scriptures is listening to God. Similarly, Christianity views the Scriptures as the revealed words of God, and the reading of them as communication with Him. Furthermore, even writings that are not Scriptures, but are spiritual in nature, can be avenues of prayer. In the Christian approach, reading becomes prayer when a person no longer reads a passage to analyze the writer or the culture in which the text originated, but instead, simply listens to what God is saying to her at that particular moment.

The reading of spiritual texts has long been a part of Christian worship. For example, Catholic monastic life has always made *lectio divina*—spiritual reading—a large part of the day. When looking at monastic life—and monks are best known for their lives of constant prayer—we find that Saint Benedict, who founded an order of monks that is still active today, recommended a *via media,* a middle road, that involved three forms of prayer: formal prayer sessions, spiritual reading, and physical labor. Spiritual reading was considered a prayerful act in and of itself.

As mentioned above, the Christian does not have to read from the Bible in order to pray with text, but the Bible is probably the most common literature used for spiritual reading. It is important to note that the Christian tradition looks to the Jewish tradition as a living part of its heritage, for it is the same God the Father that Christians and Jews worship. So the Jewish Bible is included in the body of Christian Scriptures, only it is referred to as the Old Testament. The books and stories written after Christ's death and concerned with His ministry and church are collectively referred to as the New Testament. The following discussions focus on the two areas of the Christian Bible from which many of the sacred readings are drawn—the four Gospels and the Books of Psalms.

Also please note that Christian teachers recommend slow, open-minded reading of spiritual texts in order to attain effective prayer. They

Friendship and Fear

In the Christian perspective, God certainly exercises authority over the universe. But in addition to His kingly role, the Christians' God bears a deep longing for a loving relationship with each of His creations. To express this desire, He came to earth and lived among humanity, touching them, talking to them. In the Gospel of John, we learn that soon before His death, Jesus told His chosen companions, "I do not call you servants any longer, because the servant does not know what the master is doing; but I call you friends, because I have made known to you everything that I have heard from my father" (John 15:15). The Christian is encouraged to think of her prayer relationship with God— the three-part God—as one of intimate closeness and comradeship, not simply one of master and servant.

While Christianity does promote an intimate, familial prayer relationship with God, this religion does not by any means take away from the sublime, awe-inspiring nature of God. In fact, as a Christian progresses in her prayer life, she not only becomes more familiar and comfortable with her God, but also grows in amazement of God's timelessness, boundlessness, and incomprehensible goodness. This is what is meant by a Christian's "healthy fear of God." Fear, in this sense, is not an emotion that would make a person hide in a corner, but a sense of awe in the presence of something that cannot be grasped by the human mind.

suggest taking a small passage, reading it patiently, and dwelling on it for a while. The reader can then apply the words of the passage to her specific situation.

The Gospels

We can consider the four Gospels biographies of Jesus Christ. Because these first four books of the New Testament are so Christ-centered and so informative, quoting Christ and detailing His actions, they are a wonderful source of spiritual readings. The Gospels tell the stories of Jesus' lineage, His teachings, His love, His social action, His religious ideals, His death, His resurrection, and His promise to be with His followers always. The Gospels are also blueprints for the Christian life. Each one is unique in presentation and emphasis.

The first Gospel is the Gospel of Matthew. The author is thought by many scholars to have been an original disciple of Christ—one of the twelve men to whom Jesus initially passed on His ministry. This Gospel was written in Hebrew, the language of the Jewish people, and is heavily influenced by the Jewish tradition. It highlights how Jesus fulfilled the Old Testament prophecies.

The Gospel of Mark appears to have been written for Romans of the early centuries of the Common Era. Mark seems to have traveled with Paul, an early evangelist who started converting Romans to Christianity very soon after Christ's death. He also is believed to have written down the teachings of Peter, the apostle whom Jesus specifically asked to head His community. In his Gospel, Mark concentrates on communicating the power of Christ as a savior for *all*, in order to reach non-Jews who had little knowledge of Jesus' culture and traditions.

Luke's Gospel is the third book of the New Testament. Luke was a physician, and his scientific background is evident in his detailed account of the stories he gathered on Christ's life. His telling of Jesus' life is beautiful and thorough, involving a wealth of information on the real-life people involved in the Christ experience, such as shepherds, townspeople, and friends. This, too, was written with a non-Jewish audience predominantly in mind.

Finally, the Gospel of John is the most radical account of Christ's ministry and future purpose. The source is believed to have been another of Jesus' original and carefully chosen followers, and is the self-proclaimed "beloved" apostle of Christ. Historically, John is thought to have had an especially close relationship with Jesus, having been taken under Jesus' wing as though he were a little brother. John the Apostle was the youngest of the original group of twelve ministers with whom Christ worked, and the only one who wasn't killed for his faith and ministry. Many scholars suggest that the tract we know as John's Gospel today is actually John's words recorded by faithful followers late in the first century. So it is not necessarily the actual written account of John himself. Nonetheless, it holds mystical and complex understandings of Jesus not only as a divine man, but also as the source and future of humanity. Symbolism and metaphor enrich this Gospel account. Poets and writers find this one especially moving!

The Psalms

Just as it is often used as a medium for prayer in the Jewish tradition, the Book of Psalms is a popular avenue of prayer for the Christian. The 150 Psalms cover everything from despair to rejoicing, and from poverty to prosperity. Many Christians claim that they have found a direct response to their needs in the Psalms, and turn to them regularly in prayer life. For a more detailed discussion of the Book of Psalms, see page 71.

Jesus quoted the Book of Psalms quite often in His ministry. In fact, many of His last words were actually rooted in lines from the Psalms. Since Jesus Christ found satisfaction in praying the Psalms, His followers are guided to this portion of the Bible for both help and celebration.

Traditional Prayer

Clearly, among Christian sects, there is much variety in liturgical and personal prayer practices. This makes it impossible to provide a common ritual of observance when it comes to traditional Christian prayer. However, the focus on salvation through Jesus; the belief in the three-part God; and the mission to uphold Jesus' love and teachings is shared by all Christians. And these elements can be found in the several fixed prayers studied below. The following prayers are not exclusive to any group, but are shared by Christians of all denominations.

The Lord's Prayer

The Lord's Prayer, also known as the Our Father, is said both in community and individually. This prayer was given to Christians by Jesus Christ Himself, in response to the question, "How should we pray?" Thus, by analyzing the words of the Lord's Prayer, which is presented in the inset on page 108, we can learn a great deal about Christian belief, prayer, and practice.

First, Jesus tells His followers to address God as "our Father." Note the recognition that all people share the same God through the use of the plural pronoun "our." Also note the familial tone that Jesus encourages. The word used in Jesus' own Aramaic dialect was *Abba*, which is an endearing term for a father who protects and cares for his children. It was a title that was used with reverence, respect, and admiration, but also with great warmth.

In the Lord's Prayer, praise is given to God. In addition, God is asked to bring His kingdom—which is a life of peace and love in union with

The Lord's Prayer

As explained on page 107, the Lord's Prayer, also commonly called the Our Father, was Jesus Christ's response to His followers' question: "How should we pray?" Through this prayer, Jesus Christ taught His listeners to address God in an endearing, familial way. He also taught them to implore God's active presence in their daily lives.

━━━━━━━━━━━━━━◄○►━━━━━━━━━━━━━━

Our Father, who art in Heaven,
hallowed be thy name.
Thy kingdom come, thy will be done,
on earth as it is in heaven.
Give us this day our daily bread,
and forgive us our trespasses,
as we forgive those who trespass against us.
And lead us not into temptation,
but deliver us from evil.
For thine is the kingdom, and the power, and the glory,
now and forever, Amen.

His spirit—to us here on earth. This prayer also confirms that the Christian's first intention is to observe the will of God, and to serve that will. Therefore, the prayer does not ask God to alter the natural course of things or to observe the Christian's personal desires, but only that His will be done. The prayer practitioner also asks that simple, daily needs be attended to by God, including sustenance and forgiveness for transgressions, so that she may remain a healthy and effective individual. Again, note the plural nature of this request, which asks that the entire community, not just the individual, be granted basic needs.

The concept of evil—destructive forces or events—is also addressed in the Lord's Prayer. The individual asks God to protect her from bad things and from personal temptations that may lead her into harmful living. The last phrase of the prayer concludes with praise, once again, of the sublime nature of God and His creative force. The Christian recites this prayer with confidence that God hears the individual's voice, and with certainty that this way of prayer is pleasing to God because Jesus Christ composed it.

In *Simple Prayer,* John Dalrymple challenges the reader to perform a specific prayer exercise with the Our Father. Although a person can recite this prayer within a few seconds, Dalrymple suggests prolonging the reading for fifteen minutes. Digest every word; dwell on every concept; and note the various beliefs confirmed through recitation of this prayer.

The Nicene Creed

The majority of denominations that consider themselves Christian accept certain fixed creeds that present the basic tenets of the faith. One such prayer is the Nicene Creed, composed during the early years of the Christian Church and still recited today, individually and communally. As you read the text of the Nicene Creed, found in the inset on page 110, note how it lists the fundamental concepts of Christianity, including the use of the plural "we" to emphasize community among Christians.

The Jesus Prayer

The Jesus Prayer is a very short, yet truly meaningful prayer that, centuries ago, was born from and popularized by the Eastern Orthodox Church—or, more specifically, the Russian Orthodox Church. It can be found in several versions. Three popular ones are: "Lord, Jesus Christ, Son of God, have mercy on me"; the more simple "Lord Jesus Christ, have mercy on me"; and finally "Jesus, Son of God, have mercy on me, a sinner." Repeated recitation of this prayer throughout the day, as the Christian goes about her regular activities, is a realistic way to remind herself of God's constant presence. In addition to its rather spontaneous recitation, the Christian may also count repetitions on traditional prayer beads, which are discussed on page 119.

Holy Communion

For many Christians, Holy Communion is a significant part of prayer life. In fact, the central activity of many Christian religious services is the Liturgy of the Eucharist, or Holy Communion. During this liturgy, Jesus' last Passover supper is reenacted. Jesus lifted bread, blessed it, and said, "Take, eat; this is my body" (Matthew 26: 26). He did the same with wine, thanking God and saying, "Drink from it, all of you; for this is my blood of the covenant, which is poured out for many for the forgiveness

The Nicene Creed

This creed, fixed in the fourth century of the Common Era, states the basic beliefs and principles of the Christian faith. It begins with the oneness of God, proclaims His three-fold nature, and expresses the truths that the Christian Church recognizes in light of Jesus' coming to earth.

———————————————◄O►———————————————

We believe in one God, the Father, the Almighty,
Maker of heaven and earth, of all that is seen and unseen.

We believe in one Lord, Jesus Christ, the only Son of God,
eternally begotten of the Father, God from God, Light from Light,
true God from true God, begotten, not made,
of one Being with the Father.
Through Him all things were made.
For us and for our salvation He came down from heaven:
By the power of the Holy Spirit
He was born of the Virgin Mary and became man.
For our sake He was crucified under Pontius Pilate;
He suffered, died, and was buried.
On the third day He rose again
in accordance with the Scriptures; He ascended into heaven
and is seated at the right hand of the Father.
He will come again in glory to judge the living and the dead,
and His kingdom will have no end.

We believe in the Holy Spirit, the Lord, the giver of life,
Who proceeds from the Father and the Son.
With the Father and the Son He is worshiped and glorified.
He has spoken through the Prophets.
We believe in one holy catholic and apostolic Church.
We acknowledge one baptism for the forgiveness of sins.
We look for the resurrection of the dead,
And the life of the world to come. Amen.

of sins" (Matthew 26: 27–28). Some Christian groups believe that when a priest or minister resides over bread and wine—or bread and juice—and repeats the words that Jesus said, Christ mystically enters the substances, and they literally become the presence of Christ. Other Christians view Holy Communion as a symbolic act, a memorial.

As discussed previously in this chapter, if they wish, members of such denominations as Roman Catholicism and Eastern Orthodoxy can attend a daily Mass, which contains the Liturgy of the Eucharist and sacred Scripture readings, among other prayers. Protestant denominations vary in their practices. The Liturgy of Holy Communion may occur weekly, biweekly, or monthly. In any case, the Christian can make efforts to ingest the Body and Blood of Jesus and meditate upon union with Jesus during that act. Holy Communion is a practice that brings the Christian closer to God.

For those who believe that Jesus' presence literally enters into the Eucharist, visitation of the blessed bread is considered another form of prayer. For example, a Roman Catholic Church will always have blessed communion bread—which is, for Roman Catholics, the actual Body and Blood of Christ—locked in a *tabernacle* on the altar of the church. Roman Catholics can enter the church during open hours and sit in meditation or other prayer before what they call the "Blessed Sacrament." According to Sister Briege McKenna, a Catholic nun and healer, the Blessed Sacrament offers a focal point for the prayer practitioner, enhancing concentration and inspiring reverence.

Meditation

There are quite a few techniques that fall under the heading of Christian meditation. Some include reading about and dwelling on God—or, in the case of certain Catholic churches, dwelling on one of the righteous souls whom God offers as an example. Meditation may also involve fixating on an image or word that draws us closer to God. Or meditation may take the form of breathing exercises performed either alone or as an accompaniment to spoken prayer.

Meditation was a spiritual practice even during the earliest years of the Christian Church. According to Barbara Gawle in *How to Pray*, this early form of prayer centered on a number of steps, forming "a rhythmic process of prayer": receive the Word, ponder the Word, respond to the Word, unite oneself with the Word. In this process, the "Word" refers to Jesus as revealed in the universe, through the Scriptures, and in one's daily life. Several meditation approaches are discussed below.

Scripture Meditation

The goal of Scriptural passage meditation is to find personal revelations in the Holy Scripture. It is important to note that in Scripture meditation, the Christian does not "study" the text, analyzing it for historical content or literary skill. Instead, she reads Scriptures to hear the words of God, and discover how a particular prayer or passage applies to her at that very moment. Beyond reading the words, there are periods of silent dwelling upon the message received. The section "Sacred Reading," which begins on page 104, discusses Scriptural texts that are especially prominent in Christian meditation.

Word Meditation

The rhythm developed in word meditation, which is a form of chanting, is a very effective means of prayer. The prayer practitioner can meditate upon one word, such as "Lord," "Father," or "Love"; or can meditate on a phrase, such as "Come, Holy Spirit" or "You are my God." Regardless of the chosen word or phrase, or whether the recitation is vocal or silent, the rhythmic repetition encourages continued focus on God, diminishes distractions, and enhances awareness in the moment, as well as providing solace in the sound of the chant.

Breathing Exercises

Various exercises are available to the Christian who is interested in breathing meditation. One technique involves breathing in a paced manner while mentally reciting spiritual phrases. Take, for example, the Jesus Prayer, discussed earlier: "Jesus, Son of God, have mercy on me, a sinner." On the inhale, the prayer practitioner would mentally and slowly recite, "Jesus." On the exhale, "Son of God" would be mentally articulated. On the following inhale, "have mercy on me" would be the concentration. Finally, "a sinner" would close the prayer and coincide with the ensuing exhale. In this technique, body, mind, and spirit work in union to pray. The intention behind the words becomes more significant as the practitioner slowly paces herself and dwells upon each phrase. And the act of breathing—something so simple and innate to us—becomes holy service.

Nonlanguage breathing mediations involve simply concentrating on the breath and its relation to God. The Christian might choose to view the breath as divine, creative energy, and attain a state of union with God by becoming aware of its ebb and flow inside her own body. Each respiration is an opportunity to study how God maintains our earthly lives.

Visualizing God

Another form of meditation involves dwelling on an image of God, or on a saint or angel who draws the Christian closer to God. Some Christian denominations are opposed to using physical representations, such as statues and icons, to aid this process. They feel that this practice borders on idol worship. But for many Christians, a statue, cross, crucifix, or other visual aid proves very helpful. The "Prayer Accessories" discussion, which begins on page 118, provides more information on statues and icons.

Whether you use an actual physical item to enhance your imaging, or you form an image in your mind without the use of an aid, there are a number of popular images for dwelling upon the Christian God. First is a triangle with an eye inside. This represents the three-sided nature of God, as well as His ever-watchful presence. The second is the image of Christ on the cross. Someone who isn't used to this practice may find it upsetting to meditate on such a sad image. However, the Christian who studies this depiction of her God is reminded of Christ's selfless love and His shared suffering with humanity. Another commonly used image is that of the dove of peace that gently floats in the air, reminding the Christian of the soft inspiration of the Holy Spirit. These are only a few of many effective images on which the Christian can meditate.

Contemplation

Quite different from Christian meditation, which involves dwelling on a specific image or phrase, Christian contemplation does not involve thinking about anything. It simply consists of basking in God's presence. Perhaps an effective way to describe contemplation is that it is not a dwelling *on*, but a dwelling *in*.

> *"To be alone with Him, not with our books, thoughts, and memories but completely stripped of everything, to dwell lovingly in His presence—silent, empty, expectant, and motionless."*
>
> From "On Prayer," Mother Teresa of Calcutta

It can take some time to get used to the practice of contemplation. It is not intellectual; it is intuitive. Those who have accomplished it say that at first, the relinquishing of mental control that is necessary can be a bit frightening or uncomfortable. The person has to rely totally on faith as

Prayer With Nature

*"The next morning, Jesus awoke long before daybreak
and went out alone into the wilderness to pray."*

Mark 1:35

Christianity is often associated with its pretty churches and its vibrant singing. What many people don't recognize is that Christianity also promotes communion with nature, and encourages prayer time within the sacred outdoors. Jesus Himself often chose to pray in a secluded garden. Christians can follow His example and find time with God in the quiet of a beautiful landscape or an inspiring seascape.

Christians believe that God communicates with His creatures in a number of ways, and that the beauty and power of nature is one of them. Therefore, the Christian can come to know God better through interacting with nature. In *The Cloister Walk*, noted Christian author Kathleen Norris writes the following description about the sacredness of her Dakota home environment: "I noticed the sky was doing glorious things. Quickly, I pulled on my boots and a jacket and began

she enters this state. But the enjoyment of this form of prayer is immeasurable. Those who have effectively contemplated, even for several seconds or minutes, say that it is a very fulfilling form of prayer. No thought processes or selfish motives mar the experience, and the union that is achieved with God feels like a return home.

ENHANCING THE PRACTICE OF PRAYER

Over time, Christian teachers and prayer practitioners have developed a number of approaches that can help the Christian conduct more effective prayer. For example, putting oneself in a Christ-like state of mind can help, as can the use of certain postures and prayer aids. Whether or not you subscribe to Christianity, the following ideas may assist you in making your own prayer time more fulfilling.

walking west, toward one of those sunsets in which both the eastern and western sky are vivid with color. . . . And as I walked I began to have a biblical sense of God's presence in the sky, of God speaking through the colors."

Many Christians who dedicate the majority of their lives to prayer—namely, monks and cloistered nuns—make nature prayer a regular part of their day whenever weather permits. For example, they may pace through gardens with a prayer book in hand, reading Scriptures and using the environment of nature to listen to God even more fully. Furthermore, a good many Christian organizations promote retreats, during which participants visit designated nature-oriented locations and dedicate several hours or days largely to personal devotion. But simple dwelling on the power and glory of God in nature is an easy meditation at any local park or peer.

Lastly, the Christian Church teaches that God has appointed human beings to be stewards, or caretakers, of His earth. Therefore, caring for natural settings—tending to a garden or feeding birds, for example—can also be viewed as a form of prayer. This is something to consider if you are looking for new ways to pray.

Adopting the Right State of Mind

The following are suggestions for developing a calm and reverent state of mind during prayer. These approaches can help you focus on the love and peace of God, making prayer time more fulfilling.

Pray in Christ's Example

The Christian generally prays with the example of Christ in mind. Christ not only articulated certain ways to pray, as discussed throughout this chapter, but also taught by the example of His daily life how we should live in God. Therefore, the Christian who wants to enhance her prayer life might continually hold herself up against Christ's example. She might remember to be peaceful at heart, to release anxieties, to pray with great trust, and to dwell on love above all things.

To place herself in a more enhanced state of prayer, one Christian explains that she recites the following prayer to Jesus: "Jesus, please teach me to see with your eyes, to hear with your ears, to speak with your voice, to touch with your hands, to know with your knowledge, and to love with your love." This simple prayer reminds her to use Christ as her guide and example during her prayer sessions and throughout her daily life.

Enjoy God

In his book *Enjoy the Lord: A Path to Contemplation,* author and priest John Catoir teaches that at the bottom of every Christian prayer should be the enjoyment of God. Catoir writes, "Just knowing that you are made to enjoy God can change the direction of your thinking. You will want to live in the presence of God and enjoy all aspects of the life he gives you: walking, resting, working, playing—all of life becomes infused with his loving care." By delighting in God, we come to understand that the goodness of God will overcome all pain and harm. It brings peace and happiness in prayer.

Practice the Presence of God

When praying, and when going about daily life, it is helpful to constantly call attention back to God by using short, one-line prayers. Examples are the Jesus Prayer (see page 109) or simple statements such as, "I love you, Lord," "Thank you, Lord," or "Be with me, Lord." Even if the Christian is reciting fixed prayers or practicing image meditation, these short exclamations can enliven and impassion prayer. The goal is to make prayer feel vibrant by directly addressing God in the moment.

Prayer Postures

It is not believed that God demands any specific bodily posture in prayer. And in today's practice of Christianity, simple sitting in a chair seems to be the posture of choice. With the back straight and pressure distributed healthfully throughout the body, the Christian can attain a comfortable and productive position for prayer. However, liturgical prayer does have prescribed protocols for standing, sitting, and kneeling. In addition, during personal prayer, some Christians choose body postures and hand positions that inspire further reverence and respect in their own minds.

It is a well-known Christian practice to kneel while praying, whether in church or at home. This posture was derived from the custom of kneeling before a king. But for the Christian, more than an attitude of submission is involved. By getting down on her knees, a person automatically feels humble. Humility is constructive in prayer, as it calls us to let go of our notions of ego and to submit to a greater Source. Similarly, kneeling makes the person feel slightly vulnerable. This less-stalwart position, again, fights off egocentrism. And kneeling brings the person physically into closer contact with the organic earth, through which God breathes life into all of His creations. So yes, it does traditionally stem from a culture that would kneel before political and economic rulers as an act of submission, but kneeling during prayer can encourage so much more than that limited understanding.

While considering respectful gestures, it is helpful to mention head-bowing as well. Some Christians practice slightly bowing the head when the name of Jesus is recited, audibly or mentally, during prayer, and even during discussion. This activity is a simple but significant reminder of the holiness of Christ.

Whether sitting, kneeling, or bowing the head, several traditional hand positions may be used during Christian prayer. The most common one involves bringing the palms together, and then folding the fingers down and between each other. In other words, the hands are clasped, with fingers interlocked. A similar hand position involves simply placing the hands palm-to-palm, allowing the fingers to remain upright so that the hands resemble triangles. Both of these hand positions symbolize unity—a coming together of God and the individual, of the spiritual and the earthly realms. They also demonstrate respect and humility.

Some Christians like to pray with their hands held out slightly to the sides, palms cupped and facing upwards. This position communicates receptivity—the opening of the self to God. Symbolically, the hands are open to receive the blessings that pour down from God. Both this hand position and the other positions and postures detailed in this section, enrich the practice of prayer by making the body an active part of the experience.

Prayer Accessories

Several common prayer aids can be used to further enhance the Christian's prayer experience—or, actually, anyone's prayer experience. From the visual stimulation provided by statues and paintings, to the tactile aid of prayer beads, to the calming and sacred scent of incense, the accessories discussed below offer help for the prayer practitioner.

Statues and Icons

As explained earlier in the chapter, many Protestant sects—especially those that have their roots in the Puritan Revolution of the sixteenth and seventeenth centuries—do not believe in using representations of holy figures. They fear that veneration before such items leans toward idol worship, which is strictly prohibited in the Ten Commandments. Therefore, it must be clarified that certain prayer aids are used in only some Christian denominations. Within those traditions, however, they are an important part of prayer life.

First and foremost, the depiction of the cross is considered a prayer aid for many Christians. Whether in a church or in a private prayer space, it is common to see a simple cross hanging on the wall or sitting on a table, reminding the worshipper of Christ's sacrificial death for humanity's sins. Some Christians prefer a crucifix—a cross that bears a representation of the Christ figure.

Many Catholics find that statues and other religious art pieces, such as religious paintings, also aid concentration on God, the Blessed Mother Mary, and various saints. In prayer, a Catholic might sit down or kneel before a depiction of Jesus and focus on it. The prayer practitioner then has an object upon which to dwell—an object that leads her away from other distractions while feeding her with a concept of God that is understandable to the human being.

The Eastern Orthodox Church promotes the use of *icons*—two-dimensional representations of sacred people and events. Christ, the Blessed Mother, saints, and angels have all become popular subjects of icons. The point of the icon is not to convince the viewer that the person portrayed actually looked like that, nor are these pieces of artwork looked upon as simple paintings. Rather, through line and color, the icon is intended to put the viewer in touch with the transcendent and life-enhancing attributes of the subject. For instance, an icon of Christ would introduce an element of reverence and holiness through the colors and shapes used; through the depth of the eyes; and through the cultural coding—the placement of the hands, for instance—that literally tells a story.

Icons are necessarily two-dimensional. In fact, Eastern Orthodox Churches are opposed to the practice of using three-dimensional artwork—that is, statues—in prayer. These churches teach that statues concentrate too much on the physical recreation of the subject, while icons capture qualities that lead the viewer to a transcendent understanding of their faith. Icons are so valued that they are always present in traditional Eastern Orthodox households, where faithful observers kiss the icons and bow before them.

Prayer Beads

Certain fixed prayer techniques require a specific number of repetitions of prayers. The *rosary*, for instance, is a Catholic form of devotion that mainly involves repetitions of the Our Father and Hail Mary prayers. Prayer beads, also called rosary beads, are used to keep count of these repetitions.

The main loop of the prayer beads consists of fifty small beads, punctuated by a large bead at intervals of ten. An additional line of beads branches off this loop. At the end of the line is a small crucifix, and between the crucifix and the main loop are a large bead and three small beads, all of which are associated with the recitation of particular prayers. While the prayer beads were traditionally arranged to suit the recitation of the rosary centuries ago, some Christians like to use them for other prayer forms. Some recite the Jesus Prayer on every bead, and others use the beads to guide them on meditative recitations of personally composed prayers or phrases.

Incense

Incense was traditionally used during rituals in the early Church, and it is still used during such events as funerals and high holy days in certain Catholic Churches. The rising of smoke from an incense holder symbolizes the rising of prayers to God. Following this practice, some Christians choose to burn incense during their private prayer sessions. The pleasant fragrance helps to relax the prayer practitioner, putting her in a reverent state of mind. Although any scent can be used, heavy, spicy scents, like frankincense and myrrh, best mimic the incense used in traditional church ceremonies.

CONCLUSION

Prayer practices vary among the Christian Churches. But the one thing that is common to all Christians is that prayer is centered in a three-person understanding of God—the Father, the Son, and the Holy Spirit. Christians pray to a God who is an all-present creator, an all-loving brother, and an all-inspiring spirit. Prayer is always performed in the recognition that God loves humanity and wants them to turn always to an awareness of His presence. In this presence, the Christian finds peace, hope, and rest.

6

Islam

In Arabic, the word *islam* means submission. When used as a name for the religion, *Islam* refers to submission to the one true God, Allah. Followers of this faith are called Muslims—ones who submit to Allah. This religion developed from the great prophet Muhammad's revelations, occurring in the earlier half of the seventh century.

The God of Islam is the same God as that of Judaism and Christianity, but the Muslims believe that only Muhammad's revelations have been faithfully recorded and remain untainted. These revelations teach the absoluteness and unity of God, the Creator of all things. Yet the Muslim views Allah as removed from His creations. He is a ruler, not a father, albeit a benevolent ruler to those who willingly obey Him. And obedience involves beautiful traditions of prayer that demonstrate submission and devout praise. This chapter discusses those traditions, and presents other basic information on Islam.

A BRIEF HISTORY

To understand the spiritual, social, and political significance of Islam, it is necessary to first trace the story of Muhammad's life. There, the religion of Islam had its roots, and began to blossom into a faith marked by a passionate devotion to Allah.

Muhammad's Early Life

The prophet Muhammad was born in 570 CE, in the city of Mecca, located in today's Saudi Arabia. Although Muhammad was a member of the wealthy tribe called the Quraysh, his family was quite poor. Both of Muhammad's parents died while he was very young, and so he remained under the protection of an uncle and worked for a wealthy widow, Khadija. Muhammad led a rather normal early life, marrying Khadija at twenty-five and having several children—although all of his sons died. However, tradition does note that even as a child, Muhammad was exceptionally spiritual and even may have had supernatural experiences.

For many years, Muhammad was faithful to local Arabic religious practices. He would, for instance, retreat into the desert during Ramadan—the time of the year when fasting would occur in remembrance of the poor and in honor of the local gods. But in the year 610, his usual routine was changed forever. According to Muslim history, the Angel Gabriel—who is also recognized by the Jewish and Christian faiths—appeared to Muhammad and began revealing the Qur'an (pronounced *kuh•rahn'*) to him. This work was to become the sacred word of God for the Muslims.

At first, Muhammad kept the revelations to himself and his immediate family. Within a few years, however, he began to preach about Allah as the one Creator, and began to warn listeners about a future judgment day. Thus, the seeds of Islam were first sown.

The Development and Growth of Islam

Muhammad's doctrine of one God was contrary to the local religion. Therefore, his teachings angered many Arab traditionalists. Muhammad talked of equal rights. He taught that the Arabs now had a mission from Allah to form an ideal community in which all people would be treated with respect and value—the rich, the poor, male, and female. This enraged those listeners who were happy with their personal economic progress. Meanwhile, Muhammad's wife and uncle died, and he lost the protection of his immediate relatives. Furthermore, his enemies grew in number, and eventually, Muhammad and his faithful followers had to escape from Mecca. Fortunately, a city to the north—then called Yathrib, but later renamed Medina, meaning "the city of the Prophet"—had invited Muhammad to make his home there. The year of Muhammad's escape to Medina and the start of his formal community there is called the *Hijrah* or *Hegira,* and marks the first year of the Islamic calendar. Therefore, it also signifies the formal beginning of the religion known as Islam.

The Name Allah

Allah is the Arabic word for God. Prior to Muhammad's revelations, the highest-ranked local god was known as al-Ilah. Interestingly, poets of the time would call this god Allah. Thus, it is not difficult to understand how the present title for Islam's one, supreme God was formed. And according to *Islam: An Introduction for Christians,* edited by Paul Martinson, the term *Allah* is also linked to the Hebrew *elohim* or *eloah,* which is a Jewish name for God. Furthermore, Arab Christians call God by the name *Allah.* So the title actually enters into all three monotheistic religions studied in this book.

Muhammad united the warring tribes in the city that welcomed him, and thus gained power over many aspects of the people's lives—religion, politics, economics, and social dynamics. He continued to fight enemies, such as local Jewish tribes who sided with Mecca, and threatening opponents in Mecca itself. Although Muhammad's followers were, at first, not large in number, they enjoyed victory in the majority of their battles. Eventually, Muhammad and his troops gained access to the Ka'ba (or Kaaba), Mecca's ancient temple dedicated to pagan idols, and turned its former fasting rituals into service toward Allah. Within just two years after the taking of the temple, the city of Mecca decided to yield to Muhammad's growing influence. As a result, Muhammad formally took Mecca without a battle. He cleansed the Ka'ba, and it became the primary site of Muslim pilgrimages—and remains so to this day. He even traced the original establishment of the Ka'ba back to Abraham—the first of the Hebrew patriarchs—whom he considered one of the great prophets of God. In fact, Muhammad understood himself to be only one of a long line of prophets, but significantly, the last prophet that God would send.

Why would God send yet another prophet? After all, Moses had given the Torah to God's people, while David gave them the Book of Psalms, and Jesus revealed the Gospels. According to Muhammad, these were all valid sacred texts originating from the same God. However, he taught that the authentic message brought by the other prophets had been distorted over the years—tainted by human interference. The

Qur'an, once and for all, would offer the true message and record it accurately so that it would be preserved forever. The Qur'an would reveal a lifestyle code that would show the Arab people how to please Allah and how to attain a heavenly afterlife.

The community that Muhammad maintained was known as the *umma(h)*. Its members followed Muhammad's code of law, called *shari'a*, which he formed from his revelations. Muhammad became a leader of the Muslim people in every way. He could rightfully be called a political and military leader, a warrior, an economic leader, and a social reformer. He waged war against powerful nonbelievers. He collected taxes from Muslims, and even offered protection for non-Muslim people who would contribute to his community. He led raiding expeditions, which were, at that time, a common Arabian practice when a tribe needed sustenance. And he expressed firm opinions on issues ranging from marriage, to children, to slavery, to inheritances.

Of course, in addition to being a strong political leader, Muhammad was a holy messenger. He continued to receive Allah's words in dramatic revelations. And in accordance with Allah's words, he created a religion that required very specific behaviors of its followers. These can be summarized in the Five Pillars of Islam. The first pillar is to proclaim the *Shahada*, discussed in detail on page 136. This prayer confirms the oneness of Allah and the position of Muhammad as Allah's holy prophet. The second pillar is to perform ritual prayer—*salat*—five times daily (see page 136). The next three pillars involve obligations for giving alms, fasting, and making a pilgrimage to Mecca. Orthodox Muslims add a sixth pillar—to spread the faith of Islam worldwide.

Muhammad did not claim divinity, or even supernatural powers. He was simply God's messenger to the Arab people and was, therefore, a servant to Allah. But legends grew around him, declaring Muhammad holy. Even today, many Muslims believe that the recitation of Muhammad's name has a blessing effect on them. They view Muhammad as a great saint who can intercede on their behalf. Some legends even report that Muhammad possessed supernatural powers since childhood, and that he ascended into heaven in a glorious display.

Islam Today

Muhammad died in 632 CE. His position as the leader of Islam would be passed on, but not without eventual disagreements concerning legitimate successors. These disagreements led to splits among the Muslim people. And then there were simply cultural developments that yielded various sects of popular Islam.

Today, there are many Muslim groups throughout the world, and each has developed its own form of Islam. Presently, the most well-known Muslim groups are the Sunni, Shi'ite, Sufi, Ahmadiyya, and Nation of Islam. Many Americans are aware of the strong presence of the Nation of Islam in the United States. It is especially popular within the African-American culture. Each Muslim sect follows a different leader, has its own interpretation of the Qur'an, and also has its own version of the legal code. For example, according to orthodox Islam, Muhammad was the last prophet. Therefore, orthodox communities do not recognize sects that claim modern-day prophets. The Ahmadiyya and the Nation of Islam are examples of such sects. However, all of Islam's groups share certain common elements. All Muslims observe the Five Pillars of Islam; share deep reverence for a God who is master over all creation; recognize the Qur'an as Allah's revealed word; and believe that obedience to Allah is critical to gaining Paradise.

THE CONCEPT OF GOD

It is important to note that the Arabic word for God—*Allah*—cannot be assigned gender. In addition, it is not capable of being pluralized. This confirms that the Muslim God is not subject to human attributes, and that God is one and absolute. Muhammad, the great prophet of Islam, did not consider himself to be revealing a new god to the world, but, instead, revealing the God of monotheism to the Arab people. Muhammad did not stray much from the teachings of the ancient Jewish prophets, nor from those of Jesus Christ, when it came to doctrines of the oneness of God, to sin and atonement, and to reward for righteousness.

Allah is one, eternal, and omnipotent. The Arabic term for this oneness is *tawhid*. Allah knows everything, observes everything, and is the creator of everything. The Muslim strives to be constantly aware of this presence. The very center of Islam is submission to Allah. So a Muslim's goal is to become an *abd Allah*—a servant or laborer of Allah. In doing so, he will fulfill his determined role on earth and attain peace.

The Muslim understands Allah to be merciful to those who are obedient to His will, and a harsh but righteous judge of those who aren't. He forgives the sorrowful and submissive; to them, He is beneficent and generous. But Allah expects those who have received many gifts to share with others. This is partly why Allah asked Muhammad to reveal the rules for a better society to the Arabs—because mercantilism had triggered greed, and therefore extremes of wealth, that hadn't been a problem among Arabs previously. The Qur'an, in the thirtieth chapter, verse 38, states, "Give to kin, to the poor and the traveler what they need; that is best for those who seek the face of God."

Interestingly, in the Qur'an, Allah refers to Himself using the pronoun "we." That pronoun seems to imply that Allah is all-encompassing. But Allah is not to be looked for in nature or in others. He is removed from His creations.

Although Allah cannot be found in human beings or in other facets of nature, there are ninety-nine names of Allah that identify His characteristics. However, while these names can be useful in meditative prayer, the Muslim recognizes that they are simply superficial ways to grasp something ungraspable. If it helps at the time, that's fine. But in the orthodox understanding of Islam, no human truly develops a personal relationship with Allah. This God exists far above His creations, judging, but also leading, humankind.

Allah is never called "Father." In *Muslim Devotions: A Study of Prayer-Manuals in Common Use,* Constance E. Padwick states that Islam is "a religion in which the tenderer couplet father-child is excluded from worship." Traditional Muslim ways do not assign poetic descriptions to Allah. However, great emphasis is placed on Allah's position as the Creator. Islam teaches that the world is Allah's, and therefore Allah has supreme rule over it. Allah is the master of the universe; humans are Allah's servants. This dynamic is understood quite literally. Because Allah has given human beings the highest place of all creatures, humans carry the responsibility of caring for the earth. They are also intelligent enough to be accountable for their actions. Thus, the Muslim submits by free will, with confidence and desire. In fact, the term *Islam* signifies not only submission, but submission borne out of one's own will.

Under the tenets of Islam, humans are not born with inherited sin. However, humans are weak, and they sin out of that weakness. To make up for their offenses, Muslims should perform good acts; should proclaim the Shahada, which is the formal profession of faith (see page 136); and should otherwise practice the Five Pillars of Islam. Such observances teach the Muslim to rely on Allah, and therefore gain His forgiveness.

Muslims believe that those who obtain Allah's forgiveness will enjoy a most pleasant afterlife. Allah allows only Muslims to enjoy Paradise in the afterlife, where spiritual and physical ecstasies are constant. For the grave sinner, hell is a burning, putrid punishment. Yet most Muslims believe that if a spirit is sent to hell for sin, the banishment is not permanent. There is only one sin that remains unforgivable, and that is *shirk*—putting other gods before or alongside Allah, or worshipping another. Furthermore, every individual is responsible for his own actions. A person cannot make up for another person's sins, as Christians believe Jesus did for them.

Whereas some schools of Jewish and Christian thought teach that humankind is created in an image or likeness of God, Islam holds no such doctrine or mode of thinking. Allah is unfathomable, and certainly doesn't hold a physical form that resembles a member of humanity. Allah is cloaked in mystery. He does not raise humanity to holiness by crafting humans in His image.

Allah wants the Muslim people to entrust themselves to His care and His plan. As a result, many Muslims train themselves to find contentment in daily life, believing that everything which occurs is of the will of Allah. While Allah runs the universe, there is also a strong belief that humans are responsible for the way they individually respond to Allah's plan, and for the way they worship their God. The result of these beliefs is a delicate balance between predestination and human free will.

> *"Islam is a religion with a transcendent God, Allah, with stated beliefs and creeds, with various rituals and ceremonies, with a system of law for all of life, and with ethical norms for governing behavior. Islam also includes a personal and devotional side to religion within and beyond rituals of prayer and pilgrimage. It is a religion of revelation, reason, faith, and faithfulness."*
>
> From *Islam: Its Prophet, Peoples, Politics and Power*,
> George W. Braswell, Jr.

THE CONCEPT OF PRAYER

Submission and obedience are the only ways to please Allah. Yet the Muslim *enjoys* serving Allah, and this means that he enjoys obeying and praising Him through an extensive tradition of prayer. It is true that the Muslim recites certain prayers out of religious obligation. But it is also true that he does so with joyous intensity. Also, countless Muslims perform additional prayer practices out of a personal longing to communicate further with Allah.

Muslim prayer is built on the fundamental intention to obey and honor Allah. In addition, prayer holds elements of fear and reverence before Allah. But the Muslim trusts that Allah will be merciful and generous to those who come to Him with mindful, good intention. With these perspectives in mind, let's further study Muslim prayer traditions.

Where Did the Prayer Traditions Begin?

The obligatory prayer traditions of Islam stem directly from the revelations given to Muhammad, and can be found in the Qur'an. Allah issued prayer instructions, and these changed over the years of revelation. For example, early in the Qur'an, Allah instructs His people to perform ritual prayer and accompanying prostrations three times per day. Later, this requirement increases to five times per day.

In addition to performing the prayers required by Allah, many Muslims have developed private prayer practices out of a desire to develop more individual relationships with Allah, to make personal entreaty, and to meditate upon Allah's greatness. Many of the personal prayer traditions stem from *Sufism,* the mystical branch of Islam. Sufis believe in truly enjoying the presence of God, not in praying out of fear of hell, nor to gain entrance to Paradise. They concentrate on *feeling* or *experiencing* Allah's presence.

While reveling in Allah's presence, Sufism still maintains the primary notion of Allah as master. The difference is that emphasis falls on understanding Allah as a loving, tender master. In Sufi poetry, the speaker often approaches Allah as an infatuated lover would approach the object of his desires—with great adoration, passion, and longing. Very conservative Muslims do not support the concept that the human being can love God as he loves another person. They claim that the only way to truly *love* Allah in this world is to love His law and to serve Him willingly. But Sufi prayers are rich in emotion, and imply a perception of Allah as a benevolent lover of sorts.

How Important Is Prayer in the Muslim Tradition?

Prayer is so central to Muslim life that it is a religious obligation—a mandatory way to display submission and obedience to Allah. As mentioned previously, one of the fundamental principles—or "pillars"—of Islam is to perform a specific prayer service five times a day.

But prayer's importance moves beyond the concept of obligation. Prayer helps the practitioner to purify himself, contributing to the forgiveness of his sins. It also strengthens his ability to carry out his obligations on earth. Prayer allows the Muslim a time and space to focus solely on Allah's transcendence, goodness, and mercy. In doing so, he gains confidence in Allah's general plan and faces his daily life with less anxiety.

How Is Prayer Practiced?

Muslim prayer involves a variety of forms and techniques. There is certainly a strong fixed prayer tradition. Some fixed prayers are said under obligation, while others are chosen at a person's own discretion—perhaps regularly, perhaps in a moment of joy or sorrow. In addition, personal requests might arise spontaneously and be spoken freely to Allah. Attentive reading and recitation of sacred texts is yet another practice of prayer in Islam.

The fixed, obligatory prayer repertoires are referred to as *salat*. As mentioned previously, they are traditionally conducted five times a day. These prayer rites involve not only reciting praise and thanks to Allah, but also expressing submission to Him through gestures and prostrations. (For a detailed discussion of salat, see page 136.) Importantly, the salat prayers are always performed in Arabic. Allah transmitted the Qur'an to Muhammad in Arabic, so that language is considered especially sacred, and therefore appropriate for formal prayer.

Since Islam teaches that Allah is all-present—that He sees and knows every occurrence and thought—the observant Muslim makes efforts to remember His presence throughout the day. One way to call forth this mindfulness is to practice additional personal prayer, whether it takes the form of meditative sayings or petitions to Allah composed in the moment. Therefore, nonobligatory prayer is important for bringing the Muslim into constant mindfulness of Allah.

Personal nonobligatory fixed prayers of praise and thanksgiving fall under the title of *dhikr*. Dhikr involves repetition—aloud or mental—of certain phrases or words. (See page 141 for more information.) Many of the traditional dhikr prayers are in Arabic, but it is not considered a transgression for the worshipper to recite personal prayers in his native tongue.

Prayers of personal request—called *du'a', du'ā,* or *da'waā*—are also not included in the formal prayer rite. They are recited whenever an individual desires, in his own language. If the person who is praying feels moved to implore Allah with his own words, du'a' can be spontaneous and suited to the moment. Alternatively, the Muslim can turn to a variety of helpful collections. Du'a' is further discussed on page 142.

A lot of the nonobligatory forms of prayer grew out of Sufi practices. As mentioned earlier, Sufism is the mystical movement of Islam that aims to go beyond ritual prayer and to develop a spirituality based more heavily on the experience of God's presence. According to Jacques Jomier in *How to Understand Islam,* Sufism includes any prayer practice that exists outside the strict obligatory and formal prayers, covering such prayer activities as dhikr, du'a', the recitation of poems and other post-Muhammad teachings, and even political activism to some degree. Sufis are best known for their ecstatic dancing, and for the composition and recitation of passionate poetry.

As noted previously, praise and thanksgiving are also offered to Allah through the memorizing and reciting of sacred texts. This text-oriented form of worship allows the Muslim to both receive Allah's words and thankfully return them to their source. See page 143 for a further exploration of this topic.

What Are the General Intentions of Prayer?

The greatest intention behind Muslim prayer is to demonstrate obedience to Allah. The Muslim heeds the instructions that Allah provided in the Qur'an when he performs salat five times per day. In addition, the various types of Muslim prayer address four other intentions toward Allah: praise, thanksgiving, confession, and petition. These objectives are identical to those of Jewish and Christian prayer.

Praise and thanksgiving are essential to Muslim worship. All prayer is recited with these intentions. And all prayer contributes to the forgiveness of a worshipper's sins; it purifies him. So every form of prayer can be considered prayer for confession and atonement, as well.

Quite differently, petition is conducted only through personal prayer. Some Muslim groups discourage prayers of personal request—they believe in relying solely on Allah's plan and care. But for those who practice prayers of supplication, how effective are they believed to be? Can such prayers change or sway Allah's will?

Muslims ultimately believe that Allah follows no one's design, and certainly is not bound by human prayers or actions. He has established a plan, and no person's pleas will be powerful enough to change that plan. However, Allah does appoint human beings as caretakers of the earth and allows them certain decisions. For this, He has equipped them with free will. In addition, He wants the human being to earn Paradise by demonstrating obedience and submission. That, too, should be a result of the person's free will. So Allah does leave certain choices up to the individual. Within this space, humans might request Allah's guidance and mercy. That's where the intention of personal request comes in. The worshipper asks Allah to actively manifest in his life, providing mercy and aid. Some Muslim theologians propose that the decisions that humans make have already been anticipated by Allah and are worked into the large scheme of things.

So, because Allah's overarching plan has already been put into place and cannot be changed, Muslims do not suggest that they can alter Allah's will through prayer. In fact, Muslims are often taught to be content with what they have, not to pray for more or for something different. If they do conduct prayers of personal request, the hope is not to sway Allah. The intention is to please Him—to display submission, reliance, and trust so that Allah will continue to permit certain beneficial occurrences to take place. In keeping with this attitude, prayer is first an act of loving obedience; then an act of praise and thankfulness; next a way of attaining pardon for sin; and last, petition. Such an approach avoids egocentrism and the offense of seeking to impose one's will upon Allah.

Does Muslim Prayer Involve Saints and Angels?

Those who practice popular Islam, as opposed to orthodox Islam, tend to admire and meditate on the lives of especially holy and learned Muslims of the past. For example, a group may form around the memory and teachings of a certain inspiring figure. The person whom the group remembers and emulates is a saint to them. It is not uncommon for these admirers to pray to the saint for intercession on their behalf. They might visit the gravesite and even dedicate a shrine to that Muslim saint. Some might toss money at depictions of the saint at the tomb. In some locations, devout Muslims can even pay a shrine staff member to write a prayer of intercession to that saint. These practices are not rare or limited to small numbers of Muslims. For example, the Shi'ites—one of the largest and most recognized sects of Muslims—are known for their practice of venerating saints.

It shouldn't come as any surprise, then, that many Muslims also pray to Muhammad, who is considered God's beloved—*habibullah*. Countless Muslims view Muhammad as a high saint who can intercede for his people. Therefore, to gain both favor and blessings, they might repeat Muhammad's name in an act of praise and petition. Great celebrations on Muhammad's birth date are common, as well. There are even specific prayer techniques developed around devotion to Muhammad. Consider the techniques of *naat* and *darud*. According to editor Azim Nanji in *The Muslim Almanac*, naat is "the a cappela melodic recitation of devotional verse about the Prophet Muhammad in Arabic and vernacular languages." The practice of darud involves performing fixed Arabic blessings to Muhammad in order to obtain certain benefits, such as a vision of him in a dream. It is believed that Muhammad personally hears his adorers' prayers, as his spiritual presence is as active today as it was hundreds of years ago. Some Muslim folk groups even claim that Muhammad was divine.

Furthermore, members of Muhammad's family and successors to his leadership are venerated as saints. This devotion is particularly important in Sufism. The Sufis refer to the spiritual descendents of Muhammad—his passed-on family members, his successors, and the greatest of the Sufi spiritualists—as *awliya*. In service to Allah, these spiritual presences are aware of all the goings-on of the people under their dominion, and report these events to Allah. Humans can pray to the awliya for intercession, and the awliya can directly affect humans' lives.

> "Unlike God, who transcends time and space and whose attributes are largely abstract, the Prophet is a human being. Thus, the events of his life can be recounted and serve as paradigms for human action. Devotion to the Prophet, like that centered on the Qur'an, provides a concrete focus for a Muslim's religious fervor."
>
> From *The Muslim Almanac*, edited by Azim A. Nanji

While only popular Islam recognizes saints, all forms of Islam recognize invisible beings. After all, the Qur'an discusses angels, as well as another group of beings called *jinns*, or *genies*. The jinns are spirit-like and are gathered into communities. Some are Muslim and some are not. They can cause great problems among humans, or they can be completely benign. The bad ones are non-Muslim, and work against Muslim ideals.

Angel life has played an important role in Islam from its start. You may remember that the Angel Gabriel brought the revelations from Allah to Muhammad. It is also believed that each person has two guardian angels, and that these angels stand to his right and left, observing every action. Angels serve as Allah's servants, carrying out Allah's orders throughout heaven, earth, and hell. But importantly, Allah has ranked humans higher than angels; humans are at the top of the spiritual chain, under Allah. Therefore, guardian angels are not to be worshipped. Remaining in good community with them by wishing them peace at prayer time and by maintaining a life of good will is a constructive endeavor. But simply stated, since angels and jinns are less powerful than humans, venerating them would serve no purpose.

Satan figures into Islam as an angel who refused to bow to Adam—the first man—once he was created. Satan also was the force behind Adam's sin of eating the fruit that Allah forbade him to ingest. Some Muslims consider Satan a bad angel, while others consider him a bad jinn. Either way, Satan and his allies are believed to actively work to defile humans. Those who live in obedience to Allah are under Allah's kind protection, but must avoid falling to the corruption of bad forces.

PRAYER TECHNIQUES

It is important to mention that some orthodox Muslim groups take issue with performing prayer practices outside of the prescribed rites. This is taken so seriously in some regions, that prayer outside of the daily rites is illegal. But many Muslims, including the majority of American Muslims, see additional prayer practices as a confirmation of their continual allegiance and submission to Allah.

Both obligatory and nonobligatory prayer practices are covered in this section on prayer techniques, as are spiritual readings. In addition, we will first look at a traditional method of preparing for prayer. However, it should be noted that the following discussion is by no means designed to recommend a change in the set prayer life of any Muslim individual who has decided to strictly observe the salat only.

Preparing for Prayer

Muslims must observe a specific way of preparing for prayer—or, at least, of preparing for the five obligatory daily prayers referred to as the salat prayer. Traditional Muslims follow a rather extensive protocol that prepares them for prayer. These rituals are intended to cleanse the Muslim for communication with Allah, and to encourage a focused, reverent state of mind.

First, the Muslim conducts ablution, or cleansing, in order to come to Allah in a purified state. It is felt that the cleansing of the body is an outward sign of the intention to cleanse oneself of internal impurities. In addition, by coming before Allah with a clean body, the worshipper shows respect to his God.

Cleansing rituals vary widely among Muslim groups. In general, though, it is believed that minor sins or wrongs can be washed away with a quick, rather easy ablution or bath, called *wudu*. A simple rinse with water on the feet, forearms, hands, head, face, mouth, nose, and so on, can be accomplished without removing too much clothing or taking too much time. (See the inset below for details about wudu.) Larger sins, such as those having to do with sexuality, require a full body wash, called *ghusl*.

A Cleansing Ritual

The discussion above explains the meaning behind ritual cleansing that Muslims use as a means of preparing to pray. Called *wudu*, the most common cleansing practice involves washing body parts that are exposed to the external environment. Although this custom varies from group to group, it is helpful to look at one way in which wudu can be performed.

First, the practitioner makes sure to find clean, fresh water, and to dwell upon the intention of the act of cleansing. Then, a few blessings to Allah are recited, followed by the rinsing.

The washing begins with the hands, which are rinsed up to the wrists three times. Next, the mouth is cleansed with a toothbrush or the finger, after which gargling is performed three times. The nostrils are then rinsed out with water three times. The practitioner washes his entire face three times. The right arm is rinsed up to the elbow; then the left arm is rinsed in the same manner. This is performed three times, as well. Wet hands are run over the head, and a wet finger is placed inside the ear, while a wet thumb cleanses the outside of the ear. Then the other damp fingers rinse the nape and sides of the neck. Finally, the right foot is rinsed up to the ankle, followed by the left foot, with each being washed three times.

When wudu is complete, the worshipper is ready to come before Allah in prayer. He can form his intention, and continue his ritual.

Next, the Muslim must select an appropriate place to pray. He may, of course, pray in a *mosque*—a house of Muslim worship. However this is optional, except for the Friday afternoon service, which men are required to attend. Although the environment of the mosque is conducive to uninterrupted, focused prayer, it is not believed that the mosque holds an enhanced presence of Allah. If the Muslim cannot or does not pray at a mosque, he must select clean ground space for his prayer rite. In addition, shoes should be removed before entering the selected space, unless the shoes are very clean.

It is common for Muslims to use a personal prayer carpet. These carpets are small and easy to carry; spread out, they are only a few feet long. The carpets come in handy because it can be difficult to find a clean space during work, a social function, and the like. Thus, the carpet allows the Muslim the opportunity to establish an appropriate prayer space at virtually any location.

Next, the Muslim must turn and face the direction in which the city of Mecca lies or, if in the city of Mecca, must face the Ka'ba, the ancient temple. Once the Muslim orients himself accordingly, he forms his "intention"—that is, he mentally recalls what he is about to do before Allah, and why he is doing it. (For more on this significant part of prayer preparation, see page 146.) Once all of these steps have been accomplished, the Muslim can begin his prayer rite.

Obligatory Prayer

The prayers discussed in this section are said prior to or during the obligatory prayer rite known as salat, but also during many individuals' personally designed private worship practices. When it is time for a salat rite to be performed, a "call to prayer" is issued from a highpoint at the local mosque, or, in predominantly Muslim countries, over the radio. That's when certain fixed prayers start to be recited. The rite continues with a number of traditions that are carried out with precision and heartfelt devotion.

Allahu Akbar

Allahu akbar is translated as "God is greater." Another translation is, "God alone is great, the greatest." This one-line prayer is used at every call to prayer. But Allahu akbar is also repeated during salat, and is said repeatedly in private prayer and during group gatherings. It is an essential prayer of the Muslim's life.

Unfortunately, the Allahu akbar has become associated with battle, as some Muslims use it while entering into combat. But its original, beautiful intention was to declare the supremacy of God over all other things, and possibly also to declare that other gods and demons—meaning pagan spirits that were formerly worshipped or feared—are by no means on the same level as Allah.

The Shahada

The *Shahada* is the basic creed, also called the confession, of the Muslim. It sums up the foundational beliefs of Islam: "La Ilaha illa Allah, Muhammad rasul Allah," translated as "There is no god but Allah, and Muhammad is His Prophet." Under Islam, there are no sacraments necessary to obtain God's grace. There is no baptism into the faith. The sole requirement is that two witnesses observe the recitation of the Shahada. Then the person who recited this creed is considered to be in Allah's service. While the Shahada is a formal profession of faith, it is also a common daily prayer. Muslims say it both during prayer rituals and during their personal prayer practices.

Salat

Salat traditionally refers to the five daily prayer sessions that are obligatory for Muslims, and carried out every day of the week. The prayers of salat call out to Allah and praise his transcendence. According to Muslim belief, the performance of salat can also counteract the prayer practitioner's weaknesses and bad actions, purifying him and reinforcing his spiritual strength. Salat is so central to Muslim worship that the prayers and accompanying gestures are the first elements of Islam that the Muslim child learns. The gestures are critical because by physically demonstrating submission to Allah, the mental or spiritual submission is reinforced and enhanced.

The prayer practitioner must meet certain requirements to be permitted to perform salat. He must be Muslim; he must be clean in mind, body, and clothing; he must say the prayers in a pure place; he must appropriately cover the body (for women, this means that only the face, hands, and feet can be visible); and he must pray with his face in the direction of Mecca or, if in Mecca, the Ka'ba—the ancient temple that is now the seat of Muslim worship.

As previously mentioned, there are five set times to perform the ritual prayers, and each session consists of elements—*rakats*—that are repeated two, three, or four times. The first ritual of the day is *al-fajr*, which is recited at dawn. Its elements are repeated two times. The second service, called *al-zuhr,* is said at noon. Its elements are repeated four times. Next is the afternoon prayer, *al-ásr,* which is performed in the middle of the afternoon. Its elements are repeated four times as well. Then comes the evening prayer, *al-maghrib,* said immediately after the sun sets, with elements repeated three times. Finally, a night prayer, or *al-'isha,* is recited at approximately ninety minutes after sunset. The elements of this prayer service are repeated four times. There is some variation among traditions.

The time for salat is signified by a call to prayer, as mentioned earlier. Whether broadcast over loudspeakers or the radio, the call can be either a live chant or a recording, and is always spoken in Arabic. The words are fixed. In response, the worshipper begins salat by facing Mecca and repeating his own personal call to prayer. Next, the Muslim states his intention in prayer. For this, he stands with raised and open hands. Palms should be turned forward and held at ear level, with the

Call to prayer position.

thumbs placed behind the earlobes. An example of stating intention would be to say, "I intend to offer ____ rakats of the ____ prayer, and face the Ka'ba for the sake of Allah and Allah alone." The first blank would be filled in with the number of elements required during the particular prayer session, and the second would be filled in with the name of that session: al-fajr, al-zuhr, al-ásr, al-maghrib, or al-'isha.

The worshipper may then recite the Allahu akbar, discussed on pages 135 and 136. According to Jacques Jomier in *How to Understand Islam,* when recited in salat rituals, it is referred to as the Allahu akbar of sacralization, because it brings the person into a holy mindset. Once all of this is completed, the worshipper brings his hands to his sides or crosses (folds) his arms, and salat prayer formally begins.

Standing, the worshipper recites the first chapter of the Qur'an, titled the *Fatiha.* (For the text of the Fatiha, see the inset on page 139.) Afterwards, many Muslims follow a practice during which, still standing, they recite a few passages of their own choice from the Qur'an. This occurs at least during the first and second rakats. Sometimes, but not often, a Muslim group recommends fixed verses during this part of the ritual.

A Muslim next performs a full bow, bending from the waist, with palms on the knees. He may recite the Allahu akbar again during the bow. Upon straightening, some sources translate that the person declares, "Lord, to You be the praise." Others explain that the Muslim says, "God has mercy on those who praise him," or a variety of other similar phrases. Additional bows and declarations of Allahu akbar are common at this point.

The full bow.

The formal prostration.

After the bows, a formal prostration is performed, but not before declaring "Al-hamdu lillah" once. Translated as "Praise be to God," this is a phrase of thanks to Allah. Then the traditional Muslim gets down on his knees and, with his hands palm-down below his shoulders, places his forehead on the ground, saying a prayer—in Arabic—such as, "Glory to my Lord, the Most High. God is great." Another example of a prostration phrase is, "Glorify the name of God most high." Next, the person sits back on his heels and, maintaining a kneeling position, says Allahu akbar. Once again, the head is placed to the ground and the prostration is repeated, along with the accompanying phrase. There is a return to kneeling, and another Allahu akbar. Then the Muslim returns to standing position. The whole process is repeated for a designated number of times, starting again at the Fatiha. Some traditions hold that before concluding each set, the head is turned to the left and right.

The kneeling position.

The Fatiha

The *Fatiha* is literally the "opening" of the Qur'an. The first chapter of the sacred book of Islam, it is recited at the beginning of every prayer rite.

◄○►

In the name of God, the Compassionate, the Merciful,
Praise be to God, Lord of the Creation,
The Compassionate, the Merciful,
King of Judgment-day.
You alone we worship, and to You alone we pray for help.
Guide us to the straight path,
The path of those whom You have favoured,
Not of those who have incurred Your wrath,
Nor of those who have gone astray.

After the second and the last rakat, the worshipper recites the *Tashahud*. These ritual words are meant to call forth God's help. (See the inset on page 140.) At the conclusion, while still on his knees and sitting back on his heels, the worshipper recites the *Salawat*, also contained in the inset on page 140. He then greets any other prayer practitioners to the right and left, wishing peace upon them: "As-salamu alaykum wa rahmatu-Llah," or "Peace be with you and God's mercy." This is called the *taslim*. At a mosque, handshakes are also exchanged as a sign of brotherhood. If the worshipper is not at a mosque service, but rather is praying privately, he will greet his two guardian angels. Ultimately, the salat involves praise, thanksgiving, proclamation of Allah's lordship, remembrance that there will be a day of judgment, and requests for Allah's guidance. The whole sequence often takes five to ten minutes.

Friday afternoon salat services, which are obligatory for men, include not only the usual salat prayer rituals, but also a lengthy reading from the Qur'an and a sermon. At each service throughout the week, an *imam*, or prayer leader, heads the communal prayer. An imam is not a member of the clergy. Rather, he is a person who is very well studied in the Qur'an. Any such man can serve an imam at a mosque service.

It is important to note that Muslim law does not allow a Muslim to per-

Prayers of the Salat

Salat—the Muslim obligatory prayer ritual—includes several fixed prayers that are piously recited. Two of these prayers are printed below. The Tashahud is said after the second rakat (or part) and the last rakat of the salat. The Salawat is performed after all of the rakats have been completed.

―――――――――――◄○►―――――――――――

The Tashahud

I bear witness that there is no god but Allah. He is one and no one is like Him, and I bear witness that Muhammad is His conformer and His messenger. O'Allah send greetings to Muhammad and the Family of Muhammad.

The Salawat

O Allah, bless our Muhammad, as you have blessed Abraham and the people of Abraham. Surely you are the Praiseworthy, the Glorious. O Allah, be gracious unto Muhammad and the people of Muhammad, as you were gracious unto Abraham and the people of Abraham. Surely You are the Praiseworthy, the Glorious.

form a salat ritual before its designated time. However, the prayer ritual can be performed late if there is good reason for the delay. Men and women share the same prayer obligations, except that only men must attend the Friday service. In addition, there are certain times when women are exempt from their prayer responsibilities, such as during menstruation.

Nonobligatory Prayer

After an obligatory prayer ritual, many Muslims perform further prayers. In addition, many Muslims carry out personally designed prayer sessions—be they regular or spontaneous—over the course of the day. These personal prayers may be repeated phrases endeavoring to praise Allah, or may be prayers of petition.

Dhikr

When not engaged in obligatory prayer, a Muslim may choose an effective phrase or prayer litany and recite it repeatedly to enhance his mindfulness of Allah. In fact, many Muslim brotherhoods—or social/prayer groups—prescribe litanies of prayers to be said on prayer beads to create constant awareness of Allah's presence. This meditative chanting of fixed phrases is commonly known as *dhikr*. The Arabic root of the word *dhikr* refers to remembrance and mindfulness.

The prayer-bead loop used to count dhikr contains ninety-nine beads, which coincide with the Ninety-Nine Holy Names of Allah. So a Muslim may meditate upon the various characteristics of Allah by chanting each one of His ninety-nine names—one for each bead. One tradition quotes Muhammad as saying that anyone who repeats all of Allah's names by memory will be sure to gain entrance to Paradise in the afterlife. According to Braswell's *Islam: Its Prophet, Peoples, Politics, and Power*, these names yield "power and God consciousness" to the worshipper. Braswell reports that the characteristics highlighted by the holy names include majesty, generosity, beauty, essence, action, power, wisdom, fear-provoking, and goodness. The inset on page 142 lists a few of these names.

Another dhikr technique is to repeat three fixed phrases, saying each one thirty-three times, so as to complete count on the prayer-bead string. In English translation, the three phrases are: "Praise be to God! Every thanks is due to God! God is greater!" After these meditations, a person's own requests can be made. Called *du'a'*, these personal requests are discussed on pages 142 and 143.

Dhikr is traditionally performed in group, but the technique can be extended to personal prayer devotions. Also, the repetitive recitations can be accompanied by breathing techniques and designated movements. Dhikr might be done in any position—standing, sitting, dancing—according to a worshipper's traditions. The result is that the person who prays in this manner actually puts himself in a type of trance, removing himself from distractions and forming a highly focused state of awareness.

The Sufis perform great dances during their dhikr. Those who follow the practices of Jalal ad-Din ar-Rumi, a great Sufi master and poet, throw off their black cloaks in order to symbolize the shedding of burden and darkness. They then whirl around in white garments to symbolize life in Paradise. They may turn about individually, or form a ring and dance in an open circle, as though revolving around Allah. This type of mystic practice is gaining in popularity in Western culture.

Allah's Holy Names

Islam assigns ninety-nine formal titles to Allah, with each one empha-sizing a certain characteristic. Most of these names are found in the Qur'an. As explained on page 141, a common dhikr practice is to recite each of these names, dwelling on the meaning of every title. The prayer-bead loop contains ninety-nine beads for this reason—to allow the prayer practitioner to keep count. The small selection of names provided below suggests the wide range of characteristics addressed in the Ninety-Nine Holy Names of Allah.

al-Batin, Hidden	Al-Hasib, Reckoner
Ar-Ráuf, Compassionate	al-Wadi, Governor
al-Malik, Ruler	al-Muqit, Nourisher
al-Qahhar, Dominant	al-Muhyi, Giver of Life
al-Latif, Kind	al-Mumit, Giver of Death

Du'a'

Du'a' has come to signify the personal, extraliturgical prayers that a Muslim performs outside of salat obligations. This type of prayer is also referred to as prayer of supplication or petition. Dhikr, discussed above, can be considered a type of du'a', or personal prayer practice. Du'a' and dhikr are not truly distinct from each other. A possible way of distinguishing the two is to consider dhikr as simple, focused praise and mindfulness of Allah, whereas du'a' involves personal request. Prayers of intercession—that is, prayers said on behalf of another person—are included in du'a', and are called sdlā li'ajli in Arabic.

Whereas the fixed prayer rituals are to be recited in Arabic, du'a' can be spoken in each Muslim's native language. This form of Muslim prayer can be spontaneous and informal—more along the lines of a con-versation with Allah. But while the nature of du'a' is the individual's articulation of needs, we all know that sometimes words don't come flu-ently in prayer. For such situations, the Muslim can refer to texts that print du'a' prayers of an admired saint, poet, or spiritualist. An example of such a text is *The Complete Book of the One Who Constantly Prostrates*

Himself in Prayer, translated from the Arabic, *As-Sahifat al-kamilat as-saj-jadiyya*. This book contains the prayer collection of Zayn al-'Abidin, a famous Shi'ite prayer leader, or imam, who lived during the seventh to eighth centuries.

Spiritual Reading

Certain texts are given great significance in the practice of Islam. Among these is, first and foremost, the Qur'an, which Muslims believe to contain the actual words of Allah. Second to the Qur'an in textual importance is the Hadith. When discussed in full, the Hadith is a multi-volume collection of stories, legends, and lessons about Muhammad's life. Reading from the Qur'an and the Hadith, and meditating or dwelling upon the messages found therein, is considered prayerful activity. These two sources of Muslim tradition are further discussed below.

The Qur'an

Islam considers its sacred book, the Qur'an—also commonly spelled Quran and Koran—so holy that someone in ritual impurity should not touch it, nor should anything be placed on top of it. The passages are literally taken as the word of Allah, articulated through the Angel Gabriel

Using Muhammad's Words

When a Muslim is praying to Allah outside of the obligatory prayer rituals, he can voice his praise and supplications in his own language and words. For those times when personal prayers don't come easily to the lips, however, the worshipper has the option of turning to prayers composed by famous spiritualists, teachers, and saints—including the words of the prophet Muhammad himself. Here is an example of a beautiful prayer recited by Muhammad.

————————————◄o►————————————

O God, make a light in my heart and a light in my tongue;
Make a light in my ear; and make a light in my eye;
Make a light in back of me and a light in front of me;
Make a light above me. O God give me light.

to Muhammad, and thus sent out to the people. *Qur'an* is actually an Arabic word that means "reading" or "recitation." Reading and reciting the passages of the Qur'an signifies the accepting of, and then the thankful returning of, Allah's words. Certain verses can call forth blessings and protection. (See the inset on the Throne Verse on page 145.)

The Qur'an was revealed to Muhammad over a period of twenty-two years—from 610 to 632 CE, the last year being that of Muhammad's death. It was fully compiled about twenty years after the Prophet's death. The text explains that life on earth is a time to prove oneself; it is a temporary exam that will assess whether or not a person is worthy of an enjoyable afterlife. Therefore, upon death in this world, each person will experience either reward or punishment. The Qur'an supports a definite belief in life after death, in a final judgment day, in resurrection, and in every person's responsibility for his own actions. It addresses the problem of human weakness by constantly reminding the human consciousness of its necessary submission to Allah. All laws for Muslim living can be found in its pages.

> *"The Qur'an not only functions as a sourcebook of prayer but is itself the central prayer in the daily life of Muslims. That second dimension focuses on the notion of remembrance as a key to understanding the scripture as living prayer and as divine word now addressed back to God."*
>
> From *Seven Doors to Islam*, John Renard

The Qur'an is made up of chapters, each chapter being a *surah*. There are times when the Qur'an seems to correct itself, or further develop. According to the revelation, this isn't because Allah's words are sometimes wrongly communicated, but because Allah knows that the human being cannot handle all of the truth at one time. The entire concept of Islam unfolds over the course of the book. It has been said that some of Muhammad's earliest followers were drawn to Islam by the strikingly beautiful, poetic verses of the Qur'an.

The Hadith

There are thousands of *hadiths*—stories about Muhammad, his words, his actions, and the events of his life. At one point, these stories were oral tales

The Throne Verse

The following passage, taken from the second surah—or chapter—of the Qur'an, verse 255, is often referred to as the Throne Verse. Many Muslims believe that the recitation of this verse offers strong protection against evil.

◄◦►

Allah! There is no god
But He—the Living,
The Self-subsisting, Eternal.
No slumber can seize Him
Nor sleep. His are all things
In the heavens and on earth.
Who is there can intercede
In His presence except
As He permitteth? He knoweth
What (appeareth to His creatures
As) Before or After

Or Behind them.
Nor shall they compass
Aught of His knowledge
Except as He willeth.
His Throne doth extend
Over the heavens
And the earth, and He feeleth
No fatigue in guarding
And preserving them
For He is the Most High,
The Supreme (in glory).

passed down through the generations. Each story is attributed to an eye-witness to Muhammad. The whole collection of these stories is formally called the *Hadith*, and makes up fifty or sixty large volumes. The hadiths discuss a large variety of topics, from Muslim obligations, to Allah's generosity, even to the devil. Because of the traceable authenticity of the hadiths, they are considered second only to the Qur'an in importance.

One body of these stories is known as the Prophetic Hadith. These tales are specifically attributed to Muhammad himself. It is not uncommon for Muslim communities to claim that the Prophetic Hadith is inspired by Allah but is in the Prophet's own words, rather than direct reiteration of Allah's message. Then there is the Sacred Hadith, which is considered by some to be directly communicated to humanity by Allah. These are rather emotional tracts, expressing God's intense love for humanity and His presence in all things. Because of the emotional content, many conservative Muslims find these passages offensive. They believe such hadiths diminish the transcendence of Allah. However, the beauty and sweetness of these hadiths have made them valued texts among those who allow themselves an emotional perspective. Reading such passages on the love and benevolence of Allah reinforces the prayer lives of such Muslims.

ENHANCING THE PRACTICE OF PRAYER

Muslim prayers are always performed with the notions of submission and obedience in mind. Yet they are also enjoyable experiences, allowing Allah's servants to bask in His presence and focus their attention on their God. Even if the prayer practitioner no longer observes all of the strict obligations required of orthodox Islam, he can choose a number of traditional ways to enhance his spiritual practices, making his prayer time more effective. This can involve keeping certain attitudes in mind, and using helpful prayer postures and aids.

Adopting the Right State of Mind

By adopting the proper attitude when approaching prayer, the practitioner can increase his mindfulness of Allah, as well as the joy he experiences by acting in service to Allah. The following approaches have proven effective for many Muslims, and may also be helpful for any prayer practitioner, regardless of his religion, who wishes to enjoy all the benefits that prayer has to offer.

Form Niyyat

In Arabic, *niyyat* or *niyah* refers to *right intention*. The Muslim is supposed to form niyyat in his mind before reciting prayer. During this gathering of intention, he reminds himself that his prayers are said solely to Allah. He then declares the number of prayer elements he will perform, and which specific service he will conduct.

For an act of prayer, or any act, to be beneficial, the right intention must be behind it. Each prayer service—obligatory or optional—should be performed willingly and decisively, not simply by rote. Niyyat puts the person in a reverent and clarified state of mind, locking out distractions and organizing thoughts around service to God.

"Mindfulness is therefore the soul and ritual prayer the body of a believer's grateful surrender (islam) to God."

From *Seven Doors to Islam*, John Renard

Have Gratitude

A non-Muslim might wrongly assume that Muslims pray largely out of fear and submission. But the truth is that the Muslim delights in his God. Gratitude, not fear, is very likely the fuel that drives worshippers. Expressing thankfulness to Allah in prayer makes a person more aware of the everyday gifts from Allah—of how precious the world around us is—bringing a happiness and sincerity to prayer. That is why salat, the daily prayer rite, includes thanksgiving.

Emphasize Obedience

Islam teaches that every prayer should be said with the intention to obey Allah. This is comparable to the "Thy will be done" approach found in Judaism and Christianity. Muslims continually focus on their obedience to Allah, and also the joy that they experience in obeying their God. They trust that if they remain obedient to His commands and practice devout praise and thanksgiving, Allah will be merciful and generous to them. This emphasis on obedience helps put the prayer practitioner in a good state of mind by diminishing the egocentrism, or self-centeredness, that is so prevalent in human life.

Prayer Postures and Gestures

To enhance the experience of prayer and also to further display submission to Allah, the Muslim practices certain postures and gestures. It is evident that the body is very much considered a tool of worship in Islam. Prayer postures and gestures prevent prayer from lodging solely in the mind; the dynamism of prayer is further manifested through the body.

The prayer prostrations that became obligatory for the Muslim were not meant to degrade humanity. In *Islam: A Short History,* author Karen Armstrong explains, "The prostrations were designed to counter the hard arrogance and self-sufficiency that was growing apace in Mecca. The postures of their bodies would re-educate the Muslims, teaching them to lay aside their pride and selfishness, and recall that before God they were nothing." Therefore, Muslim prayer is rooted in the desire to wipe away egocentric attitudes and to become mindful of the true center, Allah.

The term *rakat,* also written as *rak'a* or *rakah,* refers to the entire repertoire of prayer gestures and words that are repeated during Muslim prayer. *Qiyam* is "the standing," during which the worshipper faces Mecca, recalls Allah's supremacy, and turns to Allah for protection from evil. *Rukū* is the term, translated as "kneeling," for the kneeling/bowing gestures. *Sujūd,* or *sajda,* is a prostration. (See page 138.) These postures performed before Allah are acts of adoration and service. They outwardly express the submission that is taking place on a spiritual level.

Hand gestures are also a part of Muslim prayer. The du'a' are often performed with open hands turned so that palms face upwards. Some prayer practitioners cup the hands, as well, to symbolize that the Muslim is set to receive the blessings which Allah will send in response to his prayers. It is also traditional to wipe the hands over the face once prayers are completed to spread the received blessings onto the body.

Prayer Accessories

As in other religious systems, certain Muslim prayer aids can contribute to the practice of prayer. Not all Muslims use the accessories discussed below, but many find that one or more of these aids can make the experience of prayer even more significant.

Prayer Beads

The Muslim prayer beads, which are discussed quite thoroughly in the section on dhikr, beginning on page 141, contain ninety-nine beads in a loop. This prayer aid is used to keep track of the worshipper's declarations of the Ninety-Nine Holy Names of Allah, and/or to keep count of phrase repetitions of any sort.

Prayer Carpets

As mentioned earlier in the chapter, many Muslims who perform the salat carry a prayer carpet with them throughout the day. This carpet, upon which prostration is performed, is called a *sajjāda.* It can be used in the mosque, on the street, on the grass—anywhere. Often, a sajjāda contains inscriptions of Qur'an passages to enhance the prayer practitioner's awareness of Allah. Some carpets are highly decorative, displaying intricate symbolic artwork.

Artistic Writing

Visual triggers for prayer, through artwork, are also a part of Muslim prayer life. This artwork can be found on buildings, books, prayer carpets, and many other articles that Muslims see and use both in prayer and in other daily activities.

Epigraphy is the inscription of sacred writing on mosques, buildings, tombs, and even smaller articles like prayer carpets and lamps. The complex inscriptions, usually spelling out Qur'an passages, are sometimes so highly artistic that they become coded, capable of being read only by a very trained eye. The selected texts often address the largest of issues—death, judgment, resurrection, and Allah's mercy through forgiveness. The Shahada, described on page 136, is a popular phrase for epigraphy, as well. These inscriptions are meant to trigger mindfulness of Allah, and also to provide the worshipper with beauty. Therefore, for example, when a Muslim simply glances down at the prayer carpet as he is about to kneel, he will see the epigraphy on that carpet and be further reminded of the purpose and beauty of his prayers.

Calligraphy is very popular in the Muslim culture; beautiful types of lettering have been designed throughout the history of Islam. Calligraphy is used in epigraphy, yet in a stricter sense, calligraphy refers to artistic writing done by hand, with pen or paints. It is considered one of the highest prayerful activities to write out passages from the Qur'an or the hadiths in calligraphy.

Finally, a technique referred to as *illumination* is often used to embellish works of epigraphy and calligraphy. This art entails carving or penning geometric and floral designs around the sacred passages to enhance visual appearance. The artwork created through epigraphy, calligraphy, and illumination affects the prayer lives of worshippers by bringing the presence of visual beauty and artistic adoration of Allah into their prayers.

Wazīfa

In some Muslim communities, individuals sometimes turn to an imam—a community spiritual leader—or an inspirational spiritualist to guide them on their personal prayer journeys. A spiritual guide can organize a daily prayer ritual specifically around a person's needs and wishes. Designed to be performed during prayer practice outside of salat, such a ritual is referred to as *wazīfa* or *rātib*. A fixed prayer plan, it eventually becomes a natural routine.

CONCLUSION

Above all, the Muslim performs prayer out of the desire to submit to and please Allah. The obligations of salat are met with joy of service, and additional personal prayers are recited with zeal to further communicate with Allah. Clearly, Muslim prayer life is rich with numerous traditions.

Islam appreciates the aural and oral aspects of prayer—listening to Allah's word, and reciting that word back to Allah, along with other prayers. Gestures and postures are also a significant part of Muslim worship, making prayer a total effort, not just one of the mind. And prayer can even be found in sacred text and artistic writing. Religion permeates every part of the Muslim's life—political, economic, and social. And a highly developed practice of prayer is essential to the Muslim religion.

7

Buddhism

 So far, we have studied the prayer practices of religions that worship one supreme God. Prayer is a natural part of these religions, serving as an avenue for communication with the divine. But what of a life philosophy that doesn't worship a supreme God? What of a belief system that considers the powers of liberation from suffering to be within the mind, not within a creator's compassion? Over five hundred years before the Common Era, Siddhattha Gotama, the "Buddha," developed such a system. Now recognized as Buddhism, its influence continues to affect many people worldwide. This chapter looks at the most fundamental elements of Buddhism, and within it, the practice of meditation. Under the tenets of Buddhism, meditation is one of the processes through which an individual moves away from ignorance and suffering, and therefore toward enlightenment—the ultimate goal of all Buddhist practice.

A BRIEF HISTORY

The story of Buddhism begins with the life story of Siddhattha Gotama. He is responsible for developing its fundamental doctrines. Sidhattha's own enlightenment and subsequent lifestyle serve as an inspiration to all who seek true peace and knowledge through Buddhism. In addition, his tenets have since been adapted to suit various cultures and individuals.

The Story of the Buddha

Scholars believe that Siddhattha Gotama, the Buddha, was born in 563 BCE. By birth, he was a member of India's warrior caste—a high, privileged

---

class. Siddhattha's father was a country squire. His mother died soon after giving birth to him, so the boy was raised by his mother's sister, who became his father's second wife.

Siddhattha received love and affection from his family, as well as material comforts. His early life was culturally routine. According to the tradition of his caste, Siddhattha was not taught to read and write; he married at age sixteen; he had a son at twenty-nine. Yet during the year of his son's birth, Siddhattha experienced an unavoidable urge to find a way to end the suffering that is inherent to life—that is, the suffering that naturally comes with birth, age, sickness, sadness, and death. So he put on monk's robes and began his quest as a wandering spiritualist.

Siddhattha started studying under one teacher, then another, and found no satisfaction. So he embarked on his own journey—one of severe asceticism. He carried out self-mortifications, extensive fasting, and strenuous breathing techniques. For six years, he followed this path, gathering five disciples who waited and watched for Siddhattha to reveal great truths. But Siddhattha finally realized that self-torture was not an effective path either, and so he gave up asceticism. And because he abandoned these ways, his five disciples abandoned him.

Alone and still searching, one day Siddhattha remembered a wonderful experience he had as a child. While simply relaxing and reflecting under the shade of a tree on his father's property, young Siddhattha had entered so deeply into solitude that he experienced no wants, no emotions. It seemed to be the ultimate existence, as desire and suffering could not penetrate his contemplative state. Recalling this event, Siddhattha considered that such a state was the way to liberate the individual from suffering and, therefore, to attain enlightenment.

Taking a lead from his childhood memory, Siddhattha sat under a fig tree and began to meditate. In pensive examination, he moved through the whole process of existence. He recalled previous lives; he comprehended how the cycle of birth and rebirth—*samsara* (pronounced *suhm• sah ´• ruh*)—occurred. He realized that every being is subject to this cycle as long as she remains ignorant and experiences attachments and cravings—that is, as long as she sees herself as a distinct and permanent self. At the moment that Siddhattha understood the whole process of suffering, as well as the way to liberation from it, he attained enlightenment or *bodhi;* he became a "Buddha." Siddhattha was thirty-five years old.

Although the Buddha was drawn to a life of solitude, he decided to embark on a teaching ministry out of compassion for beings who still suffered the pain of unenlightenment. Thus, Buddhism was born. The Buddha's first disciples were those five followers who had abandoned him when he stopped his severe asceticism. These monks were mesmerized by the Buddha's explanation of the cycle of birth and rebirth, and his conviction that self-discipline and moderation could lead to liberation. He prescribed the Eightfold Way to the Termination of Suffering, discussed on page 157. The Buddha's teachings—*dharma*, or *dhamma*—were well received, and he continued to spread his newfound knowledge.

Within a few months, sixty followers had joined the Buddha's order. He asked them to go out into the surrounding areas, and start teaching others how to seek enlightenment. And the Buddha, himself, continued his ministry for another forty-five years, wandering throughout Northern India and compassionately teaching the dharma. The Buddha died in 483 BCE; he was eighty years old. His body was cremated, and his ashes were placed in several urns and given to noted families. The families enshrined the urns in burial mounds, which have since been located. The remains are venerated to this day.

The Buddha was known for his contemplative personality, his compassion for all people and beings, his courtesy and self-restraint, his certainty in his teachings, and his magnetic effect on those to whom he preached. Siddhattha did not consider himself divine, but once enlightened, he certainly did not place himself on the same level as any beings around him. In fact, Siddhattha once instructed a monk not to address him as "friend," but as "Thus-Come, a fully Enlightened One." Yet he was not self-aggrandizing. The Buddha was very clear that the dharma itself —not he nor any other teacher—was the authority of Buddhism.

> "Once . . . a brahmin asked him [the Buddha] whether he was a god, a heavenly being, a spirit or a man. To all these possibilities he answered in the negative. The imperfections, which place a person into any of those categories, had been exterminated in him; he was a Buddha."
>
> From *Buddhism: An Outline of Its Teaching and Schools,*
> Hans Wolfgang Schumann

Siddhattha is not the only Buddha to ever exist. A Buddha is anyone who understands the truth of reality without having it imparted or taught to him; he discerns it through his own nature and insight. And those who become enlightened under the schooling of Buddhas are called arahants, or saints. But Siddhattha is often referred to as the Buddha, because he not only found the path to enlightenment, but also crystallized and articulated it to others, becoming the father, so to speak, of Buddhism.

Buddhism Continues to Develop

Many schools of Buddhism have developed over time. The three main branches of Buddhism today are Theravada Buddhism, which traces back to the time immediately after the Buddha's death and is largely followed in Burma, Cambodia, Indonesia, Laos, Sri Lanka, and Thailand; Mahayana Buddhism, which was established in the first century of the Common Era, and is mainly practiced in India, Indonesia, Japan, Korea, mainland China, Nepal, Taiwan, and Tibet; and Vajrayana or Tantric Buddhism, which formed between the third and seventh centuries of the Common Era, and took a strong root in Tibet. Buddhist schools generally stem from these three traditions. Most Asian regions have their own schools of Buddhism, such as Tibetan Buddhism, Burmese Buddhism, etc. One of the better known schools is Zen, a subschool of Mahayana Buddhism that developed in China and Japan, and is now widely practiced even in the West. (See page 172 for more information.)

Quite significant differences arise among the branches of Buddhism. For example, Theravada Buddhism does not include a belief in a great Absolute that exists before and within every being—in other words, something akin to God and heaven in Western religion. After enlightenment, a being is not immersed in a greater union, but simply ceases to be. However, in the Mahayana school, there *is* a proposed Absolute—a fundamental state of perfection and unity into which every being is immersed. In fact, that Absolute is always in existence, infused into samsara and tying everything together in a perfect oneness. In the Mahayana school, the Buddha is viewed as a projection of this Absolute, whereas in Theravada Buddhism, he is viewed simply as a wonderful teacher.

Obviously, there are some crucial differences among the types of Buddhism practiced. However, there are also fundamental concepts shared by all Buddhist groups. First, all Buddhists believe that life is suffering, and that liberation is necessary to end that suffering. Second, all groups believe in rebirth and hold that there is karmic law—a law neither brought about nor maintained by a god—that affects these rebirths. Also, all Buddhists believe that this world has no real substance. Nothing in this world is permanent. As a result, there is no transcendent self or soul. Therefore, extinguishing notions of the self is necessary for enlightenment. Overcoming greed, hatred, ignorance, and attachment are the only paths to liberation from suffering. Finally, there is great respect for and confidence in the Buddhas, whether a given school believes them to be human, superhuman, or divine.

THE CONCEPTS OF THE DHARMA

While Siddhattha Gotama did not leave any written documents behind, his followers recorded and compiled his teachings, referred to as the dharma. The dharma is based on Four Noble Truths: life is suffering (*dhukka*); suffering is the result of ignorance about reality and of attachment, which includes craving, greed, hatred, and other selfish phenomena; suffering can be terminated by conquering ignorance and attachment; and the termination of suffering can be achieved through the Eightfold Way, discussed later. The fact that life is suffering is obvious when the individual encounters illness, pain, anxiety, and death. But Buddhists believe that even what "feels good" continues the cycle of suffering. For example, love leads to desire, attachment, and ultimately loss. And lust is essentially a state of want, which is suffering. True happiness can be found only in the permanent, and nothing to do with this life is permanent.

Buddhism teaches that there is no self, no transcendent soul, for that would suggest something permanent, and therefore something that would warrant attachment. If a being is not attached to anything, nothing can disturb her. She becomes calm and kind, not to earn a pleasant life the next time around, but simply as a result of liberation from the craving and anxiety caused by attachment. It is this kind of nonattachment—this moving away from the delusion that a self interacts with objects, beings, memories, and the like—toward which the Buddhist works.

If a person can overcome ignorance and attachment, which essentially allow the notion of selfhood to be maintained, "she" will no longer exist. There will be no "self" to perpetuate. At that moment, *nirvana* or *nibbana*—extinction—takes place. Loving kindness, compassion, sympathetic joy, and composure characterize the being who has attained nirvana. Some ancient texts describe nirvana with poetic terms such as bliss, peace, deathlessness, and truth. But the more philosophical descriptions of nirvana explain it in terms of negation. Nirvana is the termination of suffering—the destruction of all elements that keep the being bound by samsara.

As evident in the information above, nirvana is attained while the being is alive. Then the enlightened being simply waits to pass out of the body, never to be reborn again. Once the being has been freed from the body, the state of nirvana is called *parinirvana* or *parinibbana*. However, according to Mahayana and Vajrayana Buddhism, some enlightened beings decide to remain in compassionate service to others during this lifetime and even past it, rather than be altogether extinguished. Such beings are called *bodhisattvas*.

Until nirvana is attained, the being remains in samsara. The type of rebirth that a being experiences is designated by the *law of karma*, or the *law of kamma*. This law states that if a being accomplishes largely good deeds in her lifetime, she will be reborn in better conditions, and vice versa. That doesn't mean that the human is always reborn as a human. There are many realms of existence—gods, humans, spirits, animals, and hell. Some sources site an even lower realm of demons. Humans actually are in the best realm for enlightenment. Why? According to Buddhist teachings, the gods have it so good that they are not likely to see the need for enlightenment; while the spirits, animals, beings of hell, and demons lack the intellectual sophistication to search for and attain it. All of these beings must become human before they can hear the Buddha's teachings and become liberated.

When rebirth occurs, there is no soul that travels from one body to another. Instead, the concept of rebirth is maintained by *conditionism*, which means that one birth conditions the next. In his book *Buddhism: An Outline of Its Teachings and Schools*, Hans Wolfgang Schumann offers a helpful metaphor. During a game of pool, one ball strikes another ball, which then sets another ball in motion, and so on. No material is passed along in this process, but the proceeding movements aren't random, either. By its force and direction, each ball sets the next one on a specific path. So it is with rebirths. Each one stimulates the next to proceed in a specific manner, but does not transfer any material.

If a being has performed many good deeds, the subsequent rebirth occurs in a more favorable sphere or a more favorable situation. And if a person commits harmful deeds, rebirth occurs at a more disadvantageous level. There is no concept of sin or guilt. There is only a belief that deeds which lead toward liberation—compassionate deeds, for instance—are helpful to the being, while those that lead away from liberation are harmful. It is actually not the deed itself that affects the practitioner, but the intention behind the deed.

Note that any deed performed with intention will affect the cycle of samsara in some way, good or bad. The way to liberation is to act without *any* intentions, whether harmful to others or helpful to the self—to act compassionately, but without purpose for the self. Once a being masters this system, she is enlightened and attains nirvana. Enlightened beings still perform good deeds, but not to maintain enlightenment. The good deeds of enlightened beings are simply a result of a perfect state that can yield only goodness.

The path to nirvana is a good deal harder than it may seem. For most beings, many rebirths are necessary. Desire, which is inextricably linked to the "I" or the ego, and ignorance keep a being from detaching herself from this world. So how does she get rid of desire and ignorance? The answer lies in the Eightfold Way.

The Eightfold Way is the Buddha's prescribed path to end suffering. It includes right view, right intention or resolve, right speech, right action or conduct, right livelihood, right effort, right mindfulness or awareness, and right meditation or concentration. Obviously, for some of the elements of the Eightfold Way, there are varying translations. But the various terms provided imply the same general concepts.

Certain ancient Buddhist texts group these eight elements into three categories. The first two fall under wisdom or comprehension; the next three, under morality or virtue; and the final three, under meditation or concentration, in the large sense of mental discipline. It is this last group with which we now concern ourselves, as we continue with a discussion of meditation. But one point is necessary to make. It is not the Eightfold Way that triggers enlightenment. Enlightenment is gained by shedding ignorance and desire. The Eightfold Way is simply a means to achieve that end. Many people have attained enlightenment without following the Eightfold Way.

THE CONCEPT OF MEDITATION

Meditation is a general term that refers to the practice of mental exercises which bring an individual closer to nirvana. The practice of meditation helps the practitioner to know the mind, to gain control over the mind, and therefore to finally free herself from the mind. Below, we further investigate the role that meditation plays in the Eightfold Way. We then examine the role of meditation in the Buddhist's life.

What Role Does Meditation Play in the Eightfold Way?

In the previous discussion of the Eightfold Way, we identified the umbrella category of meditation—exercises of mental discipline—and assigned three elements under it: right effort, right awareness, and right concentration. The last of these, right concentration, is sometimes called right meditation, and refers to the specific application of meditation methods according to a person's particular needs. For example, a person who struggles with a scattered and nervous mind might choose to practice a meditation technique that encourages stillness of mind. The decision to do this, and the action of accomplishing it, falls under right concentration or right meditation. It is important to note that the umbrella category applies not only to specific meditation sessions, but to the entire lifestyle of a person. By looking at the three elements of the Eightfold Way that occur under the general topic of meditation, we will better understand how crucial meditation is on the path toward nirvana.

What Is Right Effort?

Right effort involves working toward control over the senses so that they allow only that mental activity which works toward enlightenment, while avoiding perceptions and thoughts that work against enlightenment. This is not to suggest that a person will not, or should not, notice or respond to certain sense triggers. As you will learn in the discussion of right awareness, below, it is crucial that the individual be fully aware of all sensations and objects. But every individual can work to diminish her emotional response to them, and can get better at this diminishment with practice. So instead of reacting emotionally to someone or something—feeling hatred or desire, sympathy or repulsion—the meditation practitioner should make an effort to simply observe the object and make a mental analysis of it. Eventually, that analysis will chip away at any personal attachment, good or bad, to that object. The meditation technique of guarding the senses, which is an important part of right effort, is discussed later, starting on page 162.

What Is Right Awareness?

The terms *right awareness, mindfulness,* and *attentiveness* all refer to the individual's full awareness of everything within and around her, including the body, the mind, and all sensations and objects. By becoming mindful of even the most common of things, like breathing, the mind's tendency to wander, to jump, and to pass ridiculous judgment is greatly diminished, allowing the individual to let go of anxiety and to exist in a calm, productive state. The mind is then able to take control of the moment and the object of its attention. Obsessions with the past and the future fade away, and the practitioner is better able to act appropriately in the present.

What Is Right Meditation or Concentration?

Right meditation, or *concentration,* allows a person to understand techniques of meditation, and how she can apply them to gain calm and insight. According to Hans Wolfgang Schumann in *Buddhism: An Outline of Its Teaching and Schools,* techniques include guarding the senses (right effort), awakening the senses (involved in right awareness), focused observation, trance, contemplation, and abiding. Most of these are discussed under "Meditation Techniques," found later in the chapter. Trance is not further discussed because it involves levels of realization about perception and consciousness that are too complicated to be responsibly handled here.

Where Did the Practice of Meditation Begin?

Clearly, the basic intentions and techniques of Buddhist meditations can be traced back to the Buddha and the very first teachers of the dharma. That's not to say that Buddhists have not further developed techniques and modified them to form new traditions. But the Buddha himself included "right meditation" in his Eightfold Way to Termination of Suffering and practiced meditation exercises.

Interestingly, though, there was an established tradition of mental-discipline exercises *before* the Buddha, and some of his thinking was drawn from these practices. The ancient Indian tradition of Yoga, which influenced Buddhism and, at the same time, Hinduism, involved many highly developed mental exercises. A short history lesson will give you an idea of how far back the discipline of meditation goes.

In the ancient culture of what is now India, the indigenous people based their way of life on Yoga. A term that means "yoking," *Yoga* refers to the gathering of the mind's powers through disciplinary concentration exercises, and thereby increasing the force of the individual's inner world. In the cultural sense, Yoga applies to an entire lifestyle, from breathing, to eating, to understanding the cosmos and the individual's place in it. The concept of karma existed in the Yogic tradition. So did the idea that each person is responsible for her own spiritual progress, rather than being subject to the whims and judgments of the gods.

Scholars have discovered that in the seventeenth century BCE, the Aryan people, who came from the region known as Iran today, invaded the Indus Valley region (India). The Aryans conquered the natives of the land and impressed their religious beliefs upon them. Identified as the *Vedic* tradition, these beliefs are chronicled in the *Rig-Veda* text. The

Aryans recognized many gods, most of which represented forces of nature. Very early on, there were signs that worshippers had a general concept that the various gods were all expressions of one Divine. But myths allowed discussion of the mystery that no one could solve.

By the eighth century BCE, the Vedic religion was no longer satisfying for the population, and traditions from the Yogic belief system resurfaced. The concept of karma was met with great interest, as was the concept of an individual's responsibility for her own spiritual progress. The gods that had been implanted by Vedic traditions were further understood to be mythical explanations for one great reality. A return to Yogic postures, breathing techniques, and concentration exercises now became widespread. Buddhist meditation practices are rooted in Yogic mind techniques that resurfaced when Vedic beliefs were no longer satisfactory.

> *"When Buddhists experience bliss or a sense of transcendence in meditation, they do not believe that this results from contact with a supernatural being. Such states are natural to humanity; they can be attained by anybody who lives in the correct way and learns the techniques of Yoga."*
>
> From *The History of God*, Karen Armstrong

How Important Is Meditation in Buddhism?

Meditation is very important to the person who is working toward enlightenment. It is part of the path that is believed to bring an individual into nirvana. Meditation teaches a person to understand the processes of the mind, from which craving and delusion stem, and therefore to control these processes and ultimately eliminate them. It is only in freeing oneself of a desirous and deluded mind that liberation from suffering is possible.

Does Meditation Change a Person's Karma?

You probably remember that karma actually refers to the intention behind deeds, both good and bad, and is necessarily a part of the whole cycle of birth and rebirth in suffering—samsara. The individual's intentions determine the conditions into which she will be reborn—and whether she will be reborn at all.

The purpose of meditation is actually to eliminate karma, not to improve it. Meditation should be geared to end craving and ignorance—even the craving to do good things in order to better one's own state, because that is ultimately a selfish drive. Acts of meditation allow the individual to shed the notion of individuality, not to work toward improving her "self." Therefore, rather than being viewed as a means to obtain better karma, meditation should be understood as one of the necessary elements of the Eightfold Way (see page 157), which terminates the karmic process.

That being said, as a person develops a life of meditation, she naturally becomes more compassionate and balanced. If she does not attain enlightenment in this lifetime, she will at least have achieved good intentions that will produce positive karmic effects.

Does Buddhist Meditation Involve Prayer to Saints and Spirits?

As implied by this chapter's earlier discussion of the various spheres of beings, the Buddha did not refute the existence of gods, spirits, demons, and the like. He just confirmed that they, too, were bound by the cycle of samsara. In traditional Buddhist philosophy, there are gods, humans, spirits, animals, beings of hell, and, according to some sources, a separate sect of demons. Humans are actually in the most desirable position because they are most likely to understand the need for enlightenment, and they are the beings who can be exposed to and observe the Buddha's teachings. So there is no need to pray to other samsaric beings for aid or guidance.

However, saints—called *arahants*—and Buddhas are beings who have reached enlightenment. Remember, a Buddha differs from a saint in that he attained nirvana on his own, without the tutoring of a dharma teacher. Mahayana and Vajrayana Buddhism schools state that help can be obtained from saints and Buddhas who have compassionately committed themselves to remaining in connection with the samsaric cycle in order to aid others in their quests toward enlightenment. Such beings are often referred to as *bodhisattvas* (pronounced bo•dee•saaht'•vaahs). Some Buddhists who are working toward enlightenment practice prayer to these beings. They often dwell on images of these saints and Buddhas for inspiration, asking them for additional instruction on the dharma and for help in attaining the discipline necessary to achieve enlightenment.

Of course, Siddhattha Gotama is worshipped by countless Buddhists as a savior who spiritually helps those who turn to him, above all, in faith and confidence. Once Buddhism started breaking into various schools, the idea arose among many of them that the Buddha was super-human, even divine. Folk religions mixed with Buddhism to yield practices in which pilgrimages to shrines of *the* Buddha—as well as other Buddhas—were encouraged. Such pilgrimages are thought to bring blessings upon faithful visitors, thus heightening their chances for better samsaric experiences and for more quickly reaching nirvana.

There are also deities within certain Buddhist schools of thought. These deities, which were never human, are gods of enlightenment, and serve to remind people of certain qualities that are necessary for enlightenment. In fact, their role is pretty much the same as that of saints and Buddhas—they can be depicted and dwelled upon—except that they are mythical, not historical, figures.

So within some types of Buddhism, there are prayer practices to saints and Buddhas. But prayer is not the purpose of meditation practices. The goal of true meditation is to actively work toward emptying the mind of attachments, and prayer is born from attachment. Therefore, there is a distinction between traditional Buddhist meditation and the folk prayer traditions that have arisen over the centuries in some schools.

MEDITATION TECHNIQUES

Several meditation techniques are described in the following pages. It is important to note that proficiency in these techniques develops with practice, over time. The first goal that the individual must work toward is the attainment of calm or tranquility. But as the meditator becomes more advanced, the techniques actually serve as tools for insight, or increased knowledge. The meditator begins to see and comprehend the subtleties of life, understanding things as they really are. Ultimately, she realizes the impermanence of everything and the futility of attachment. These realizations, in turn, yield a sense of detachment and, finally, the disintegration of the ego or self. It is in this way that the meditator moves toward nirvana.

Guarding the Senses

The purpose of the guarding the senses technique is to make oneself aware of the way the mind judges objects and, therefore, imposes personal prejudice onto everything around it. In Nyanaponika Thera's *The Heart of Buddhist Meditation*, we learn, "Normally man is not concerned with a disinterested knowledge of 'things as they truly are', but with 'handling' and judging them from the viewpoint of his self-interest, which may be wide or narrow, noble or low. He tacks labels to the things which form his physical and mental universe." Ultimately, the meditator who guards the senses moves away from using labels. She avoids passing judgment, a habit that comes so naturally to the human in response to sense stimuli. As she conquers the habit of judging both physical objects and her own thoughts and perceptions, she achieves detachment.

The practitioner begins guarding the senses by making a conscious effort to observe only simple facts when encountering stimuli. For example, if she sees a man, her natural tendency might be to regard him as attractive or unattractive. But in guarding the senses—eyesight, hearing, smell, taste, touch, and mind—she attempts to see him more objectively. She tries to put aside thoughts of personal desire or repulsion, and to make objective observations instead: he has dark hair; he is slender; he has a quiet voice. As the practitioner develops this form of meditation exercise, in which she learns not to see things in light of the self's desires, she achieves greater composure and levelheadedness; she is not dominated by personal greed or distaste. This brings her forward on her journey toward nirvana.

> "In what is seen there should be only the seen; in what is heard, only the heard; in what is sensed (as smell, taste or touch), only the sensed; in what is thought, only the thought."
>
> The Buddha, *Udāna* 1, 10

Let's take another example, just so we don't limit ourselves to thinking that this type of meditation is people-oriented. Consider the example of a thick, soft blanket that appeals to the sense of touch. A person might automatically think, "This blanket is comfortable and warm." This simple thought is actually loaded with self-centered perception. The person understands the blanket not as a thing in and of itself, but as an object that will feel good on *her* skin. Practicing the guarding of the senses would help the practitioner keep the self out of her observations. The practitioner would make the effort to simply notice the color, the size, the texture. Eventually, she would see the blanket not as an object that has potential to affect her, but just as an object consisting of many elements.

A little earlier, you may have noted that in Buddhism, the individual's world is created by *six* senses: eyesight, hearing, smell, taste, touch, and the activity of the mind. Guarding the mind from mental phenomena is the highest level of guarding the senses. The practitioner actually works on diminishing attachment to states of mind, such as happiness and fear. She analyzes even subtle perceptions, seeking to empty them of personal involvement. The goal of meditation, in general, is to clear away the clutter of mental "objects." Guarding the mind helps to achieve that goal. Note that guarding the senses can be practiced at any time; it is not designed specifically for use during sitting meditation sessions.

Awakening of Awareness

Some of the most ancient Buddhist texts contain a meditation exercise known as *satipatthāna*, or awakening of awareness. The aim of this exercise is to become mindful of activities that are usually performed unconsciously or semiconsciously. The exercise can thus enhance sensitivity and control of the mind, and help develop better concentration. Because by enhancing sensitivity, this technique also enhances alertness and clarity, it may be referred to as "sharpness of the mind." Upon practicing it, the individual becomes levelheaded and calm.

The Three Refuges

Some Buddhist meditators like to recite the Three Refuges, or the Threefold Refuge, at the beginning of their meditation sessions. It serves as a type of creed. Note that the *sangha*, mentioned in the third phrase, refers to the order of monks and also, for many, to the saints. Through recitation of the Three Refuges, the meditator reminds herself that her path is recommended by the Buddha himself, and that it has been shown to be viable through the monks and saints. Therefore, she gains confidence in the practice she is about to begin.

◄◉►

I take refuge in the Buddha.
I take refuge in the dharma.
I take refuge in the sangha.

Awakening of awareness can permeate all levels of existence. Generally, the practitioner starts with awareness of bodily activities by examining breathing, standing, lying down, and walking. She then moves to feeling; state of mind; and, finally, all of the minute mental contents such as perceptions that arise unconsciously. Below, you will learn about two of the most basic forms of this technique—breathing meditation and walking meditation.

Breathing Meditation

In her book *The Heart of Buddhist Meditation,* Nyanaponika Thera discusses mindfulness of breathing. She clarifies, "It is an exercise in *mindfulness,* not a 'breathing exercise'. . . . there is no 'retention' of breath or any other interference with it. There is just a quiet 'observation' of its natural flow."

Beginners are advised to focus on breath awareness for a short but quality "sit" at first—maybe ten minutes—and to gradually increase the length of the meditation over time. The meditator sits either in a firm chair, on a mat, or on a cushion. She should be comfortable and maintain good posture. (For more information on ways to sit, see the "Postures and Gestures" section on page 175.) Whichever sitting technique the meditator chooses, pressure should be well distributed along the spine, and hands should rest comfortably either on the knees or cupped in the lap.

> "*Breath stands on the threshold between the voluntary and the involuntary bodily function, and thus offers a good opening to extend the scope of conscious control over the body.*"
>
> From *The Heart of Buddhist Meditation,* Nyanaponika Thera

To begin, the meditator generally takes a few deep breaths to cleanse the body and mind, release tension, and gather her attention. Some teachers instruct that attention should be placed in the abdominal area, below the navel. This is considered the seat of energy in Zen and other meditation schools, as well as in Yoga. But other forms of Buddhism instruct meditators to focus simply on the place where the breath first makes contact with the body—the nostrils. Regardless of the meditator's focal point, she proceeds with natural breathing performed in a comfortable rhythm.

In Mary Heath's "The Benefits of Zen Meditation in Addiction and Recovery," we learn about two methods of breathing meditation. The first is "breath counting," a technique that's great for beginners. The meditator keeps track of the number of breaths, gearing herself for counting ten breaths at the most. She simply takes a full breath and, upon exhale, mentally proclaims, "one." After the second breath, she thinks, "two," and so on. This method helps the meditator remain focused on breathing as the sole intention of the moment. When her mind strays, it is best for the practitioner to gently call her attention back to breathing, without getting angry at herself, and to restart the counting. Once the

The Practice of Naming

According to Mary Heath in "The Benefits of Zen Meditation in Addiction and Recovery," both Zen and Vipassana Buddhism use a technique called *naming*. This practice involves acknowledging any stress, pain, or tension as it arises during a meditation session—or at any other time, for that matter. By identifying any invasion on your calm, you may recognize that it is unnecessary or avoidable, and therefore be able to let it go.

So when sitting or walking in meditation, don't get anxious about occurring thoughts and tensions. Instead, name them. If an annoying thought arises, mentally say, "Annoyed mind!" If you feel scared by a passing thought, say, "Scared," or "I'm fearful." If you experience a moment of grief, acknowledge it with a phrase like, "I grieve." And by the way, Heath suggests naming your *good* thoughts as well, and then allowing them to drift away and leave you in unattached meditation. So if you think of a loved one, say, "Love." If you feel a surge of healthy energy, proclaim, "I am well." Then return your attention to the focus of your meditation. By bringing your thoughts—good and bad—to a conscious level, giving them a moment's attention, and then letting them fly away, you may find that you are calmer, more focused, and better able to benefit from whatever meditation technique you have chosen to practice.

desired number is reached, the meditator begins again at "one," or ends the meditation session.

The second method is simply to experience the breath. The meditator notices the subtleties of the breath—if it's warm or cold; how it feels as it is drawn down into the abdomen; if there is a change in its characteristics as it goes deeper into the body. The mind doesn't fixate on set answers to these questions, but simply becomes aware of the intricacies of the process. Eventually, the meditator loses awareness of everything but the breathing. She becomes so immersed in the breath that it seems the only thing that exists or matters in those moments. The notion of the self disintegrates as the breath becomes all-pervasive.

Walking Meditation

Walking meditations are sometimes interspersed with sitting meditations, but can also be performed alone. Beginning meditators who find sitting meditation troublesome may benefit from first trying walking meditation. The technique is quite simple; the practitioner walks slowly around the meditation room or over a carefully selected outdoor spot. Concentration is placed on breathing and footsteps—on how each movement is orchestrated, coordinated.

As a way to enhance subtle awareness abilities, many meditators like to perform walking meditation in bare feet, in order to experience textures. Some like to walk on a consistent texture, while others like to step from hard floor onto mats or grass, and then back, moving across different stimuli. Environmental sounds and visual distractions fade away as the walking becomes the sole focus of the moment.

During walking meditation, the head should remain rather upright so that the practitioner can see where she's going, though eyes are most appropriately downcast to guard against visual distractions. The shoulders should not be tensed, nor the hands clenched. Hands are best held over the navel, cupping each other. Another good option is to leave the arms down by the sides, but touch the thumbs to the index fingers. The slight touching sensation seems to enhance sensitivity by providing a subtle stimulation, while encouraging the arms and hands to remain relaxed.

Many Buddhist temples have designated areas for walking meditation. Some of the meditation "courses" actually resemble mazes. Walkers find these paths very relaxing, and appreciate the fact that the already-carved paths allow them to trust the environment and concentrate more fully on each step.

Object Focus

Object focus involves attentive observation, or *bhāvanā*, of an item. The practitioner simply sits before an object, in a meditative posture, and focuses on it. It is a challenge to maintain mindfulness solely of that article, and not let various and sundry thoughts invade concentration.

Like other meditation techniques, object focus has great practical benefits. It quiets the mind, allowing it to develop concentration and one-pointedness. It drains away any excess mental activity. And it helps the meditator leave stresses behind, at least for a period of time, offering a nice break from the day-to-day rush.

Any item can be used in object focus, some of the most common ones being flames, stones, and the spiritual art objects called mandalas. Some sources even suggest focusing on clods of earth or other organic materials. Two forms of object focus are discussed below.

Flame Focus

The technique of concentrating on the flame of a candle has permeated every culture. Everyone knows that there is something inherently relaxing about candlelight. However, practitioners of meditation also know that when practiced properly, fixed attention on the flame is stimulating and enlightening. The meditator grasps the impermanence of the flame, noting how it jumps and swells, only to diminish and rise again. Yet on a deeper level, the meditator mentally enters the flame. She loses the sense of self as everything is drawn into that small tongue of light. For the Mahayana Buddhist, this is a wonderful opportunity to contemplate the oneness of everything as she merges her consciousness with the constantly changing flame.

Use of Mandalas

The Buddhist meditator can also focus on visual art objects that are mounted on a wall or placed on the ground. Among the Buddhist art forms used in meditation are the *mandalas.* These meditation aids— whether printed, painted, or designed in sand art—consist of an outer circle and a variety of geometrical designs within it, plus any symbols or figures that the creator decides to include. The meditator studies the mandala to gain knowledge about the universe and its processes. In fact, one of the translations of the Sanskrit word *mandala* is "whole world."

The simplest mandalas contain geometric shapes in patterns that resemble a maze. The simplicity of shapes encourages the meditator to avoid distraction, and the maze pattern helps the meditator consider the paths of existence—how they are confined within samsara, and yet are constantly changing and moving. But mandalas can become very complex, holding symbolic depictions of life elements, celestial spheres, and more. Ultimately, meditation on the mandala is intended to trigger the spiritual energy inside of the meditator, making her more capable of insight.

Chanting

Chanting could be considered another type of object meditation. The focus, however, is not visual, but aural—that is, it is perceived by the ear. And aural focus is another way of quieting the mind. When the practitioner channels the mind's energy into monotonous, vibrating sounds—chants—she trances herself into a deep concentration, shutting out all distractions and occupations with the self.

In *The Power of Prayer's* essay "The Common Ground of Healing," author Paul R. Fleischman, MD, discusses his experience with a gong used in an Indian Hindu temple. During meditation, someone kept banging a gong at consistent intervals. At first, the sound was terribly painful to the ear. But the disturbing noise then began to drown out the "noise" or tension within the body. In doing so, the sound of the gong actually created silence within. Buddhist chanting, like the sound of the gong at the Hindu temple, calls the mind away from internal noise. And the lulling vibration creates calm.

The phrases or sounds that a Buddhist meditator chants are called *mantras*. Mantras can be as simple as "Om," or as complicated as long phrases recited in traditional Sanskrit or a regional Asian language. The *Om Mani Padme Hung* mantra is a very popular mantra. It was apparently developed by the Buddha of Compassion, also known by the names Avalokiteshvara and Chenrezi. In Tibetan, the pronunciation of that specific mantra is *Om mani peme hung*, and in Sanskrit, a traditional Indian language, the pronunciation is *Om mani padma hum*. This mantra can be understood in a number of ways. It can, for instance, be broken up into syllables, with each syllable being assigned an emotion from which the practitioner is to be purified. "Om" is associated with pride; "Ma," with jealousy; "Ni," with desire; "Pe," with prejudice; "Me," with possessiveness; and "Hung," with hatred. As each syllable is recited, the chanter contributes to purification of negative karma due to the represented vice. A different way to understand the mantra is to assign a samsaric realm to each syllable, such as gods, humans, spirits, animals, beings of hell, and demons. Concentration upon each realm develops insight into existence. These methods of interpreting the mantra are only two of many.

Many practitioners of Buddhist meditation like to chant this mantra or other mantras 108 times, in accordance with the number of beads of the prayer-bead loop. (See page 178 for more information on prayer beads.) The repetition helps the power of the mantra to develop within the individual.

Abiding

The technique of abiding is actually a progressive development of loving kindness, compassion, joy, and composure, and involves emitting these positive states in six directions—north, south, east, west, above, and below. This practice is believed to have a marked effect on everyone around the practitioner, producing an environment that is conducive to enlightenment. People become kinder, calmer, and more open. Animals are soothed. It has been recounted that the Buddha even subdued an attacking elephant by emitting loving kindness! (Don't try this at home, though.)

The technique of abiding can be practiced in group or individually. The practitioner simply concentrates on allowing love and calm to manifest through her, toward others. It is interesting to note that compassion, in the Buddhist sense and in the way it is used in abiding, refers to knowing how to appropriately help another person. The term does not really apply to emotion or sentiment.

Abiding is a specific practice that takes great focus, and should be approached like any other sitting meditation; it is not just an attitude for life. However, abiding will become natural with practice and will generally help make the practitioner a pleasant, balanced person, in addition to benefiting surrounding beings.

Contemplation

The Buddhist practice of contemplation is quite different from the Christian practice of contemplation, discussed on page 113. In Christian practice, contemplation is an imageless dwelling with God—a basking in God's presence. Buddhist contemplation, however, involves choosing a certain concept of Buddhism, as found in the ancient texts and the teachings of various masters, and then dwelling upon that concept. For example, the Dalai Lama, the political and spiritual leader of Tibetan Buddhism, suggests considering the concept of impermanence as a contemplative meditation. The impermanence of all things was first recorded in ancient texts, and then confirmed by countless Buddhist teachers.

In contemplation, the practitioner's goal is to gain familiarity with the concept being considered, and then, ultimately, realize the truthfulness of it. The Dalai Lama calls this final state *spontaneous realization*, meaning that the meditator no longer has to use reasoning to grasp the concept. Instead, she achieves understanding without effort because her mind has actually merged with the concept under contemplation.

The meditator who wants to study ancient texts in order to enhance her contemplation practice can turn to what comes closest to scriptures in Buddhism—the *Tipitaka*. This is made up of three books: the *Sutra Pitaka*, which consists of discourses attributed to the Buddha; the *Vinaya Pitaka*, which contains the monastic code; and the *Abhidharma Pitaka*, which offers discourses on philosophical, psychological, and doctrinal issues, and also serves as a type of glossary. Theravada Buddhists rely heavily on these writings, believing that they come directly from the Buddha. The Mahayana Buddhists, however, place less emphasis on these ancient texts.

Zazen

Zazen, meaning "awakening," is a particular type of meditation practiced in the Zen tradition. Zen Buddhism was developed in China and Japan, and is now quite popular in the United States. (For more information on Zen, see the inset on page 172.) The Zen Buddhists look upon meditation as the study of the self. Yet, paradoxically, this study is believed to yield the forgetting of the self, which ultimately leads to enlightenment. Zen Buddhists are popularly recognized as the "meditation Buddhists" because of the heavy emphasis they place on the ritual of zazen.

To practice zazen, a meditation cushion or a doubled-over mat is placed on the ground, generally in front of a wall. The practitioner stands in front of the cushion, facing the wall, and places her hands in *gassho* position. That involves turning the palms inwards and pressing the palm and fingers of one hand to those of the other hand. The coming together of hands symbolizes the oneness of everything and the one-pointedness—or perfect focus—of the enlightened mind. With hands in the gassho position, the practitioner bows, bending at the waist. She then turns clockwise to face the direction that was directly behind her, and

The Way of Zen Buddhism

Actual enlightenment is not something that a teacher can impart; it is not passed on, inherited, studied, or read. Quite differently, it is simply experienced. And it is already there, attainable, for anyone who pursues it. Thus, in Zen Buddhism, when a practitioner reaches a new level of awareness through meditation practices, this change is referred to as *zazen,* or awakening. (For more on zazen, see pages 171 and 173.) It is as though it has always been there—and, in fact, it has. But delusion and dependence had to be shed in order to find it.

It is interesting to briefly focus on Zen Buddhism—a subschool of Mahayana Buddhism that developed in China and Japan—because it takes a unique approach. As this chapter explains, many Buddhists seek the aid of ancient texts, inspiring images, and various meditation accessories on their paths to enlightenment. But the practice of Zen attempts reliance on nothing—not even the dharma. Masters of Zen have been known to burn Buddhist texts and to make diminishing remarks about the Buddha: "If you see the Buddha in the road, run him over." Some have even been known to hit their meditating students in order to shock them out of dependence on comfortable surroundings. None of these methods are done to suggest disrespect, and any force used on the students does not afflict significant pain. The purpose is to open a clear path that avoids all reliance, even on history and images, because such reliance is a source of attachment and dependency, and thus will prevent the individual from attaining enlightenment. In fact, Zen teaches that even words become vehicles for unenlightened behavior because they are merely symbols, labels—nothing real. So silence is crucial to Zen practice.

Zen places emphasis on the master's personal guidance techniques and on full awareness of the moment at hand, rather than on past teachings and figures, or on future gains. Once the Zen practitioner is able to break away from false comforts—whether intellectual, spiritual, or physical—and practice her zazen meditation or any other activity with plain dwelling in the moment, a high state of clarity is reached. Only then does an awakening occur—a rise out of the deluded slumber that the human being typically knows as life.

bows again. In a Buddhist temple, this bow offers greetings to people who are seated behind the practitioner.

Once the bows in gassho are complete, the meditator sits upon her cushion and assumes her chosen leg and hand positions. She then sways the upper part of her body from side to side, decreasing the range of the sway as she continues, until she comes to rest in a balanced, centered position. She breathes naturally, easily, and silently, inhaling and exhaling through the nose. Effort is made not to concentrate on anything—neither on an object nor even on the intention to discipline her own mind. Traditionally, this position is maintained for thirty to forty minutes.

After meditation, while still sitting, the meditator performs a bow, puts her hands on her knees, and repeats the swaying process. Once she centers, she rises to a standing position, bows in gassho toward the wall, and bows in gassho again after turning clockwise to face the opposite direction. The zazen session is then complete. If the practitioner decides to perform another term of zazen, she is advised to take a break of approximately five minutes.

Emptiness Meditation

As detailed above, zazen accomplishes an emptying of the mind; the practitioner exists in peaceful nonattachment. It may be unique in its specific protocol, but is not unique in its intention. Some non-Zen Buddhist meditators, for instance, practice *emptiness meditation*. Also referred to as *shikantaza*, as well as other names, this advanced form of meditation has the same goal as zazen. In "The Basics of Buddhist Meditation," Dr. C. George Boeree describes emptiness meditation: "You hold your mind as if you were ready for things to happen, but don't allow your mind to become attached to anything. Things—sounds, smells, aches, thoughts, images—just drift in and out, like clouds in a light breeze."

Most people must learn to control the mind through techniques such as guarding the senses and awakening of awareness before they are able to successfully accomplish emptiness meditation for an extended period of time. However, some practitioners with natural talents for stillness and mindfulness can practice this meditation technique without much trouble.

Once the techniques of meditation are understood, the person who is working toward enlightenment should focus on the ones that help her with her particular challenges. Different people find different techniques more helpful, due to their personal qualities and their personal needs. For example, if a woman has problems with scattered and desirous thoughts, she might work on awakening of awareness and on object focus. If she struggles with anger, she might find the practice of abiding very helpful. A large part of right concentration or meditation involves knowing which techniques must be developed into exercises, and then understanding how those exercises must be honed to move toward liberation.

ENHANCING THE PRACTICE OF MEDITATION

A number of practices and accessories can make meditation more effective, either by enhancing concentration or by reducing physical discomfort. By considering the following suggestions and adopting those approaches that you find personally appropriate, you may be able to greatly increase your success not only in Buddhist meditation, but in meditation practices of all types.

Comfortable Clothing

The clothing that is worn during meditation should be comfortable and nonrestrictive. For effective practice, the meditator must be able to sit in a contemplative position easily, without blood circulation being diminished. Otherwise, "pins and needles," cramping, and other irritating if not painful conditions will result. So it is important to avoid stiff or tight belts, restricting elastic, and the like. It is also best to remove your shoes, and to meditate barefoot or wearing only socks.

Although it may sound unnecessary to mention the need for proper clothing, in our culture, where "comfortable" clothing is often denim jeans and heavy sweatshirts, this issue requires some attention. The bunching of thick material behind the knees, under the arms, and in other "bent" areas reduces blood and energy flow. The rough and heavy materials can also be distracting and cause the need to constantly shift. Take a lead from the monk's meditation outfit—a loose robe and bare feet. Such clothing maintains modesty while causing few restrictions and no discomfort.

Diet

Diet is another issue that, unfortunately, is often overlooked in our culture. Traditional Buddhist monks ingest no solid foods or heavy liquids after midday, so that the body is not laboring with digestion during periods of meditation. This would be a difficult practice for most of us, and is unnecessary for the typical meditator, but it teaches us to be mindful of our eating habits prior to meditation.

Because the body and mind become fatigued when digesting food, meditation is not as effective when performed after a meal. However, taking a light snack or a refreshing beverage prior to meditation may actually aid concentration, as it insures that the stomach won't spasm in hunger, and that electrolyte balance won't be impaired.

In addition, keep in mind that the Buddha promoted moderation in all things. So even when not preparing for a meditation session, a person who is interested in a Buddhist lifestyle should continually maintain moderate food and drink intake. This keeps the body and mind healthy.

Postures and Gestures

A variety of postures can benefit the meditator by placing her in a concentration-enhancing position. It is important to note that none of the following positions has mystical significance. Rather, these postures have been designed by master meditators to produce the discipline and comfort needed to carry out effective meditation. Over time, they have been shown to foster stability, to improve blood and energy flow, to allow deep breathing, and to promote mind clarity and focus.

Regardless of how the legs and hands are situated, certain basics should be kept in mind throughout the meditation process. For instance, the back should always be kept straight. It is healthiest to allow a slight, natural curve inward of the lower spine—that is, a slight outward pushing of the stomach area—in order to maintain good posture and comfort. Shoulders and arms should be situated to avoid tension. The head is best fixed straight ahead and tilted slightly downward. It is also a good practice to keep the mouth closed, with the tongue slightly pressing against the roof of the mouth. This reduces salivation, thereby cutting down on the need to swallow, and thus lessening distractions. Finally, the eyes can either be closed, half-open, or entirely open. But it is often suggested that the meditator keep her eyes cast downward and ahead a few feet, thus remaining half open. This diminishes the need to blink, while avoiding the sleepiness that can often come with closed eyes.

If sitting in a chair, it is important to remain in an upright position; the meditator should not allow herself to rest on the arms of the chair, or to slouch against the back or sides of the chair. Some meditation teachers suggest that the meditator place a meditation cushion under her buttocks. The cushion is designed to tilt the hips slightly forward, allowing a good distribution of pressure along the spine. It also encourages the

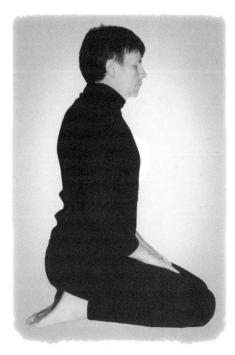

The seiza position.

meditator to keep her feet firmly on the floor, which is important for proper balance.

When sitting on the floor, most meditators find it helpful to place a mat or cushion beneath them. Kneeling is known as the *seiza position.* Some people find unsupported kneeling to be very difficult on the back and ankles. To rememdy that situation, either a cushion or a wooden *seiza bench* can be placed atop the heels or calves, allowing the meditator to rest her buttocks on it. This promotes better posture and good balance. Nyanaponika Thera states that in the East, female meditators do not sit in a cross-legged position, but rather kneel, resting on their heels, but using puffy, plump cushions as just described. Their hands simply rest on their knees.

The meditator can also choose from several floor-sitting positions. It is important for her to fold the legs in a *comfortable* crossed-leg position, not to place unnecessary strain on her joints and muscles. Over time, with consistent practice, the leg muscles will stretch and more advanced sitting positions will be possible. Regardless, it is best to use a plump meditation cushion, or *zafu*, to raise the rear and hips, drop the knees toward the floor, and distribute pressure properly along the spine. Balance, as well as breathing and mental efficiency, is better achieved in this way.

The best-recognized Buddhist floor-sitting position is the *full lotus*, which involves tucking the legs in as if about to sit "Indian style," but then placing each ankle on top of the opposing thigh. This is considered the most stable position, as it allows the body to reside in full symmetry. However, it is also the most

The full lotus.

difficult position to achieve. The *half lotus* is another option, and means placing only one foot on top of the opposing thigh, with the other foot remaining tucked under the opposite leg. Those who find both of these positions uncomfortable should simply bend their legs in a

The half lotus.

The Burmese position.

way that allows comfort and blood flow. The *Burmese* position is the simplest option. In this posture, the legs are folded in and placed one in front of the other. The tops of the feet—or the sides, depending on ability—rest on the floor.

There are, of course, a number of options when it comes to hand positions, as well. Importantly, the hands should be comfortably resting either in the lap or on the knees. For the lap, the traditional Buddhist hand position is the cupping of one hand within the other—both hands open with palms

The cosmic mudra.

up—and then the touching of the tips of the thumbs. A small oval-shaped space is formed between the thumbs and forefingers. This position is called the *cosmic mudra.*

Hand resting on knee.

For those who prefer to rest the hands on the knees, hands can be placed downward or opened upward. When palms are turned up, it is helpful to lightly press the tip of each thumb against the tip of its accompanying forefinger. This prevents tension and promotes concentration.

Meditation Accessories

The following objects can contribute to the further effectiveness of your meditation sessions. These accessories can be found in New Age stores, Tibetan spirituality stores, some online meditation sites, and appropriate catalogues. See the Resource Directory for a list of online sources.

Prayer Beads

The traditional string of prayer beads used in Buddhist meditation is referred to as a *mala*. These beads are used for counting mantras. Ideally, there are 108 beads on the prayer-bead loop. The reason for this particular number is that Buddhism recognizes 108 different types of hindrances and obstacles that must be overcome on the path to enlightenment. The loop often has a small section branching off that contains a fringed tassel. The tassel serves to mark the beginning and end of the loop, but, for some meditators, also signifies how all separate entities come together in union. Shorter malas that resemble bead bracelets are also available.

Meditation Cushions, Kneelers, and Mats

A variety of sitting accessories can be used to make meditation postures a little more comfortable. First is the mediation cushion, called a *zafu*. This is a plump, firm pillow that can be placed under the buttocks to raise the hips and thus drop the knees toward the floor. Some are round while others are crescent-shaped, and some are less plump than others to allow for a gentler tilt. The posture that results from using a zafu is healthy and comfortable. Importantly, the best way to use a zafu is not to sit on top of it like a stool, but to tuck the pillow under only one- to two-thirds of your buttocks—not under the thighs. Some meditators also place the zafu between their thighs and heels while kneeling. This helps to maintain good circulation, as well as comfort. The zafu is suggested for use atop a chair seat, too.

Some meditators employ wooden benches to ease kneeling. Called *seiza benches*, these items are not positioned under the knees, as in traditional Christian prayer practices, but instead are placed between the buttocks and the heels. The benches—which usually slope at a slight decline to support the body—allow for enhanced comfort and circulation.

Meditation mats are the simplest sitting aid. Besides the added comfort provided by the slight padding, the mat also mentally fixes a clean space for the meditator. It draws a geometrical box around the person, reducing her tendency to feel vulnerable, distracted, or even lost in a large area.

Statues and Other Depictions

Many meditators find that when sitting in a meditation position, with head bent slightly forward, it is best just to let the eyes fall naturally where they will. But some find it helpful to set up a sacred table at the proper level so that the eyes fall upon a desired object that serves as an aid. Small, uncomplicated objects are most effective. A small candle is, of course, necessary for the practice of flame focus, but there are many other options. Geometric shapes, in their simplicity, are known to be helpful to many mediators, so a simple cube, disc, or triangle is a good idea. It is best to avoid shiny or heavily textured objects, as these might prove distracting.

It is also not uncommon for the Buddhist meditator to keep a small statue of the Buddha on her prayer table. And there are many Buddhas that various cultures pray to and emulate, such as the Buddha of Compassion, who is very popular among Tibetan Buddhists. Fixating on a statue or framed depiction of a Buddha may trigger calm in the meditator, or encourage and inspire her on her path to enlightenment.

Mandalas

Mandalas are certainly beautiful works of art, but they are also much more than that. When a meditator concentrates on a mandala, spiritual energy begins flowing, and knowledge about the universe is then imparted. A mandala usually is made up of an outer circle with geometric shapes and/or symbols carefully arranged inside. Whatever the complexity, this prayer accessory promotes focus and calm, opening the mind to further insight. See pages 168 and 169 for more information.

Prayer Wheels

Prayer wheels are traditional devices used in certain Buddhist traditions. They consist of numerous copies of the mantra *Om Mani Padme Hung*, printed on very thin paper or on microfilm, wrapped around a spindle, and encased in a protective cylinder. The more mantras that are on a prayer wheel, the more powerful the wheel becomes. There are four types of prayer wheels—water, fire, earth, and wind wheels. Water wheels are spun by water, fire wheels are spun by the heat of a candle or light, earth wheels are turned by hand, and wind wheels are turned by the breeze.

A faithful Buddhist turns the prayer wheel—or allows wind, water, or heat to turn it—while reciting the mantra. Reciting it out loud or silently calls down benevolent attention and even blessings from Buddhas. Often, the hand that is not holding the prayer wheel is counting the mantra on prayer beads.

The positive power of all the mantras contained in the prayer wheel is believed to shoot out in ten directions as the wheel turns. In addition, it is said that Buddhas and bodhisattvas are manifested in prayer wheels. Their goodness radiates out, eradicating negative karma, blessing and purifying all people and creatures in the surrounding areas, and helping these beings move toward enlightenment.

CONCLUSION

The practice of Buddhist meditation is ancient, yet is as applicable today as it has always been. Meditation allows the practitioner to reap a variety of benefits, not the least of which is the ability to advance on the path toward liberation from suffering. In this way, it is akin to prayer. The meditator moves away from the graspings of this world, toward tranquility and insight. The ultimate goal is to extinguish the limited notion of the self. And if you think about it, this is also what people seek through prayer. Whether praying to Allah, God the Father, or Jesus Christ, whether reading Buddhist text or practicing zazen, practitioners have the same goal—to find liberation from the painful experience of isolation and want, and enter into a state of understanding and bliss.

PART THREE

Challenges

We covered a lot of basic topics on prayer in Part One, and then learned about specific cultural approaches to prayer in Part Two. By now, you have probably chosen what applies to you and what appeals to you, and hopefully are ready to start or re-start your practice of prayer with clarity, confidence, and vigor. As you embark upon and maintain an effective prayer life, Part Three will help you tackle the challenges by offering helpful hints for your personal prayer sessions, practical advice for the tough times, and motivational ideas for making your daily routine itself more prayerful.

Chapter 8 gets down to the nuts and bolts of arranging your prayer time. You will learn about selecting an appealing form of prayer, preparing yourself in body and mind, and heightening your experience with prayer aids such as candles, music, and incense.

Chapter 9 delves into periods of frustration and doubt—times when the spiritual drive stalls due to unanswered prayers or spiritual dry spells. Ultimately, these difficult times can lead you to a more profound prayer life. By reading through Chapter 9, you will be sure to not only get past these frustrations, but also to use them as opportunities for spiritual growth.

Finally, Chapter 10 discusses the wonderful challenges involved in making your entire day prayerful—of seeing the miraculous in the ordinary, the divine in the secular. Exploring these challenges will encourage you to climb the extra steps to a holier life endowed with a greater sense of purpose and contentment.

8

Getting Started

Although you may have grown up with a very specific notion of how prayer life should be conducted, in truth, there are many methods of prayer, from formal, fixed prayer to spontaneous prayer; from mantras to Scriptural meditations; from visualization to imageless contemplation. And there are so many ways that prayer time can be enriched and made more effective. A sacred space can provide you with the seclusion you may desire. Proper posture and breathing can create a sense of balance and harmony. Statues, candles, incense, and music can further enhance the practice of prayer.

Whether you seek to make your current spiritual life more fulfilling or are embarking on an exploration of prayer for the first time, this chapter will acquaint you with many forms of prayer, and show you a variety of ways in which you can enjoy a more successful experience. The following pages also provide a wealth of pointers—suggested by spiritual masters, teachers, writers, and prayer practitioners—that can help you approach prayer with the best possible attitude.

FORMS OF PRAYER

Remember that, above all else, prayer is prayer. You don't *have* to follow a certain regimen in order to pray more effectively. You don't have to pray just like Mr. So-and-So in order to please God. The important thing is that you pray. And your prayer life will be more productive if you shape it around *your* personality and spiritual maturity, not someone else's. So it is helpful to give yourself options.

The following discussion attempts to categorize prayer into several general types. Some people find that as they spiritually change and mature, one type of prayer style yields to another. For example, they might start with vocal prayer, move to meditative prayer, and end up practicing contemplation. However, many others are just as happy choosing a different prayer form on different days, alternating according to their own needs at a given moment. Of course, only through personal practice will you find the technique or techniques that work best for you. This discussion was designed to offer ideas and get you started, so that you can ultimately make choices that suit you best.

"How to pray? This is a simple matter. I would say: Pray any way you like, so long as you pray."

From *The Way of Prayer*, John Paul II

Fixed Prayer

Fixed prayers are prayers that have already been composed, and usually have been part of religious traditions for extended periods of time. For example, the Shema is a significant fixed prayer for the Jewish community. It dates back hundreds of years and is not only a part of religious services, but also a daily personal prayer for many Jews. Christians have been reciting the "Our Father" since Jesus taught it to them two thousand years ago. Muslims perform centuries-old fixed blessings during the daily obligatory prayer repertoire called salat. And many Buddhists like to recite the Three Refuges before entering into meditation.

Fixed prayers may be said aloud or silently recited in the mind, but whatever the choice, language is necessarily involved. And language is a highly effective means of praying. In his book *In Speech and In Silence,* author David J. Wolpe discusses the fundamental power of words: "In moments of great feeling, we search for the right words, though they elude us. Somehow experience is not full until we can frame it in language. Love unspoken in incomplete." He further asserts: "We send our voices ahead of us to probe into the heart of things, to grill them, to make the array of life comprehensible to our minds." Thus, words are truly powerful as a mode of expression, self-exploration, and release, and fixed prayer not only employs this power, but imbues it with community tradition to grant a sense of wholeness and familial love.

Sometimes you won't have the strength or feel the creative spark needed to find your own prayer words, perhaps because you are fatigued, depressed, hurting, or even overjoyed. At such times, fixed prayers offer a satisfying means of expression. Or you may find that a particular fixed prayer seems to capture your sentiments and needs so fully that it is too good to pass up. Someone else's words may become a wonderful gift for you—a gift that should be appreciated and used.

Of course, fixed prayers may already be part of your religious group practices, both during formal services and during personal prayer time. In such cases, traditional set prayers tie you to the spiritual energy of your religious community. Every religion has established prayers for the faithful to use. In fact, many religions assign certain prayers to certain times.

The recitation of fixed prayers is also a valuable way to enhance prayer time when concentrating on mental or visual images. The words become so familiar that they can be chanted while you meditate upon an aspect of your spirituality. (For more on chants, see "Mantras and Chants" on page 187.) This is not to suggest that you shouldn't focus on the words and fill them with zeal. But the truth is that the rhythms and familiarity of fixed prayers can also serve as a tool for concentration.

It is a good idea to keep copies of several fixed prayers in your personal prayer space, for times when you feel drawn to recite familiar prayers. The chapters in Part Two offer a variety of fixed prayers from different traditions, and the Resource Directory suggests prayer books that will help you locate more. But when using fixed prayers, be sure to keep several important points in mind. First, resist the temptation to use fixed prayers as magic chants. Because they often come from long-established traditions that may even have certain rituals involved, it's easy to attach superstitions or magical qualities to them. Avoid thinking, "If I say these words in just the right way, I'll convince God to answer me." Fixed prayers are aids for communicating with God, not spells. There is also the danger of fixed prayers becoming so routine that they are recited by rote. To avoid this, approach your prayers with energy; clearly form your intentions to concentrate wholeheartedly on the subjects of the prayers; and consider interspersing your fixed prayers with improvised, conversational prayer—spontaneous prayer—which is discussed below.

Spontaneous Prayer

Chapter 1 explained that the most basic definition of prayer is simply a conversation with God. In daily life, we converse in a number of ways.

But for most of us, language is the primary mode of conversation. As discussed in the section on fixed prayer, words help us find ourselves in this world. Even many of our inner thoughts occur in words. It is through words that we best know how to process, report, thank, praise, apologize, complain, and request.

So when you are communicating with God, why not simply speak to Him? Tell God about your day, about your desire and needs, about your worries. Whether aloud or silently, share your thoughts. Talk through the things that made you smile, and express your gratitude. Work out the things that are making you tense, and open yourself up for new perspectives. This honest conversation will enable your relationship with God to grow and flourish.

Spontaneous prayer not only lacks protocol when it comes to word choice, but also lacks protocol when it comes to timing. In certain cultures like Judaism and Islam, some fixed prayers are assigned to specific times of the day. But spontaneous prayer can occur at *any* moment, whenever you feel moved to reach out with your words. Thus, it makes the practice of prayer all the more personal, and has the power to infuse your entire day with a sense of the sacred.

Sacred Reading

Undoubtedly, you have moments when, instead of desiring to recite prayers, you want to listen. One way to move away from your own words and into God's answers is to perform sacred reading. Yes, you still reside within the bounds of language when you read Scriptures or other spiritual texts, but you are not doing the talking. You are being fed.

When reading from Scriptures and sacred texts, select a passage and take your time with it. Read it slowly, and perhaps several times. Digest the meaning, or various meanings, and apply the words to your own life. Allow yourself to dwell on the images and memories that the passage invokes. Sacred writings are so much more than just words. In fact, in Western religious traditions, some texts are considered to be the actual revealed words of God, and so are infused with lessons and love. For textual suggestions, consult the chapters on world approaches to prayer in Part Two.

Meditation

The term *meditation* means so many different things to so many different people. But there is a common factor. Meditation takes us away from the tendency to fill the moment with our preoccupations and analyses. It calls us to be receptive, to empty ourselves of anxiety and ego concern, and to dwell on the Divine or the Truth of the moment. Below you will find a number of meditation techniques that appeal to countless prayer practitioners. When personalized to suit your own style and needs, they can make a significant difference in your life.

Mantras and Chants

The rhythmic repetition of sacred words or phrases allows for great concentration on God or the Absolute. This prayer method calls the mind home, away from passing distractions. The voiced or even mental repetition is calming, often bringing the body into unity with the spirit through the loop of sound and energy that is constructed.

In Eastern practices, the repeated phrase or sound is called a *mantra.* A mantra is selected for the trancing sound and vibrations it produces, such as "Om," as well as the symbolism it might carry. In Western practices, the activity of repeating a word or phrase is often referred to as *chanting.* These words and phrases are chosen for the sacred concepts they encourage. Examples are various names for God; single words such as "peace" and "love"; and phrases like, "Lord, have mercy on me."

If you find it appealing to use a mantra that involves a foreign language, such as the Buddhist *Om Mani Padme Hung* mantra (see page 169), it is best to choose a pronunciation that you find comfortable. You may want to keep a copy of the mantra—its original text, its transliteration, and a good translation—in your personal prayer space for reference and inspiration. Likewise, it may be helpful to make a list of various mantras or chants that appeal to you. If you are drawn to a chanting session—in and of itself, or as a way to begin or end a prayer session—and don't have a particular favorite, you can consult several choices and decide on one that feels best at the moment. See the chapters in Part Two for a number of suggestions, including various names for God and short prayers.

Visualizing God

Visualizing, or mental imaging, is a form of nonvocal prayer. It brings the focus of prayer deeply inward, away from the world's distractions and anxieties. This is generally a Western practice. During a visualization, the practitioner moves beyond articulation and dwells on a specific, sacred image.

If visualizing God is part of your religious preferences, you know that doing so helps you identify with Him. God is technically not just a being, yet imagining Him as one may help you cultivate a relationship more easily. Jewish and Christian traditions often explain God as a loving father. And mystics from the Jewish, Christian, and Sufi (Muslim) traditions often visualize God as a lover. A familial or loving image can aid you in developing intimacy with God.

Some types of visualizations move beyond pictorial images of, say, God's face. In Judaism, this might involve mentally visualizing the letters of God's holy name. In Christianity, it could mean imagining the entire scene of Jesus Christ's crucifixion. There are also many symbolic images that can be meditated upon. The individual chapters on Judaism and Christianity provide additional ideas.

It is extremely important to select an image with which you are comfortable. If you choose an image that is intimidating or disturbing, you are likely to reduce the confidence and receptivity that is so necessary in effective prayer. So if a masculine view of God doesn't work for you, try a maternal image. If a parental image upsets you, try a brotherly or sisterly visualization. And if a human depiction seems to be holding you back, try various symbols. Many Christians, for example, imagine the Holy Spirit as a dove. And some Christians symbolize the Holy Trinity—their three-part God—as a triangle with an eye inside. Whatever you decide upon, you are likely to find that visualizations are a helpful way to dedicate time and energy to the exploration of God.

Many people also like to physically focus on an object, which in turn provides the stimulation to mentally fixate on an image or theme. Usually, this involves fixing your gaze upon a religious item and dwelling on its significance. For example, a Christian might gaze upon a cross, which is a symbol not only of the suffering that Jesus Christ endured, but also of a meeting of two realms—the heavenly and the earthly—as depicted in the intersecting lines. And a Buddhist meditator might fix his gaze upon a small statue of the Buddha, placing himself in a quiet state of mind during which the characteristics that the Buddha represents can develop. In such cases, the objects serve as prayer aids, a topic that is discussed later in the chapter. (See "Statues and Other Art Objects.")

Breathing Exercises

It seems that, universally, the breath is linked to the Divine, to the soul, to the most fundamental aspects of life. In Judeo-Christian Biblical text, God brought the first people to life by breathing into their bodies. It is therefore not surprising that so many religious approaches include breathing meditations.

Many people imagine the breath as God's divine energy, filling the prayer practitioner with life and emptying him of impurities. Just dwelling on this interaction with God is a prayer in and of itself. The breath can also be understood as a bridge between the two realms—the outer world and the inner world. By focusing on the movement of the breath between these two spheres, the prayer practitioner can learn to move away from egocentrism and realize his place in the flux of God's universe. The chapters on Judaism, Christianity, and Buddhism, found in Part Two, provide further discussions of breath and spirituality. To learn about using breathing exercises as a means of preparing yourself for an effective prayer session, see page 194.

Contemplation

Contemplation is performed in silence and solitude. It is an all-consuming prayer method that many practitioners find to be the culmination of their personal practice. Interestingly, however, contemplation in the Western tradition is very different from contemplation in the Eastern tradition. So, two separate discussions can be found below.

Western Contemplation

In Western traditions, contemplation is a communion of the soul with its Source, during which no words or images are necessary. Simply stated, the practitioner rests in God, dwelling *in*, not *on*, God's presence. Contemplation can even be defined as a spiritual immersion in God. When a person reaches this level of spirituality, there is a loss of the notion of the self. The divide between Divine and human is removed.

It strikes some people as odd that prayer can be wordless and imageless. Yet many spiritualists consider contemplation the most mature form of prayer. As Christian writer Barbara Gawle explains in *How to Pray*, there is a turning point at which we no longer seek to communicate with God, but to commune with Him—to be with Him. Saint John of the Cross, a great Christian mystic, proposed that with spiritual maturity comes the change in prayer from words to imageless silence. And as Jewish writer David J. Wolpe writes in his book *In Speech and In Silence*, "Behind all our explorations, after we exhaust ourselves in words, the silence abides, waiting for us to discover it, to return to it. . . ." There is something so natural and right about dwelling in God, without the labels, sounds, and sights of this world. Contemplation allows you this silence of body and mind, so that a spiritual conversation can take place.

"Oh, how blessed are they who fall down before you in silent worship."

From "My Trust Is In You," Jehudah Ha-Levi

Many spiritualists inform us that contemplation is a normal part of the progression of prayer life. As prayer brings the practitioner away from egocentrism, the thrill of uniting with God is a natural step forward. That is certainly something to work toward! The chapter on Christianity further discusses contemplation on page 113.

Eastern Contemplation

Finally, in Eastern practices, contemplation actually involves dwelling upon a fundamental concept that leads to greater insight. The practitioner of Buddhism, for instance, might contemplate the concept of impermanence. First, he must be well schooled on impermanence, having gained knowledge through sacred texts and teachers. Only then can he contemplate the concept in solitude and silence.

As the contemplator grows increasingly familiar with the concept, he develops an understanding of it that moves beyond laborious reasoning and logic. The truth of the concept becomes natural and effortless, as does its eventual manifestation in his life. Buddhist contemplation is further discussed on page 170.

PREPARING FOR PRAYER

Prayer is a special time of calm and communion, when you turn your attention wholly to the Divine. Through prayer, you enter into an awareness that stands apart from ordinary notions of time and space; you gain access to the Infinite. Such a significant experience warrants some preparation.

Some people follow strict preparation guidelines that are prescribed by their religious affiliations. Others have no protocol. If you would like to develop a means of readying yourself for the prayer process, the following discussion provides some ideas for your consideration. By creating a sacred space for prayer and preparing yourself both physically and emotionally for this very important portion of your day, you can infuse every prayer session with greater beauty and meaning.

Your Sacred Space

It is true that a person can pray at any time, in any place, in any language, and in any form. If you believe in a God, you are likely to believe that God is all present—not only transcendent but also immanent, in the here and the now. However, because you are in a human body, you are subject to distraction by the senses, and are very influenced by your environment. So it is helpful to establish a sacred space that provides a reverent, calming environment in which you feel safe and introspective. A place reserved for prayer simply encourages a prayerful state of mind. It by no means has to be a house of worship—although, of course, it can be. Perhaps you have a favorite local church, synagogue, mosque, or temple. That is a good place to go, consistently, for prayer time. Such a place is filled with wonderful energy and inspiration. It is often quiet and beautiful, and is likely to give you a peaceful, serene feeling. Other people find nature settings to be effective for the same reasons. Do you have a quiet local beach where you can sit? Is there a park in which you can find a secluded spot? Just remember to select a place in which you feel completely safe, and where you can remain undisturbed.

You can also create your own sacred space. Whether you have the luxury of space for a prayer room in your home, or you simply have a corner or wall along which you can erect a prayer table—sometimes called an altar—it is very easy to develop such a nook. If you design it according to your relationship with God and the type of prayer you prefer, and you place your favorite prayer aids within it, the sacred space will enrich your prayer life.

What prayer aids might you arrange in your sacred space? Objects that are commonly used on prayer tables or altars include candles, incense or other fragrant objects, plants and flowers, statues, pictures, sacred symbols such as a crucifix or Star of David, prayer beads, sacred texts, and copies of favorite prayers. And because music and hymns can be an effective means of quieting and focusing the mind when played before or during prayer, you may also want to include a CD or cassette player. If you have wall space, consider religious wall hangings and, for mediation, mandalas—concentration devices that, in the Buddhist tradition, unlock spiritual energy and foster insight into the universe. (See page 168 for more information on mandalas, and page 195 for a further discussion of individual prayer accessories.)

Your sacred space should be located, if possible, in a very quiet area. You want to have a place to listen to God. It is best to have the ability to dim the lights and otherwise create a relaxing mood. If you use a chair during prayer or meditation, you will certainly want to select a firm but comfortable one. And for floor sitting, a meditation cushion or mat is very helpful. In addition, there are small kneelers that are available for at-home use, some complete with a place to rest your arms and prayer books. These extras make sitting and kneeling more comfortable.

Your Body and Mind

There's an old expression which says that the body is a temple. It deserves respect and should be treated with dignity. In fact, many mystical traditions teach that every being carries a divine spark at its deepest core. So the body is literally a keeper of the holy. And there's also the concept of the mind being a personal sanctuary. You can retreat into your silent thoughts, completely immune to invasion. Through these perspectives, the body and mind become sacred space. And just as you would prepare a physical place in which to pray, so should you prepare your internal sacred space for more effective prayer.

Diet

Many people find it helpful to observe a light and healthy diet in preparation for prayer. Try not to burden your body with foods that are difficult to digest prior to a prayer session. If you are in a state of discomfort from fullness, food allergies, and the like, you will struggle with bodily distractions. Furthermore, if you are famished, you will be thinking about your stomach—not to mention hearing it. Such distractions take away from spiritual awareness.

It is best to use common sense when preparing for prayer. Don't indulge in substances that make you "speed," such as caffeine or chocolate, if you are sensitive to them. Likewise, avoid substances that diminish your alertness—substances like wine and liquors. Prayer is most effective when you view it as an active, dynamic quest, and mood-altering substances will prevent you from being an alert and responsive prayer practitioner.

Cleansing

Traditionally, cleansing of one or more types has been an important part of the preparation for prayer. Cleansing is a symbolic gesture of renewal, a respectful gesture of reverence, and, quite simply, a healthy and energizing practice.

Cleansing can involve any of the following: physical cleansing of the body through washing or rinsing; internal cleansing of the body accomplished through fasting; and the mental and emotional cleansing achieved through the removal of negative feelings. Let's look at each of these in turn.

Washing the Body

Both Jewish and Muslim orthodox prayer practices include very specific rituals of washing prior to formal prayer times. Consider the Muslim practice of *wudu*, or ablution, which refers to the washing of the body. The general obligation—meaning the minimum obligation—is the washing of the face, the arms up to the elbows, one-quarter of the head, and both feet to the ankles. Clean, fresh water is used, and most gestures are repeated approximately three times. The exception is the head rinsing, which is usually done once with wet hands. The wudu is performed out of respect for Allah, and is used to wash away physical impurities, while symbolizing the further washing away of spiritual impurities.

A cleansing process is certainly helpful. If you are comfortable with your hygiene, you will have one less distraction during your prayers. And the process of washing is sure to invigorate you and increase your alertness. So try taking a few moments to wash up—even if it's a simple washing of the hands and rinsing of the mouth.

Fasting

Quite a few religious observers believe that the cleansing process should include *fasting*—that is, depriving oneself of certain foods, or of food in general, for a set time before prayer. This element of spirituality should be incorporated in your prayer life with guidance and prudence; abuse of this technique is very detrimental. If you choose to avoid eating for an hour or two before prayer so that your body is not fatigued by the digestive process at prayer time, that's fine. But without intelligent control, fasting can result in physical pain, hallucinations, weakness, and other problems—problems that not only fail to contribute to the prayer process, but are also truly harmful. So seek guidance if you want to take this cleansing technique to challenging levels.

Emotional Cleansing

It is helpful to cleanse yourself of negative feelings such as anger, fear, and anxiety prior to prayer. Of course, sometimes we pray specifically to relieve ourselves of these emotions. But, as far as possible, try to rid yourself of distracting and harmful thoughts by putting yourself in the presence of love. Recognize that you are in a spiritual place where you will not be harmed. You are surrounded by God's protection. If negative feelings persist despite these reassuring thoughts, try using breathing exercises, discussed below, to better relax. Once anxiety and anger have been replaced by love and calm, you will be able to enter a deeper state of sincere prayer, not only more quickly, but also more fully.

Breathing

One of the most effective and traditional modes of prayer preparation is concentration on the process of breathing. When entering a prayerful state of mind, focus on breathing slowly and deeply, and pay attention to the rhythm of your breath. This will promote calm, as the tissues are fed with oxygen and the body successfully performs its task of respiration. Proper breathing, combined with appropriate posture and the right attitude, will create a sense of unity throughout your body, producing balance and harmony. This is a great preparation for effective prayer.

To further increase a feeling of health and vitality before prayer, try some relaxation breathing exercises. When you inhale, fill your chest cavity with air. Hold the breath for a few seconds, allowing your body to feel saturated. Then exhale very slowly, so as not to tense your body. The physical sensation of relaxation, wholeness, and fulfillment will permeate your mind and spirit. You can even picture God's energy coursing through you, healing and renewing your body and soul.

Posture

Saint Benedict and many other great spiritualists have believed that since we were born into the body, it therefore is necessarily part of our communication with God. Thus, it is not surprising that posture—sitting, standing, and kneeling—has held a place in the practice of prayer throughout history, and should be seriously considered when preparing for prayer.

Most spiritual teachers suggest that we sit during prayer. This does not mean that kneeling is wrong or ineffective. It can be an excellent posture for prayer, especially if you view it as a beautiful act of humility and a reminder of servitude in your prayer life. However, sitting in an upright position has been found best for simple concentration and comfort, and allows a balance and flow of the body's energy. A straight back distributes pressure properly along the spine. It also allows for easy breathing, and generally doesn't fatigue the body to the extent that standing and kneeling do. Images of Buddhist monks in the lotus positions—with legs drawn in "Indian style" and folded over each other—immediately spring to mind. But you don't have to go that far; there are a number of effective sitting positions (see pages 175 to 177). Whether you decide to use a hard chair or the floor, take care to avoid severe rigidity. If using a chair, plant your feet firmly on the floor to maintain good posture. Avoid soft chairs and beds, which may induce fatigue.

Posture is discussed in more detail in the various chapters on cultural approaches to prayer. In those chapters, you'll find that some techniques differ greatly from the straight-backed sitting position. Walking meditation, for instance, uses the stimulation of slow walking over textured terrain as an avenue for increased awareness (see page 167). Here, suffice it to say that posture can make a big difference in the preparation for and practice of prayer.

Keep in mind that even before settling into your chosen prayer posture, you can further prepare yourself for prayer by stretching. Teachers of and books on disciplines such as Yoga and Tai Chi can provide you with a variety of helpful stretching techniques. These arts are specifically designed to promote health, encourage balance within the body, and therefore aid you in attaining a peaceful state of harmony. Stretching releases tension that builds up during times of stress, and therefore helps to mentally prepare you for prayer. A stretching period will also make you feel more awake and alert, enabling you to enjoy greater clarity during your prayer time.

The preparation activities discussed above are not only spiritually enhancing, but also health enhancing. You can see how prayer affects every part of your being, body, mind, and spirit. Hopefully, you have now chosen a sacred place, and have selected ways to ready your body and mind. But there are still other ways in which you can enhance your prayer time. The next section looks at various objects or accessories that can help create a calming and spiritual atmosphere, and also aid you in maintaining focus as you develop your prayer life.

PRAYER ACCESSORIES

A number of items can help enhance the prayer experience. It is important to recognize that these objects are not the heart of prayer itself; they are accompaniments to the practice. Hopefully, they won't serve as distractions. Depending on your religious affiliation, on the form of prayer you choose to practice, and on your own preferences, you may wish to use one or more of them to put yourself in a more reverent state of mind and to maintain focus. Some of the following articles—candles and

Looking at the Clock

It is important to generally reserve a time during the day, or during the week, for spiritual development and communication with God. In this way, you will mentally acknowledge prayer as a priority, and will be sure to give your spiritual life the time and attention it needs and deserves. If your religion assigns certain times of the day for specific prayers, this book certainly does not imply that you should violate these codes. But if you do not already have an established routine and are trying to determine the best time for your prayer sessions, the following suggestions may prove helpful.

Begin by identifying the time of day that is most productive for you. When do you feel the most energetic and clear-headed? When do you feel most open and honest? It is important to consider these questions when putting aside a time to pray. If you are a night owl, set aside a late-night slot. If you are an early bird, consider praying before the other members of your household arise. Most important, select a time during which you can remain undisturbed—when no one else is rummaging around the kitchen, when the kids are at school, or after your noisy commute home.

music, for instance—are easy to find in a variety of stores. Other objects—prayer beads and religious statues, for example—can be found in stores that specialize in religious articles and/or meditation aids, or via a search on the Internet. In addition, some large houses of worship have religious article stores on the premises.

Prayer Beads

Several different religious approaches use beads, usually strung into a loop, to keep count of prayers. Some Christians use rosary beads when saying the rosary, because of the number of repetitions involved. They also may use rosary beads to keep track of Jesus Prayer recitations, if hoping to accomplish a certain number of repetitions. Muslims sometimes use prayer beads when reciting the Ninety-Nine Holy Names of

The Dalai Lama suggests early morning prayers. He states that too many people maintain hectic nighttime schedules, fail to get adequate sleep, and then are fatigued during the brilliant morning hours. His Holiness proposes that morning is a time of great enlightenment and clarity, when the energies of the body swell with the rising of the sun. It is a shame to miss such a beautiful and creative part of the day. Now, the Dalai Lama goes to bed at 8:30 PM, and rises at 3:30 AM. For many of us, that is an impractical schedule. However, his example shows us that we should seek a healthy balance in life—that we should get adequate sleep, and that we should take advantage of the naturally creative, energetic periods resulting from an "early to bed, early to rise" schedule.

Another important "time" issue is the amount of time you should devote to formal prayer each day or week. To avoid disappointing and overwhelming yourself, start with a brief prayer period—ten minutes or so—and master prayer to your satisfaction within that period. When you are ready for a challenge, increase your prayer time. Be realistic, and don't extend the time period to the point where the clock becomes more important than the prayers themselves, or where your prayers steal time away from other important activities, and therefore cause you greater anxiety. Let your formal prayer time increase naturally.

Allah. And some Buddhists use prayer beads to keep track of their mantras. Therefore, prayer beads are cross-cultural prayer aids.

Statues and Other Art Objects

Statues; framed artwork; mandalas, the geometric designs used in Buddhist meditation; and other sacred objects may all be used as visual aids during the practice of prayer. Some art objects help the practitioner create a helpful mental image by offering a depiction of a spiritual figure. Some simply serve as focal points, drawing the practitioner away from distractions and into the awareness of One.

In addition, certain objects have great symbolic meaning. A cross, for example, can symbolize suffering, redemption, or the meeting of the Divine and the human. It can also symbolize the entirety of the universe as understood via the four directions to which it points. And mandalas, in particular, lead the practitioner on a spiritual journey by offering various shapes and spaces—all invested with cultural symbolism—that bring him slowly into a single point.

Candles

The burning of candles is a common practice during personal prayer. There are several reasons for this. First, the flame can serve as a focal point, calling the practitioner's attention away from other distractions, and encouraging the dwelling upon Oneness. Second, light is symbolic in many cultures, representing redemption, resurrection, enlightenment, and clarity. Finally, candlelight is more relaxing than artificial light. There is less glare and more shadow, fostering a thoughtful, meditative mood.

If you feel that the use of candles would enhance your prayer practice, choose candles and candle holders that you particularly like. Perhaps a certain scented wax will help you find calm. Many people choose sandalwood, ocean, and pine scents because of the nature setting they call to mind. Others choose scents that closely align with those used in Churches and monasteries, such as frankincense and myrrh. Small votive candles can be found in all sorts of scents, and when placed in little colored-glass holders, they are safe and attractive, as well as relatively inexpensive.

Of course, the use of candles necessitates great caution. Be sure that all holders are secure, and that no objects will make contact with the flame. Extra precaution should be taken if you close your eyes during the prayer session. Make sure that the candle will remain upright, and that it is placed out of the reach of small children and pets. Your prayers can then be worry-free.

Music

Writer Aldous Huxley once stated, "After silence, that which comes closest to expressing the inexpressible is music." Music has been linked with ritual and spirituality since the dawn of humanity. Its capacity for hypnotizing rhythm and liberating beauty is a powerful addition to prayer time. So when creating your sacred space, consider adding a compact disk or cassette player, along with a supply of appropriate recordings.

Be sure to select music that puts you at ease, not melodies that overstimulate you with distracting lyrics. Chants offer solemn sounds and attractive rhythms that can enhance your concentration. Hymns often provide beautiful but soft lyrics that serve as a means of adoration. The

Resource Directory, which begins on page 231, will guide you to a variety of prayer-enhancing albums, from Gregorian chants to traditional Jewish melodies to songs by the Tibetan Tantric Choir to New Age offerings.

Finally, be aware that some people choose to make their own music as a form of prayer. Whether beating a drum, swaying and singing, ringing a bell, or playing a flute, a repetitive and comfortable sound can draw you away from the stresses of words and speech, and into a different mode of communication with God.

Incense

You may enjoy filling your prayer environment with a pleasant scent— one that is special to you because of the feelings it evokes—by burning incense. The sense of smell is strongly anchored to emotions and images. Some people like to use this link as a way to bring themselves into a peaceful, reverent state. Various scents are available at many retail stores, from drug stores to specialty shops. Some people like to match the type of incense that is used at their house of worship, while other people prefer natural scents—sage, pine, or flowers, for example.

Prayer aids can be used to make your sacred space more appealing, more calming, and more effective. Depending on the prayer aids you choose, they can help you relax and set aside the worries of everyday life, better focus on your prayers, or more easily find God as He works within you. But always remember that you and God are the only *necessary* elements of prayer.

HEALTHY ATTITUDES FOR PRAYER

You have chosen a sacred space, prepared your body and mind, and gathered together various articles for your prayer time. Perhaps you have even lit a candle and some incense. Is there anything else you can do to make this special time more serene and fruitful?

Earlier in this chapter, we discussed the importance of ridding yourself of negative feelings prior to prayer. But if you wish to enjoy a truly fulfilling prayer experience, you should go beyond the simple shedding of unpleasant thoughts and emotions. The attitude that you bring to prayer makes a big difference. Try to remember that prayer changes *us,* not God. And in order to benefit from that change, we must be open, honest, and active. There's no doubt that the following pointers will enhance your prayer experience.

Pray With Receptivity and Simplicity

If you enter prayer believing that you know what's best, you will not be open to change. A receptive and simple attitude is far more productive. Instead of fighting with the universe over what is happening, or what is not happening, be receptive to new perspectives. Be willing to receive direction instead of giving it.

The truth is that we don't always know what's best. So surrendering the ego and praying for God's will is the best course of action. In his book *Recovering the Soul: A Scientific and Spiritual Search,* Larry Dossey, MD, quotes from the literature of philosopher William Irwin Thompson: "We are like flies crawling across the ceiling of the Sistine Chapel." Although there is something striking going on, we don't have the perspective needed to understand the universe in its entirety, nor our complete and specific role in it. Someday we will have that ability; that's heaven or nirvana. But for now, we have to rely on the goodness and knowledge of God to guide us. So being receptive to God—listening, remaining open, and relinquishing control—is crucial to effective prayer.

One way to remain receptive is to pray *simply*. Clouding your receptive attitude with all sorts of complex words and wishes may damage your openness. By praying simply, you can reduce distractions and concentrate on the heart of the matter. So avoid getting caught up in impressive language or in sophisticated bargaining devices. Pray as a child would pray, with uncomplicated devotion.

Pray With Faith and Courage

It is so easy to doubt yourself—your worthiness, your effectiveness. And when you picture God as a perfect being and a critical judge—that is, when you see Him as a human—you can easily become intimidated. Maybe you doubt that you are being heard. Or maybe you have the faith to believe that God is listening, but doubt that your meager prayers can make a difference. Does that sound familiar?

There's a reason for that old phrase, " It takes a leap of faith." Faith requires a leap; you must jump in. Prayers are answered when you truly believe that they are heard. Summon up faith by remembering that intuition has led you to prayer. Intuition is honest and fundamental; it counts.

Once you find the faith to pray, pray with courage. Timidity and hesitation keep you paralyzed. When you pray with courage, you confirm your significant role in the world, as well as God's presence in your life.

Praying with bravery makes prayer a dynamic and engaging process. So have the audacity to pray.

> *"Cowardice keeps us "double minded"—hesitating between the world and God. . . . And this hesitation makes true prayer impossible—it never quite dares to ask for anything, or if it asks, it is so uncertain of being heard that in the very act of asking it surreptitiously seeks, by human prudence, to construct a make-shift answer."*
>
> From *Thoughts in Solitude*, Thomas Merton

Pray With Sincerity and Gratitude

You can fool yourself only to a point, and you certainly can't fool God, who is pure knowledge. Therefore, there's no sense in praying with a "front"—by babbling pretty but empty words, by bargaining with promises that you won't really keep. Truthfulness opens you to change and brings you closer to God, as God resides in truth. So pray from the heart, not the mind. Pray with genuine earnestness and with candor.

Part of praying sincerely and honestly is to pray gratefully. When you are honest with yourself, you begin to see all the beautiful things in life. Then you realize the selfishness of your anger and complaints, and naturally become more thankful. Some of the many benefits of your new gratitude will be a greater ability to cope with hardship, and a greater happiness with all the little joys that life has to offer.

Pray With Positivity and Confidence

In his book *How to Get Your Prayers Answered*, Rabbi Irwin Katsof tells us to pray with absolute positivity. A negative attitude can prevent you from recognizing God's guidance. Negativity results in a certain blindness in which you refuse to see change, let alone to accept it. That's why it's so important to pray with full expectation that your prayers will be answered.

Undoubtedly, there will be times during prayer when you feel that nothing is happening. Don't slip into negativity! In *Simple Prayer*, John Dalrymple reminds the reader not to evaluate the effectiveness of prayer based on how it *feels* at a given moment. Feelings constantly change. The true test is what you are like as a person—how your daily attitude has

God's No-Discrimination Policy

Studies on prayer have shown that one religious affiliation is not more effective than another when it comes to getting prayers answered. God is not prejudiced; God does not discriminate. However, what does make a difference is the amount of sincerity involved. Prayers offered with genuine devotion and love are apparently more effective. The lesson: Pray sincerely in ways that move you most, and accept the prayer practices of others as being equally legitimate.

changed. So instead of being self-critical, be confident that through it all, you are being heard. God is a real God who will answer your prayers in some way.

Pray With Energy and Love

Prayer should not be performed passively. It may be difficult and challenging, or it may be relaxing. Either way, prayer time is not the time to do *nothing*. To reap the benefits, you must put in the effort.

In *Lift Up Your Heart: A Guide to Spiritual Peace,* author and Catholic bishop Fulton Sheen teaches us that in prayer, the soul must *collaborate* with God. So, for example, a person who is suffering from an addiction must not only pray to God, "Please help me to break this addiction," but must also *really desire* to break the addiction. Therefore, he will pull his weight in the process and cocreate a change with God. This takes energy.

Add to that energy by praying with *love*—love of God, your fellow humans, and yourself. When you let go of hatred and resentment, your vision becomes so much clearer. Furthermore, your words become naturally sincere. Love brings everything to the surface—the good and the ugly. And with everything at the surface, you can begin to form a healthy relationship with God.

Pray With Perseverance and Patience

Finally, don't give up. Our culture touts the glories of instant gratification. We want answers *now*. But God's time is not our time. So persevere in your prayers and wait with patience. You will be answered, even if the response is not the one that you were anticipating. As Saint Jose of Avila, the Christian mystic, once stated, "Let nothing disturb you, let nothing frighten you. All things pass away. God never changes. Patience obtains all things. He who has God finds he lacks nothing. God alone suffices."

> *"O ye who believe! Seek help with patient perseverance and prayer; for God is with those who patiently persevere."*
>
> The Qu'ran, 2.153

CONCLUSION

It is both interesting and helpful to understand the various forms that prayer can take, as well as the many ways in which prayer time can be enhanced. If you are just beginning your practice of prayer, this chapter, hopefully, has aided you in finding a comfortable direction. If you have been praying for some time, you may have already found that certain types of prayer seem to fit you just right. But keep in mind that there's something to be said for breaking away from your routine and trying different prayer techniques and traditions. For some people, routine has a disturbing way of watering down the zeal or *kavannah*—a Hebrew term for true devotion, passion in prayer. To avoid this problem, why not add spark to your spiritual practices by trying some new patterns?

Of course, no matter how perfectly you arrange your sacred place, how conscientiously you prepare for each prayer session, and how well you master various forms of prayer, it would be unrealistic to expect your prayer life to always be blissful. Being human, we are prone to spiritual dry spells—times when the frustrations of life make prayer seem like a difficult and futile task rather than a joy. And then there are the times when we face the disappointment of seemingly unanswered prayers. The next chapter will examine such spiritual difficulties, and help prepare you for the rough spots so that you can more quickly return to a rewarding practice of prayer.

9

Unanswered Prayers
and Spiritual Dry Spells

Once you realize how positively prayer can affect your life, and you learn some of the basics of prayer practice as described in Chapter 8, it is easy to get on a prayer high and happily dive into a new prayer routine. And there is every reason to feel confident in the practice of prayer, so go ahead and get started. But it would be naive to believe that prayer will *always* be answered in the way you expect, or that prayer will *always* be comfortable and satisfying.

Frustrations naturally occur when prayers don't seem to yield the desired results. Furthermore, there are times when the spiritual drive, which may be so passionate and energetic at one moment, simply stalls. All of a sudden, the presence of God may feel like a distant memory, if not a work of the imagination. You find yourself resisting prayer. How can you overcome these situations if and when they occur? What do they mean? Let's talk about the tough times so that if and when they hit, you will know how to turn them around.

SEEMINGLY UNANSWERED PRAYERS

Note that this section is titled *"Seemingly* Unanswered Prayers." One of the most important things to realize in the journey toward a more effective prayer life is not only that prayers won't always get answered in ways that you logically understand or initially hope for, but that it's a *good* thing that they don't. Yes, sometimes prayers don't give us the answer for which we're looking. But sometimes they give us something far more precious—perhaps a greater understanding of our options and roles in life, or even a greater understanding of the true purpose of prayer itself.

Realize That Your Perspective Is Limited

At any given moment, you may truly believe that you know what's best for your life and the lives of those around you. But the truth is that no one can see the big picture in the isolation of one moment. So when prayers do not produce exactly what you desire, do not assume those prayers have gone unanswered. That is not the case. When you think about it, the lack of a perceptible "yes" is not the same as the lack of an answer. There is always an answer, whether it is revealed as a physical result, a thought, a feeling, or a new awareness. Do your best to *look* for more than "yes" answers, and try *listening* and *feeling*, as well. In other words, open yourself up to alternative answers.

Often, the lack of an answer—meaning a "yes" that we readily comprehend—is an answer itself. It means that things cannot follow your plan because your plan, in the end, is not compatible with God's design. God is not being mean; God, the Absolute, is maintaining a universe and fostering each person's growth toward divine awareness.

Through prayer, you place yourself within the timeless and infinite aspects of existence. It follows, then, that in seeking answers to prayers, some answers will have more to do with a larger scheme of time and place than with the immediate scheme. If your desires are not met in prayer, you must make an effort to further widen your perspective, and to acknowledge that there must be a reason—a good reason—why the universe is unfolding as it is. The healthiest approach is to accept that there is an element of mystery to life, and then learn to cherish that mystery as a teacher.

You will get help during your hours of need if you continue to pray, and if you accept that help may come in an unexpected form. Perhaps your prayers can't bring about, for example, the physical healing of your child or the prevention of a car accident. But they can help you understand that things happen for a reason, that every event can teach you something valuable. Plus, tragedies are easier to cope with when you have faith that you are not suffering the pain alone. The sense of interconnectedness and purpose that is fostered by the practice of prayer ultimately makes coping with "unanswered" prayers much easier.

Don't Refuse the Alternatives

If you maintain a very rigid idea of how needs should be answered, you close yourself off to countless possibilities. Let's take, for example, the case of Alice, who lost her arm in a motorcycle accident. She prayed and prayed that the surgery to reattach her arm would be successful. However, critical damage to the nerves and tissues prevented the limb from being even potentially functional. Alice, understandably trauma-tized, would not hear of any other solution. She refused an artificial limb, even though technological advances had already produced prosthetic arms that could help her do everything from driving, to cooking, to brushing her daughter's hair. Alice was furious that her devout prayers were not answered, and would not settle for any other help. Instead, she settled into the notion of being abandoned by God and cheated by fate.

Eventually, Alice realized that she had two choices. She could dwell in depression and reap further health problems, or she could once again answer that need to communicate with God. There was a wound deep inside of her that could not be healed by therapy sessions or talk show television. So she simply started "having it out" with God. Alice would sit in her room and argue with God, telling Him how upset she was over the loss of her limb, how disappointed she was that God did not answer her prayers.

Finally, when all words were used up, Alice started to listen. Her mind opened up to other possibilities, and she realized that her prayers did not go unheard. There were countless loving people who surround-ed her and became extra hands during her times of needs. Furthermore, Alice realized that she had turned her back on technological advances that were all part of a developing universe—a universe that knew her needs even before her accident! There were plenty of choices that Alice had, and she had chosen the worst one—to refuse all alternatives. Once her perspective was broadened, Alice found that she had received more than one response to her prayers. She had received a range of truly help-ful answers!

Alice now counsels people to remain open-minded to alternative answers. Although we often insist that there is one right way, there are usually several right ways. You may have to accept another solution than originally hoped for, and it may be more challenging, but you'll often learn a lot of lessons in the meantime. Upon accepting a prosthetic limb, Alice learned to highly value the work of health technicians and techni-cal engineers. She found new respect for people with severe physical challenges, and found new community with them. She learned to treas-ure the little things in life so much more, like the way it feels to hold a child within her arms, or to run her hand through the water in a warm pool. Alice's life was greatly enhanced when she decided to open herself up to more than a simple "yes" answer to her prayers.

Learn to Look for the Lesson

Have you caught yourself letting anger take you for a really long ride? Did you think God just said "no" for the fun of it? You've had a bone to pick with God on several occasions, haven't you? Sure, we all have. Now, consider this: When you are primed to challenge your notion of God— ready to take a fist to heaven—why not challenge yourself instead? Remind yourself that there's a reason why the answer to your request was not a simple "yes." And then, instead of shutting God out, look for that reason.

Alice, discussed previously, had to go through a long battle with despair, doubt, close-mindedness, and anger before reaching her ultimate state of peace. She fought alternatives tooth and nail, then directed her angry thoughts at God, and finally quieted her soul enough to listen. While that chain of events is not uncommon, and may be impossible to avoid, it can be shortened if you train yourself to look for the lesson from the very beginning.

Yes, it sounds hokey, hackneyed, and trite. Yet according to the greatest spiritual teachers, we're on this earth to learn lessons—we fundamentally *want* to love and grow and create. Perhaps the fact that the prayer was not answered exactly as you imagined is God's way of reminding you that you're trying to control too much. Maybe you are being too close-minded. Consider the story of Joe and Hannah, who prayed for years that their desire to have a baby would be fulfilled.

For eight years, Joe and Hannah begged God for a child, thinking that the right number and combination of prayers would win them this incredible gift. Later on, in hindsight, the couple realized that they used prayer specifically to get what they wanted, how they wanted. And the answer from God seemed to be a repeated "no." That didn't change. Joe and Hannah never conceived a baby.

Finally, the couple accepted the fact that they would not be biological parents. But instead of railing in permanent disappointment, Joe and Hannah looked for a message in this apparent "no." They decided that they were not being refused, but being called to learn more about themselves and their special mission—their mission as adoptive parents. All of their lives, Joe and Hannah had held strict notions of family. Both coming from large families, they had taken the presence of children as a given. Furthermore, they had understood the conception of children as a *personal* achievement. But after their experience, Joe and Hannah realized that not conceiving a child had nothing to do with how good or bad they were as people, and everything to do with the journey that they were assigned in life. God needed Joe and Hannah to give life to children who were without parents. Ultimately, they adopted two children.

The situation that at one time had caused Joe and Hannah so much grief now became a wonderful opportunity to bring a group of souls together. "We were meant to be a family. Now I know that things happened just the way that they were supposed to happen," says Hannah. Joe adds, "We were trying to design everything about our lives according to cookie-cutter mentality, as though we had to follow a blueprint that we had sketched years ago. Letting go of our strict demands in prayer helped us become more open and peaceful, and ultimately made us parents! If we hadn't decided to look for a lesson in our pain and then grow from that lesson, we never would have ended up with two children who have completely fulfilled us." The "no" answer that frustrated Joe and Hannah actually opened the door to a soul-satisfying mission.

From Joe and Hannah's story, we learn to probe *why* things happen the way they do. There will not always be a simple answer, but there will always be a lesson from which we can learn. In his book *The Problem of Pain*, C.S. Lewis explains that a certain amount of pain and need is necessary in order for us to avoid attaching ourselves to this temporary world too much. God offers us a beautiful earthly life, replete with moments of love, joy, and fulfillment. Thus, the soul knows how desirable true happiness and unity is. But if life were *too* easy, we'd want to stay here; we'd get attached to all the luxuries, and forget that we are on a search for completion. Stagnating in our satisfactions would hardly help us develop into something better. So disappointments such as "unanswered" prayers may actually be opportunities for us to reevaluate life, to avoid nestling into one place and stunting our growth, and to determine if we are still actively working toward the greater good. Thus, we are more willing to work within the cycle of life, to accept the pain with the pleasure as a more wholesome experience, and to let go of obsessive control.

Remember that we live with a limited day-to-day perspective. In the larger picture, we know, for example, that if everyone were healed from every physical sickness, the world would be overcrowded and incapable of sufficiently providing for its inhabitants. We also know that if every whim were answered, we'd incur just as many problems in the long run because we'd create new difficulties. Therefore, it makes sense that not everything we wish and pray for will turn out as we want. So try looking for the lesson *before* hitting rock bottom. It will make life a lot easier.

Remind Yourself of the Purpose of Prayer

We have a habit of telling children, "When you get older, you'll understand why I'm saying 'no.'" Well, perhaps when we become more spiritually mature, we'll understand why certain things didn't turn out the way we so desperately hoped and prayed they would. Until then, have trust and faith, and know that prayers never go to waste. Whether we believe in a God who hears and answers prayer, or a greater Absolute into which we tap when we pray or meditate, the point of prayer is to open our perspective, to expand our vision, to change ourselves. That way, prayer helps us to cope better, no matter what the outcome. When we pray effectively, we find that the answers are less about us, and more about the willingness to see more and see farther.

There is a reason for all occurrences, and a way to get through every single situation. Prayer makes it *easier*, not necessarily *easy*. Just try to remember that prayer is not about changing God's will. It is about changing our approach to reality. Take the example of Francine, a widow whose only son died of AIDS ten years after being infected by a blood transfusion. Francine admits that for the first couple of years after her son's diagnosis, her prayers were comprised of tearful begging that her son would not die. She pleaded with her God that He would allow her child to live long enough so that a cure could be found. She hoped for a spontaneous healing. Yet the virus manifested in her son's body, and after ten long years of illness and medical experimentation, he was clearly losing his battle for life.

At this moment, which seemed the most crucial of all, Francine took a sharp turn in her prayer life. Realizing that she had been praying to keep her son in a place of hardship, Francine actually began to pray, "Thy will be done, God. Please liberate my son's soul from this illness." She started to see the bigger picture, and realized that his death was not about failure on her part or science's part, but about freedom from the suffering that this world holds, in one way or another, for everyone. Francine was aware that she had been praying for the answer that would make *her* happiest. She had prayed for her son to stay alive because *she* didn't want to let go. She now knew that it would be far better to tell her son that he should allow himself to pass into the next life. And she did. One night, in the hospital, Francine whispered into her son's ear that it was okay to let go. She told him that she would be all right. Her son died that night, and Francine found herself in an amazing state of peace.

Francine confirms that her own prayer life developed through this tragedy. Without God's grace, she claims that she would have never been able to let her son go. And without conversing with God, Francine believes she would never have attained this spiritual maturity. "I was praying in a very close-minded way. But at least I was praying. That kept the lines of communication open with God. In other words, God was a real presence in my life, even when I was praying more for *me* than anything else. Over the course of time, watching my son's courage in the face of illness and hearing my own desires to keep him in this world, I began to listen as much as I spoke to God. And in listening, new vision was granted to me. I saw the temporary nature of this world and its suffering, and I was able to let go."

> "*It seems written into nature: We should not pray for a divine bailout with every catastrophe. Common sense tells us there is a time when death is natural, when it is the norm.*"
>
> From *Recovering the Soul,* Larry Dossey, MD

Try Praying Differently

If you've noticed that a great many of your prayers seem to go unanswered, and that you are not having a satisfying prayer experience, it may be time to reevaluate the way you are communicating with God. In *Why Prayers Go Unanswered,* author John Allan Lavender helps the reader look at what she may be doing wrong. First, ask yourself, "Am I attempting to barter with God?" God is not running an auction, granting favors to the highest bidder. If you find yourself slipping into that type of mentality, realize that you are praying as a means to an end. You are not growing and changing in the moment.

Second, when you fail to receive a favorable answer, stop to investigate whether your own actions caused the negative outcome. Were you being selfish in your requests? Were you being a control freak? Perhaps you even had a lack of faith that God would respond. In that state of negativity, you may not have been receptive to God's answer.

Also consider whether or not you were a partner with God in prayer. You may not have made the necessary efforts to create a positive outcome. A lot of people leave all the work to God. But God has ordained us with a divine nature to cocreate. We must take part in bringing about better and more satisfying lives for ourselves. Prayer life is not about magically obtaining favors; it's about diligent effort to seek out the right path—about combining our divine energies with those of our Source to bring about change.

And did you persevere long enough, or did you give God a few days and then call it quits? Patience and perseverance are so important in prayer life. Andrew's story of perseverance is one that inspires us to stick with the practice of prayer. At the age of thirty-two, Andrew found himself in a very common situation: He was lonely for a wife and family. So Andrew tapped into the spirituality that he had been practicing on and off since youth. He decided to put efforts toward praying for his future.

Andrew knew that he shouldn't just ask God for a wife and then wait for her to come knocking on the door. He developed his prayer life as a means of learning more about himself, his needs, and the insight into other people that is necessary to truly love someone. He thought about prayer and its power, and realized that most of the power comes from within—it's about re-finding the answers. So instead of begging, Andrew prayed to God that his eyes would be opened to the right type of woman, that he would grow in maturity and become a man who was capable of great love, and that he would know the right person when he saw her. Andrew prayed like this for four years, sometimes becoming discouraged, but always returning to prayer. Why? Because he knew that prayer was more about developing himself and learning about his role in this world, than about finding a magic answer to a desire.

At age thirty-six, Andrew married Elizabeth, a woman whom he had met just a year before. Because of the introspection and development that had occurred during his "conversations with God," and due to the patience that Andrew exercised in waiting for the right person, he found a wonderfully compatible friend and lover in Elizabeth. "It took four years of talking with God about where I should look, and when I should move, and how I would know who the right one was. But the perseverance and patience paid off. I have found the person with whom I will go through the rest of this life. Instead of making the universe abide by my timetable, I allowed the right situation to unfold over time." And by the way, at forty, Andrew now has two beautiful little boys, as well.

In Chapter 2, we discussed the approaches to prayer that have been scientifically, or experientially, proven helpful. Remember the discussions of the Spindrift experiments? (If not, turn back to page 25.) These experiments concluded that we don't need to focus on a very specific goal or fill our minds repeatedly with a certain image to have our prayers answered. What if Andrew had prayed that he would find this perfect woman—a woman of a specific size, color, and personality—within one year? At the end of that year, he would be likely to either choose a woman who was not right, or get angry at God for "not listening." It seems that the most effective prayer technique is simply to put yourself in the presence of the person or problem about which you are praying. Feel love, compassion, and sincere concern. Ask God to tend to the situation, bringing divine energy to heal or harvest, whatever is necessary. But don't lock yourself into a specific, limited answer. You are praying optimally by just blessing that being or intention with love and care. The fact that you are open-minded in your prayer approach, not negative and demanding, will help you accept the natural progression of the situation, and respect God and the universe for its greater plan.

Don't let anger get the best of you when it *feels* as if your prayers have gone unanswered. Instead, consider alternatives and learn from what at first seems denial or refusal. Try to figure out the *why* behind the "no." Often, you'll come to the conclusion that the answer is not "no," but "not yet," or "you'll see more clearly soon."

SPIRITUAL DRY SPELLS

In general, prayer becomes increasingly effective and easier to practice as it becomes a natural part of your day. Countless spiritual leaders advise that the more you pray, the better you will understand God's answers, gain insights into the prayer process, and get to know yourself. However, it is also very common to go through dry spells during which you feel that no one is listening and that your prayers are futile. These are not necessarily triggered by traumatic events or seemingly unanswered prayers. They can just occur, unprovoked and unexpected. Interestingly, a number of different cultures use the same metaphor for spiritual dryness: the desert. Another popular metaphor for this state of spiritual difficulty—one originally coined by Saint John of the Cross—is the dark night of the soul. It is during the time in the desert, or during the dark night, that prayer becomes most challenging, and that persistence and patience are the only things that keep a person going.

Realize That Dry Spells Are Common

Even the greatest of spiritual teachers had periods of doubt, moments of despair, and times when they felt utterly abandoned and alone. For example, think of Jesus Christ's words on the cross, soon before His death: "My God, my God, why have you abandoned me?" Some would argue that this man—according to Christian belief, this God-Man—had a painful and very natural moment of despair in His greatest need. Isn't it human to cry out in pain and loneliness at times? Yet, Jesus fulfilled His personal mission, and to many people today, He serves as a divine example of love, courage, and holiness.

The Bible's Book of Psalms, which is known for its insights into common human experience, addresses the "dark night" on several occasions. Consider these lines from Psalm 13, a psalm of David: "How long, O Lord? Will you forget me forever? How long will you hide your face from me? How long must I bear pain in my soul, and have sorrow in my heart all day long?" Similarly, an excerpt from Psalm 88 reads: "But I, O Lord, cry out to you; in the morning my prayer comes before you. O Lord, why do you cast me off? Why do you hide your face from me?"

And consider Siddhattha Gotama, the Buddha, who clung to several teachers during his spiritual search, and was disappointed each time. The repeated attempts at finding his way were certainly challenging. Gotama tried several paths before he succeeded. In fact, he practiced severe asceticism for a number of years, including certain forms of self-torture such as food deprivation, harsh breathing techniques, and self-inflicted pain. Eventually, he abandoned these ways for a more moderate path and, on that middle road, found enlightenment. The hard knocks were definitely "desert moments," but his persistence paid off. Gotama ended up forging a life philosophy for billions of people who followed.

All of us go through times of discouragement and moments of doubt. Sometimes this happens at the beginning of our spiritual journeys, and sometimes it happens after our spirituality has matured. Desert times seem almost natural to us, as human beings who are subject to fears, numbness, fatigue, distraction, and emotion. The best thing to do is trust that a spark of insight will ignite in due time, and that perhaps the moments of darkness will, in some way, serve us better in the long run by calling us into a deeper silence and causing a greater hunger. The greater hunger will, in turn, make us capable of greater fulfillment.

"The ravening clouds shall not be long victorious,
They shall not long possess the sky,
they devour the stars only in apparition. . . ."

From "On the Beach at Night," Walt Whitman

Understand Why Dry Spells Occur

What do these dry spells mean? Do they signify anything? First, they could be precursors to a time of spiritual growth. Often, when we move from one stage in prayer life to another, we experience pain, discomfort, or apathy. The anticipation of change—perhaps more simply called fear—causes some resistance toward prayer. We unconsciously shut down because we know that the leap ahead is going to require greater courage, effort, and responsibility. So when you come upon a dry spell, realize that it may be the trench over which you must jump to reach a better place.

A dark night of the soul might also signify a need for renewal in more than one area of life. Maybe the stresses of life are piling up—job tensions, family worries, or relationship difficulties. When we overextend ourselves physically, mentally, and even spiritually, we often cause a general malaise and fatigue that can trigger a dark night. Reevaluating our daily lives and commitments may, in turn, illuminate such periods of darkness.

Whether a spiritual dry spell occurs as a result of upcoming changes in spiritual maturity or simple fatigue, there's no doubt that the experience can be harrowing. So the following section offers a few survival tips.

Surviving the Desert

When the spiritual desert stretches out before you—when you find yourself running out of steam, words, and ideas for your prayer life—first remember that you are not personally lacking something, nor are you alone. Doubt, fear, even the temporary dulling of passions are part and parcel of being human. Furthermore, you have more power than you think to overcome such troubles.

Second, exercise persistence. Why keep praying? Why not assume that you need "some time away" from God, or that prayer is simply not working? Because the problem is not God; it is your perspective, your anxiety, maybe even your growth process. And by continuing to pray, you will give yourself opportunities to change. The lines of communication with God will remain open, and as a result, you will increase the odds that you will listen and learn where you need to go from here.

Third, try praying through spiritual readings. While in the desert of prayer life, it can be difficult, if not impossible, to put your feelings into words or to recite prayers of ardor and zeal. A wonderful alternative is to focus on the calm and beauty of spiritual readings—Scriptures and sacred texts. For example, many people find the Book of Psalms appropriate, because the Psalms discuss fundamental human struggles in satisfying, beautiful ways. You may simply want to read; or you may decide to converse with God after receiving the written words. Just respond however you can.

Sarah's story is worth reading. She had been suffering through a spiritual dry spell for several years! Sarah had trouble feeling involved during religious services; she would find herself empty and frustrated during prayer periods. But she tried to generally live in awareness of God, and to make efforts to communicate with God whenever she could find the heart. One day, Sarah received an e-mail from a Christian friend. In the letter, the friend happened to discuss one of her favorite ways to pray: "In the morning, I sit down at the breakfast table with a cup of coffee and my Bible, and I imagine Jesus sitting across from me. Then I ask Jesus questions and tell him what I'm thinking. When I need a response, I simply open the Bible and start reading. I always find some kernel of truth, comfort, knowledge, even plain commiseration. It makes me feel better, as though I just visited with a close friend. There's always an answer in Scriptures."

Two nights later, Sarah experienced a particularly difficult "dark night." She felt utterly alone and was craving God's presence. In an attempt to pray, she sat on the floor and just kept repeating, "I choose you. I choose you," aiming her words toward Jesus. Within a few minutes, the words of her friend's e-mail entered her thoughts, and Sarah went to her bookcase and pulled the Bible off the shelf.

Sarah listened inside her deepest mind, and felt directed to turn to a specific area of her Bible—the Gospel of John. Within a few pages of where she started reading, Sarah came across the following message: "You do not choose me, but I chose you." It seemed a direct answer to the phrase she had repeated only a few minutes before. Sarah received a sense of comfort that she was not alone, that her prayers were being heard, and that she did not have to continue on her own. With this new-found sense of community with the Divine, Sarah renewed her prayer life.

Another survival tip is to try concentrating on different attributes of God. If your previous picture or understanding of God is no longer working, try a new one. Teresa's story offers a good example. Teresa always had a tendency to view God as a loving father. All of her life, Teresa actively prayed to and sought God, but with this limited approach in mind. During her fifties, when her parents passed away and the notion of a father figure changed meaning in her life, Teresa found herself in a spiritual struggle. She became very doubtful and entered a great desert. This hurt her terribly.

One day, during a frustrating prayer session, Teresa came to a sudden enlightenment: "Turn to a different image of God." She felt open to understanding Him in a different way, and therefore, her prayer patterns became new and exciting. Now viewing God more as a brother, a friend, Teresa began developing new elements of spirituality. Today, Teresa claims that her prayer life is all the richer for that desert time, when she had to break old patterns and etch out new ways to communicate with her Lord.

Hopefully, you will find encouragement in the stories and suggestions above. They confirm that spiritual dry spells are natural and also survivable. In addition, these difficulties have the potential to lead to greater spiritual depth and a renewed relationship with God. We just have to remain persistent and open.

When struggling through the sands of the desert, remember to go easy on yourself. You have been given the gift of the Scriptures and spiritual writings—a gift you can use whenever you are unable to find your own words. You have also been given the gift of imagining, and can try picturing God in a new way that might help you feel more satisfied. Finally, don't be ashamed to talk to others about spiritual dry spells. You'll find that many people are willing, even wanting, to discuss these times. Together, you can find an oasis of community and comfort.

CONCLUSION

Don't let your spiritual "lows" scare you; they are worth every effort it takes to overcome them. As you advance in your prayer life, you will be developing a more mature relationship with God, and along with this growth might come growing pains. During tough times, remind yourself that unanswered prayers and spiritual dry spells are opportunities, not death sentences. They have the power to deepen your understanding of prayer. Such hurtles strengthen your prayer muscles, teaching you to look beyond simple "yes" answers and feel-good prayers, into a more profound spiritual life.

After dealing with the heavy issues of unanswered prayers and the spiritual desert, it becomes obvious that a relationship with God is not just about asking and receiving. It's about recognizing that God is in everything, in the joy and in the sorrow. That leads us to the topic of Chapter 10. In the following chapter we will discuss awareness of God that reaches beyond prayer time, into your daily activities, your job, and your contact with people and nature.

10

Making Each Day a Prayer

As we discovered at the very beginning of this book, prayer is more than words, more than images, more than movements. Prayer is a relationship with God, and any significant relationship continually changes and affects our lives. So as we near the close of this book on how to pray, it is very important to extend the notion of prayer to its fullest potential by confirming that each day can become a prayer in and of itself. This chapter explains how all of the little routine things that make up your life can be viewed as sacred, and how each moment can be lived in a fuller awareness of the divine.

BEING IN THE "NOW"

The first step in making each day a prayer is to recognize that each hour, each moment is an opportunity for learning and loving. Every experience is a step that you can use to climb toward the greater development of your soul—or a step that you can use to avoid that growth. In order to live life to its potential, you have to train yourself to become aware of the present. Unfortunately, humans have a tendency to be more comfortable living in everything *but* the moment.

In his book *Lift Up Your Heart: A Guide to Spiritual Peace,* Fulton Sheen discusses the tragedy of how human beings waste the *now,* while obsessing over the past and future. He explains that by using memory and imagination, the human mind can unite the past and the future with the present. As a result, we grow distracted, anxious, angry, and even compulsive. It is much healthier to "sanctify the moment," realizing how precious and powerful each instant is. We don't know when things will change, or how things will end. All we truly have is the opportunity at hand—right now. And we have the power to grace the *now* with peaceful intentions. That way, we will make ourselves, as well as others, happier.

Sheen asserts that God sends us personal messages within each moment. Our thoughts, our inclinations, our instincts, and our feelings are avenues through which God can work. In addition, God might send instant messages through a stranger's words, a child's smile, even the wag of a passing dog's tail. But if we are not in the moment, aware of the little things around us, how can we recognize these messages? And won't life be a more pleasant experience if we look for the divine in each occasion? Sheen continues, "Those who sanctify the moment and offer it up in union with God's will never become frustrated—never grumble or complain. They overcome all obstacles by making them occasions of prayer and channels of merit."

> *"All unhappiness (when there is no immediate cause for sorrow) comes from excessive concentration on the past or from extreme preoccupation with the future."*
>
> From *Lift Up Your Heart: A Guide to Spiritual Peace*,
> Fulton J. Sheen

Similarly, Leslie Marmon Silko captures the human condition of resistance to the *now* in her novel *Ceremony*. One of the characters in this work discusses how human beings are the only creatures who resist nature and the demands of the moment, sacrificing the present to the past and the future. The character explains that we can learn a lot by watching animals grazing in the fields. They move with the direction of the wind, and to wherever they are likely to find food and safety. It's a simple approach to existence—no resistance, just acceptance and action. Only humans ignore the vibrant power of the moment to wage futile battles against what happened long ago and what might occur in the future.

Try evaluating yourself in light of this perspective. Are you spending many of your moments living in the past or future? If so, be aware that you have the capability to change. When you concentrate on the time at hand and its potential for greater good, you live a prayer. You become aware of the divine aspects of each instant. You also become a far healthier and kinder person. Enhancing your awareness of the moment will lead you to a more sacred understanding of people, other creatures, nature, and daily activities. In fact, sanctifying the moment is the secret to life! Once you find the moment, work becomes a prayer, laughter becomes a prayer, and conversation becomes a prayer, because it is all done in love and gratitude. Fear no longer plays a dominant role because you trust that you are doing exactly what you are supposed to be doing.

Appreciation of the present keeps us in constant contact with God. Consider the traditional lifestyle of the Mohawk tribe, as described by Chief Tom Porter in "Why We're Here Today," an essay in the magazine *Parabola*. Porter defines prayer as, "When you take a moment to communicate with the spiritual life that surrounds you." He explains that upon rising in the morning, a person should greet the Creator, then brother sun, then parents, then neighbors. Throughout the day, little "hellos" should be said to keep us in touch with the Oneness that we all share. This extends to livestock, wild animals, even flowers and trees. He warns that if we do not communicate with the spiritual lives around us, we become "imbalanced, unhappy, and ungrateful." That's no way to live! So prayer is not limited to formal recitations, or even quiet time alone. It has to do with daily functioning, from the moment of rising until the moment of sleep. It has to do with the *now*.

> *"Our prayer begins within the moment of our birth in this particular lifetime. And at our death this particular version of our prayer ends. But at no time between our birth and our death do we cease our prayer."*
>
> From "Your Life Is Your Prayer," Neale Donald Walsch

CREATING SILENCE AND STILLNESS

It is hard to live a prayer when you are consumed by anxiety and noise. Have you noticed the average attitude in busy urban centers? Have you seen how many people practically trample the pigeons and run into baby strollers as they rush to make the next business lunch? That's because there is too much noise and activity both inside and outside their minds.

You may find it relatively easy to find silent prayer time, but what about a *silent life*? Now you're saying, "You've got to be kidding! Not in this world!" But silence doesn't have to be silence in the traditional, physical sense. And the same is true of stillness. Silence and stillness can be qualities of the mind that stem from practicing enhanced awareness. To achieve greater silence and stillness—which can be described as calm, balance, and peace—avoid the urge to swallow everything, attempting to control your environment and to compete with others. Instead, try to focus on the little occurrences of the moment. Concentrate on the simplest aspects of your activities and surroundings, and on the happenings to your right and left. By calling yourself away from scattered thoughts, and toward what is before you, the noise from three blocks down will fade away, and that hectic, harried feeling will dwindle.

Zen Buddhism teaches that silence can be found everywhere. Silence is timeless and ever present, if we choose to recognize it. You can find silence on the subway, in the hospital, at a concert hall, because it is simply the underlying calm and goodness that resides in creation. Beneath all the fears that you normally feel—fears of failure, competition, insignificance, hurt, and the like—the simplicity of silence and stillness waits for you. If you can tap into the simplicity through the practice of concentration on the small tasks and beings at hand, life becomes a beautiful prayer.

Even religion can cause great anxiety and noise in a person's life. There's a story about a Muslim saint who despised the fact that people prayed out of fear, instead of joy and glory in God. Such fear creates noisy minds and hyperactive lives. So the saint ran through the streets with a torch in one hand and a bucket of water in another. When people asked her why she did this, she declared that she wanted to set heaven on fire and douse the flames of hell. That way, heaven and hell would cease to exist, and people wouldn't pray out of fear or personal gain, but simply because they loved God. This story teaches that instead of being consumed by noisy and unsettling fears, we must find a quiet stillness in the happiness of the moment.

> *"Man prays and prayer fashions man. The saint has himself become prayer, the meeting place of earth and Heaven; and thereby he contains the universe and the universe prays with him. He is everywhere where nature prays, and he prays with her and in her: in the peaks which touch the void and eternity, in a flower which scatters its scent, or in the carefree song of a bird. He who lives in prayer has not lived in vain."*
>
> From *Echoes of Perennial Wisdom*, Frithjof Schuon

PRACTICING A PRAYERFUL LIFESTYLE

Once you have decided to extend your notion of prayer to your general lifestyle— to be fully present in the moment, and compassionately and calmly attentive in that moment—there are a number of ways in which you can help make your life a prayer. When combined, all of these small practices can actually help you cocreate a better world.

Blessing Others

Mystical Judaism promotes a concept called *Tikkun Olam*. It refers to maintaining and restoring the world, or doing our part to create a kinder world with God. Mystical Jewish texts suggest that at the beginning of time, the Divine was dispersed throughout the world. It entered everything. Thus, a piece of God resides in every person, creature, and object. And we are constantly communicating with and in the divine Source, even in the most ordinary activities.

To call attention more fully to the sacredness of everyday life, Jewish rabbis established certain blessings to be said at moments of awareness. Blessings were created for a magnificent landscape, the washing of hands, the mention of a good teacher's name, the eating of food, and more. (See the inset on page 67.) These blessings have become a part of traditional Jewish life, and can teach each one of us to become more sensitive to the world around us. Tikkun Olam is a challenge and a mission for every individual. Blessing the people whom we know, as well as the people who pass by, is one way to perform this divine task. And for those of us who don't follow orthodox practices, no special formulas are necessary—just the intention to love and care for the beings and things of this world as we come into contact with them.

Part of a prayerful lifestyle is being receptive to other beings. If we believe that there is a Oneness that is manifest in each of us, then each person carries something divine within him. So we should always be aware of the lessons others teach us, of the presence of others, of their feelings and difficulties. Because each person, each creature, does a service to us in our personal growth, it is helpful to bless them and to pray for them, as well.

Writing about her grandfather's practice of saying blessings throughout the day in her book *My Grandfather's Blessings,* author Rachel Naomi Remen states, "When we bless others, we offer them a refuge from an indifferent world." They don't need to know we're blessing them; we can do it in our minds. For example, when you pass a little girl on crutches, you can simply say, in your own head, "Bless that little girl for being so brave and enduring her hardships." When you pass a super-market stock person who is working hard at his job, you can think, "God bless him for his work in making our lives so much easier." Remen reminds us that we bless others more than we realize, such as when we call a friend for no particular reason, or when we smile at a stranger out of sheer good will. And through her book, Remen subtly encourages us to more widely practice such good habits by reminding us that every moment holds opportunities to appreciate and sanctify the world.

> *"And when a man sees that the God in himself is the same God in all that is, he hurts not himself by hurting others: then he goes indeed to the highest Path."*
>
> From *The Problem of Pain*, C.S. Lewis

In practicing the blessing of others, we become acutely aware of the need to avoid harming the world and its inhabitants. We learn to take nothing for granted, and we lead much more peaceful lives. So to make your own life a prayer, try practicing spontaneous blessings for the people and things you happen to pass by or think about throughout each day. Notice how life-changing this practice can be.

Saying Thank You

It is very easy to say "thank you," whether aloud or silently. What is not easy is to *remember* to say thank you. But practice will make this little technique easier, and you will find your general existence becoming more prayerful as you accomplish it.

In our rush-rush culture, we pass by so many gifts without even acknowledging them. Something as simple as saying a mental "thank you" to the creatures who offer their lives as food, to the engineers who design safer cars, to the computer gurus who have given us word pro-cessing, to our children for making us smile, makes life more precious. Practice noticing a few little things every day. This technique will increase your awareness of the divine in our world, and keep you in an ongoing conversation with God. For example, try touching the flowers on the dinner table at a restaurant, and simply saying, "Thank you for this beautiful little gift." Take the time to acknowledge a little cat that brushes by you at your friend's house, and thank God for the little cozy things in life. Say a little prayer of thanksgiving before eating your lunch—nothing special, just call to mind all that has gone into bringing that salad to your plate. You'll be surprised at how much your perspective changes—how more peaceful and content you become—when you follow your mom's advice: "Remember to say thank you."

Making Better Choices

Writer Neale Donald Walsch reminds us that the actions we choose maintain a "continual request" to God. Our formal times of request are only *part* of how we pray for things. In "Your Life Is Your Prayer," an essay in *The Power of Prayer*, Walsch offers the example of someone who is praying for a better-paying job. If that person says, "God, help me to find a new job," but then doesn't make sincere efforts to find that job, nor even encourage himself with an optimistic attitude, the prayer is not all that likely to come true. We must understand how very important every little choice is in our lives, and how each action can either facilitate or hinder the prayers that we offer to God.

When you choose your actions according to what you pray for and how you pray, your specific intentions are more likely to be answered. Don't rely 100-percent on a supernatural force. Instead, "co-pilot" with God. You have a creative force inside of you already; prayer will help you to find and use it. God *reminds* you how to go about making your personal world, and the larger world around you, a better place.

Watch your actions carefully and see if they reflect your prayer requests. This means constant reevaluation, an effort that may seem difficult at first, but will become more natural with practice. For example, if you are praying for better health, notice the little things you do during the day to affect your health. Do you take time to breathe deeply and relax your mind? Do you bombard yourself with caffeine and sugar, instead of clean water and fruits? Do you drive recklessly? Do you get enough sleep? It's the little choices that have the big effects in our lives. So practice being aware of your actions as much as your words.

Taking the Middle Road

In *The Way Into Jewish Prayer*, Lawrence Hoffman writes, "North American culture divides human activity into simple oppositions. We are either at work or at play, on vacation or on the job, in school or at recess. We instinctively treat prayer, therefore, as what you do when you are in a synagogue (or Church) but not in the office, the garden, the playground, or the car." Hoffman further asserts that Judaism encourages its followers to see all of life as holy. That means shedding the concept that we must live with a dualism that separates prayer from active life.

If prayer extends to our entire lifestyle, it certainly extends to how we make our living and how we perform our daily tasks. Yes, even the routine things we do in the office or in the classroom are part of the continual prayer we live every day. Realizing this, work becomes more sacred and less burdensome. And our bodies become actively involved in our prayers. We can understand even our paying jobs as opportunities for thankfulness, blessings, and Tikkun Olam. That makes the office like a little sanctuary in and of itself!

The idea of physical and mental labor as a form of prayer is an ancient one. In Buddhist philosophy, we are encouraged to follow the Middle Path. That means not only performing private sessions of mental discipline, but also carrying out wholesome conduct and action in the world. In fact, action is as much an element on the road to enlightenment as contemplation. Therefore, it's not surprising that, for instance, in Zen Buddhism, every action is looked upon as critical. Washing the dishes, making tea, are all paths to enlightenment. As we learn in J.A. Taylor's essay "Koans of Silence," published in *Parabola*, " Any task performed with concentration and respect is a marvel to behold. When every act is a new beginning there are no ordinary events. . . ."

Christian monk Saint Benedict promoted a strikingly similar lifestyle: the *via media*, or literally, the middle way. It involves a three-part life of prayer, comprised of formal prayer and hymns, sacred reading, and physical work. Saint Benedict taught that the body is necessarily a part of our prayer; we were born into the body for a reason. And actions that we perform with the body are opportunities to give glory to God, to appreciate the earth, and to improve our world. Therefore, harvesting vegetables is prayer. Cleaning the house is prayer. So is reading from the Scriptures. So is humming a hymn. Anything that encourages love and knowledge is prayer.

Likewise, the Muslim faith asks its followers to live in the constant presence of God. Every action is to be done with Allah in mind, so as to continually praise Allah and willingly allow His plan to unfold. Muslims are encouraged to view each action as a prayerful action, be it talking with a stranger in a store or bowing at the mention of Allah's name. Throughout history, as branches of Muslim mysticism explored various forms of praise to God, the body became increasingly involved in worship, from prostration to dances. Therefore, Islam teaches us to involve body, mind, and spirit in our prayerful lifestyles. It doing so, we generate balance in our lives and make everything sacred.

Taking the Middle Path or the *via media* means avoiding extremes such as social isolation, scorn of the body, and lack of worldly action. Having an effective prayer life involves the body as well as the mind, and can be conducted in the world as much as in the spirit. Prayer is as much about work as it is about thought, and as much about others as it is about your individual spirit. Prayer is not only conversing with God, but also expanding that conversation to include others.

CONTINUING TO RESERVE SPECIAL PRAYER TIME

Remember that while extending your notions of prayer to embrace your daily activities, special prayer times are still important. These are the periods of renewal and respite—periods during which you refill yourself, gathering guidance and creative energy. Mother Teresa of Calcutta suggests that as we grow in prayerful lifestyle, we grow in our desires to set aside special times for prayer. These prayer times become life food— we crave them. It is important to listen to those cravings.

Personal prayer sessions offer enhanced opportunities to find the silence and stillness inside yourself. They are like private lessons with God, during which you receive the guidance and inspiration that fosters compassion when you function in the world. Once you find the calm alone with God, you can make efforts to continue that calm outside of personal prayer sessions.

CONCLUSION

It takes some practice, but it is actually possible to make each day a prayer. It begins with living in the now, continues with discovering the sacred quiet and stillness that exists beneath all things, and ends up making even your job and your contact with strangers holy experiences. Thoughts and actions that involve anger, hatred, pride, greed, and other negative emotions and impulses are not prayer because they keep you from opening to love. But any activity that makes you more aware of the goodness, beauty, and divinity of this world *is* prayer. Any activity, mental or physical, that encourages the divine glimmer in another being *is* prayer. You've probably been praying a lot more than you thought you were! Your life is already an unfolding prayer!

Credits

The Shema on page 73 is printed with the permission of www.aish.com, the website of Aish HaTorah.

The Adon Olam on page 77 is found on the Talmud Torah—Center for Basic Jewish Education website at http://members.aol.com/LazerA, and printed with permission from Eliezer C. Abrahamson.

The Salawat on page 140 is printed with permission by the Threshold Society & Mevlevi Order, mevlevi.org.

The translation of the Tashahhud on page 140 is printed with the permission of Hani Emari, the Emari Islam Page at http://www.geocities.com/CapitolHill/Parliament/3555/salat.html.

Resource Directory

A wealth of resources is available to anyone who wants to learn more about a particular religious approach, to compile a collection of prayers, or to purchase prayer accessories. The following list of suggested books, websites, and albums is meant to serve only as a launching pad. You can easily expand your search for more information by consulting the Internet; your Yellow Pages; and regional churches, synagogues, mosques, and temples; as well as local religious article stores, bookstores, and libraries.

BOOKS

The following books have been chosen for both the quality of their content and their easy availability. Either turn to the specific religious or lifestyle approach in which you are interested, or consider the "General Inspiration" section for a wider discussion of spirituality.

JUDAISM

Falk, Marcia. *The Book of Blessings: New Jewish Prayers for Daily Life, the Sabbath & the New Moon Festival.* **Boston: Beacon Press, 1999.**

Falk's collection of prayers would be a great addition to your personal library, offering ample fixed prayers for numerous occasions. This book is both inspirational and truly substantial.

Hoffman, Lawrence. *The Way Into Jewish Prayer.* **Woodstock, VT: Jewish Lights Publishing, 2000.**

Hoffman's book is a must for anyone who wants to learn the ABCs of Jewish prayer without being overwhelmed. Length and language are reader-friendly, and the author's clear information and respectful tone make you want to learn more.

Robinson, George. *Essential Judaism: A Complete Guide to Beliefs, Customs, and Rituals.* New York: Pocket Books, 2000. This is a truly informative book, offering a comprehensive examination of Jewish culture and faith. The basics are covered from the concept of prayer to detailed accounts of the services, and from the Jewish Bible to the Jewish calendar.

Verman, Mark. *The History and Varieties of Jewish Meditation.* Northvale, NJ: Jason Aronson Inc., 1996. Verman is well respected by scholars and leisure readers alike. This book on Jewish meditation contains enough basic information to beautifully introduce the newcomer to meditation in the Jewish faith.

CHRISTIANITY

The Book of Common Prayer. The Church Hymnal Corporation and the Seabury Press, 1977. This prayer book not only includes numerous fixed prayers that are very useful for personal prayer sessions, but also is a general guide to the traditions and beliefs of Christian life, and a layout of standard Episcopalian prayer services. Here is an invaluable addition to any Christian's prayer table.

Collins, Michael, and Matthew Arlen Price, editors. *Story of Christianity: A Celebration of 2,000 Years of Faith.*

New York: DK Publishing, 1999. Readers rave about this book, which traces Christianity's history from its Judaic roots to its many modern-day branches. A stunning amount of information is presented in an organized, clear manner, and highlighted with illustrations, making *Story of Christianity* a treasure for any library.

Klein, Reverend Peter. *Catholic Source Book, 3rd Edition.* San Diego: Harcourt Religious Publishers, 1999. For those who want to study the Catholic perspective of Jesus and His life, this book is sure to be of wonderful service. It guides the reader through significant information on the Scriptures, lifestyle tradition, liturgy, and much more. Prayers are included, as well as fascinating explanations of common symbols used since early Christian times.

Tyson, John R., editor. *Invitation to Christian Spirituality: An Ecumenical Anthology.* New York: Oxford University Press, 1999. Read this book for a broad study of the belief systems and the practices of Christians. Tyson offers a comprehensive overview of Christianity. Both long-held traditions and modern-day issues are discussed, from fixed prayers to feminism, and from spiritual leaders of the past to personal grace today.

ISLAM

Armstrong, Karen. *Islam: A Short History.* **New York: The Modern Library, 2000.**
A handy book in size and content, this text offers primary information in a concise, sophisticated manner. Every major area of Islam is tackled, from the beginning of its history, to the evolution of its politics, to its modern-day practices. Helpful time lines and maps are also included.

Barks, Coleman, and Michael Green. *The Illuminated Prayer: The Five-Times Prayer of the Sufis.* **New York: Ballantine Publishing Group, 2000.**
Working from the teachings of Sufi master Bawa Mihaiyaddeen, who was heavily influenced by Rumi, the authors offer a beautiful interpretation of the Muslim salat as practiced in the Sufi tradition. This text explains inspiring ancient rituals for today's prayer practitioner, including preparation, words, and movements.

Braswell, George W., Jr. *Islam: Its Prophet, Peoples, Politics and Power.* **Nashville: Broadman and Holman Publishers, 1996.**
This text reads much like a friendly history book. It's a sure source for gaining a fundamental understanding of the world's fastest growing religion. Braswell offers a wealth of interesting facts, yet strategically organizes the text so that the reader is not intimidated.

Jomier, Jacques. *How to Understand Islam.* **New York: Crossroad, 1989.**
Here is an easy-to-use learning tool that not only covers the basics of Islam, but also provides considerable details to whet the appetite of those who do a full reading. Jomier discusses history, practice, mysticism, and much more.

BUDDHISM

Dalai Lama, and Howard Cutler. *The Art of Happiness: A Handbook for Living.* **New York: Riverhead Books, 1998.**
The author's name, His Holiness the Dalai Lama, says it all. Easterners and Westerners alike turn to this spiritual leader for guidance and inspiration. This encouraging book has helped many people who wish to apply Buddhist principles to everyday life.

Easwaran, Eknath, translator. *The Dhammapada.* **Berkeley, CA: The Blue Mountain Center of Meditation, 1999.**
Here is a collection of the Buddha's sayings, all of which can serve as inspirational tools in your personal prayer life. Easwaran's version contains historical information on the Buddha's life, as well.

Kapleau, Roshi Philip. *The Three Pillars of Zen: Teaching, Practice, and Enlightenment.* **New York: Anchor Books, 1989.**

Roshi Philip Kapleau's book is considered a classic among well-read Buddhist practitioners. A fascinating study of Zen Buddhism, *The Three Pillars of Zen* offers accounts of personal enlightenment experiences, background on meditation techniques, and much more.

Nairn, Rob. *What Is Meditation? Buddhism for Everyone.* **Boston: Shambhala Publications, 1999.** If you want to tuck a pocket-sized hardcover into your pocketbook or suit jacket for pleasant reading in a café or airport, this is the book for you. A basic introduction to everyday meditation, *What Is Meditation?* addresses and simplifies such complex issues as the major branches of Buddhism and the general mindsets that are necessary for leading a Buddhist life.

GENERAL INSPIRATION

Salwak, Dale, editor. *The Power of Prayer.* **Novato, CA: New World Library, 1998.** Every essay in this collection is a gem. Many faiths and approaches are represented, and the writers' words are heartening and positive. This is a truly worthwhile read.

Stern, Anthony, editor. *Everything Starts From Prayer: Mother Teresa's Meditations on Spiritual Life for People of All Faiths.* **Ashland, OR: White Cloud Press, 1998.**

A beloved figure of faith and prayerful living, Mother Teresa of Calcutta continues to touch the spiritual lives of countless people, even after her death. This collection of her wise thoughts is an appropriate aid to personal prayer life, as it is both encouraging and beautiful.

ONLINE SITES FOR INFORMATION

The Internet sites suggested below provide high-quality, easy-to-access information. Visit them to investigate religious beliefs and traditions, to find prayers and prayer instruction, to read fascinating articles, and more.

JUDAISM

Explore Judaism: AISH.com Website: aish.com This educational and fun site offers helpful information both for those who have background in Judaism and for those who don't. A variety of topics is explored, from Kabbalah to Jewish prayer services, and from international politics to family and personal life. You can even click into a live camera view of Jerusalem's Western Wall for a focal point during your own prayers.

Talmud Torah—Basic Jewish Education Website: members.aol.com/LazerA

Many of your basic questions about Judaism will be answered by this site, which is maintained by Eliezer C. Abrahamson. Find out about Jewish laws and lifestyle, read and learn traditional Jewish prayers, and click into other great links. This site's suggested books will guide you to further sources of information.

CHRISTIANITY

Catholic Online
Website: www.catholic.org
This is an invaluable site for Christians, and especially Catholics. A wealth of prayers can be found here, including litanies, prayers of request, prayers to saints, the rosary, and much more. Just click into the page for basic prayers. Foundational Catholic beliefs are discussed on this site as well, including information on the sacraments, which are central to Catholic lifestyle and ritual.

ChristianityToday.com
Website: www.christianity today.com
This site links to pages on all major issues of Christianity, and is interestingly arranged to spark your curiosity. Find information on Bible studies, instructional seminars, suggested schools and books, and other topics of interest. ChristianityToday. com will also keep you abreast of the latest issues concerning modern Christian culture.

ISLAM

Emari's Islam Page
Website: www.geocities.com/ CapitolHill/Parliament/3555/
Here is a simply beautiful website that provides a bounty of information. Click into instructions on salat prayer, complete with photos; guidelines on the pre-prayer bathing ritual; and interesting articles on various Islam topics. This is a truly informative and artistic site.

IslamicNet
Website: www.Islamicnet.com
IslamicNet is a truly excellent educational source for those who want to be introduced to the various aspects of Islam. Friendly and helpful, this site is a great place to begin a study of Muslim living.

BUDDHISM

Buddhism 2001, Index
Website: www.geocities.com/ buddhism2001
This website triggers lots of questions and supplies lots of answers on basic Buddhist concepts. You couldn't ask for a more comprehensive collection of information—or for a more friendly and inspiring presentation.

Exploring the Magic of OM MANI PADME HUM in Tibetan Buddhism: The Dharma-Haven Home Page.
Website: www.dharma-haven.org/ index.htm.

This Internet site is an interesting means of delving into Buddhist traditions, such as mantras and prayer wheels. It is developed primarily around Tibetan Buddhist practices, but is informative for students of Buddhism in general, as well. Plus, it provides great links to other topics and essays on Buddhism.

ONLINE STORES FOR PRAYER AIDS

The following websites offer accessories that can enhance your prayer sessions. Keep in mind that when shopping online, it is always smart to consult several sites, comparing prices and products, before making a purchase.

JUDAISM

The Judaica Collection
Website: www.thejudaica collection.com/judaica
Traditional prayer accessories—personal and home items—are offered at this site, including tallitit, tefillin, yarmulkes or kippahs, jewelry, candles, music, and much more.

CHRISTIANITY

Catholic Shop Online
Website: www.cathshop.com/ store/merchant
Among the many Christian prayer products offered at this Internet location are prayer beads, prayer books, candles, cards, statues, and crucifixes.

ISLAM

Islamic Bookstore.com
Website: islamicbookstore.com
Click on "Islamic gifts" to access information on many Muslim prayer products, including but not limited to prayer carpets, Muslim prayer books, Muslim history books, music, clothing, and spiritual wall ornaments.

BUDDHISM

Shasta Abbey
Website: www.obcon.org
Shasta Abbey sells traditional Buddhist books and various meditation supplies. Look for prayer beads, meditation cushions and benches, statues, gongs, altars, incense, and more.

MORE FOR MEDITATION AND PRAYER

Amida: Means for Meditation
Website: www.ami-da.com
All sorts of prayer and meditation aids are available at this website. Fountains, stones, bells, books, incense, and cushions are just a few of the many prayer items offered.

Samadhi Cushions
Website: www.samadhi cushions.com
If you are in the market for prayer or meditation cushions and kneelers, this is a great site. A large variety of different sized and shaped posture/sitting aids will give you plenty of options.

MUSIC TO ACCOMPANY YOUR PRAYERS

The following list presents just a few of the many albums that can enhance your prayer time. The albums are listed by religious approach or, when applicable, by retail category. Be aware, though, that there is some crossover between these categories. For instance, some music typically considered "prayer," such as Gregorian chants, can be correctly categorized as classical music, as well. So when browsing in a music store, be sure to look in several areas or to ask a salesperson for aid.

JUDAISM

London, Frank, et al. *Nigunim.*
Surround yourself with the intoxicating sound of Hassidic music. *Nigunim* is a wonderful collection for your sacred space.

Statman, Andy, and David Grosman. *Songs of Our Fathers: Traditional Jewish Melodies.*
Highly recommended by numerous listeners, this album is an enchanting one for those who want to learn more about the Jewish culture, or simply to be moved by reverent devotional songs.

CHRISTIANITY

Capella Gregorian Orchestra.
Lost in Meditation—Meditative Gregorian Chants.

Whether used as background music or as a dynamic part of your personal prayer experience, *Lost in Meditation* provides the soul-satisfying sounds of traditional Christian chanting. This album is soothing to the mind and stimulating to the spirit.

Cathedral Choral Society.
Hymns Through the Centuries.
If you want a collection of traditional hymns to prepare you for prayer or to inspire you during prayer time, consider this comprehensive album. You are more than likely to find several appealing hymns that meet the needs of any prayer session.

ISLAM

Celestial Harmonies Series.
The Music of Islam.
The series titled *The Music of Islam* includes a number of beautifully accomplished albums. It may be best to start with the *sampler*, which offers a variety of traditional Muslim sounds and songs. This album is highly recommended by listeners.

BUDDHISM

The Gyuto Monks. *Tibetan Tantric Choir.*
The Gyuto Monks are well known for their Tibetan Buddhist chanting. This collection captures the depth, the concentration, and the mesmerizing patterns of traditional Buddhist chanting.

The Lama Gyurme and Rykiel.
The Lama's Chant—Songs for Awakening.
With its orchestral background, this Westernized version of Buddhist music and chanting is a comfortable introduction for the Western ear. Here is a strikingly beautiful album that is recommended by numerous listeners.

CLASSICAL

The Vienna Boys Choir.
The Vienna Boys Choir—Portrait.
Many people close their eyes and picture a choir of angels when listening to this group of young male singers. The lilting, beautifully directed songs lend a reverent, inspirational feeling to prayer time.

London Symphony Orchestra.
Complete Mozart Edition, Volume 20—Litanies, Vespers, etc.
This traditional classical album is more sacred than secular, although it is treasured equally in both areas. It is an awe-inspiring collection.

NEW AGE

Eno, Brian. *The Pearl.*
An entrancing album with meditative sound, *The Pearl* promotes a calm and introspective state of mind.

Vas. *Offerings.*
Vas is widely known for the transcendent qualities that make their music more sacred than secular. *Offerings* includes a combination of profound music and vocals. Interestingly, the vocals are in singer Azam Ali's own improvised language, helping the listener to avoid any dependence on analytical, inherited language.

GENERAL

Safared. *Three Cultures— Jewish, Christian & Muslim Music in Spain.*
This is a great addition to your spiritual music collection—one that will familiarize your ear with a variety of traditional religious approaches.

References

BOOKS AND PERIODICALS

Adler, Eric. "Prayer Helps Sick in Mysterious Ways, Study Suggests," *The Kansas City Star*, October 24, 1999.

'Alī, 'Abdūllah Yusuf. *The Holy Qur'an: Text, Translation and Commentary*, New Revised Edition. Brentwood, MD: Amana Corp., 1989.

Allison, Alexander W., Herbert Barrows, Caesar R. Blake, et al., editors. *The Norton Anthology of Poetry*, 3rd Edition. New York: W.W. Norton & Company, 1983.

Armstrong, Karen. *A History of God: The 4000-Year Quest of Judaism, Christianity and Islam*. New York: Ballantine Books, 1994.

Armstrong, Karen. *Islam: A Short History*. New York: The Modern Library, 2000.

Associated Press. "Studies Link Religious Belief With Good Health," *USA Today*, February 11, 1996.

Backman, Milton V., Jr. *Christian Churches of America: Origins and Beliefs*. Provo, UT: Brigham Young University Press, 1976.

Barrett, Marvin. "Inviting Hell Into Heaven: An Interview With William Segal," *Parabola: Myth, Tradition, and the Search for Meaning* 24, no. 2 (Summer 1999): 58–65.

Bender, Sue. "A Lesson in Prayer." In *The Power of Prayer*, Dale Salwak, editor. Novato, CA: New World Library, 1998.

Book of Common Prayer, The. The Church Hymnal Corporation and The Seabury Press, 1977.

Braswell, George W., Jr. *Islam: Its Prophet, Peoples, Politics and Power*. Nashville: Broadman and Holman Publishers, 1996.

Bruchac, Joseph. "Why We're Here Today: An Interview With Chief Tom Porter," *Parabola: Myth, Tradition, and the Search for Meaning* 24, no. 2 (Summer 1999): 43–46.

Buxbaum, Yitzhak. "Praying for Real: Hasidic Teachings." In *The Power of Prayer*, Dale Salwak, editor. Novato, CA: New World Library, 1998.

Caffrey, Jim. *On Prayer: An Interview With Sr. Briege McKenna, OSC.* Dublin, Ireland: Veritas Video Production, Ltd., Co., 1990.

Campbell, Sally. *A Primer of Christianity for Pew Sitters and Other People.* Cold Spring Harbor, NY: Springs, 1999.

Capital-Journal Editorial Board. "Study: Prayer Works," *The Topeka Capital-Journal*, October 26, 1999.

Carter, Jimmy. "Prayer Without Ceasing." In *The Power of Prayer*, Dale Salwak, editor. Novato, CA: New World Library, 1998.

Catoir, John T. *Enjoy the Lord: A Path to Contemplation.* New York: Alba House, 1988.

Chopra, Deepak. *Ageless Body, Timeless Mind: The Quantum Alternative to Growing Old.* New York: Three Rivers Press, 1993.

Cleary, Thomas, translator. *Dhammapade: The Sayings of Buddha.* New York: Bantam Books, 1995.

Comstock, G.W., and K.B. Partridge. "Church Attendance and Health," *Journal of Chronic Diseases* 25 (1972): 665–672.

Coomaraswamy, Rama. "An Elevation of Our Soul," *Parabola: Myth, Tradition, and the Search for Meaning* 24, no. 2 (Summer 1999): 53–55.

Currie, David B. *Born Fundamentalist, Born Again Catholic.* San Francisco: Ignatius Press, 1996.

Dalai Lama. *Spiritual Advice for Bud-*

dhists and Christians. Donald W. Mitchell, editor. New York: The Continuum Publishing Co., 1999.

Dalrymple, John. *Simple Prayer.* London: Darton, Longman and Todd, Ltd., 1984.

Dossey, Larry. *Recovering the Soul: A Scientific and Spiritual Search.* New York: Bantam Books, 1989.

Drury, Keith. *Holiness for Ordinary People.* Indianapolis: Wesley Press, 1983.

Dulles, Avery. "Authentic Prayer." In *The Power of Prayer*, Dale Salwak, editor. Novato, CA: New World Library, 1998.

Gawle, Barbara. *How to Pray: Discovering New Spiritual Growth Through Prayer.* Englewood Cliffs, NJ: Prentice-Hall, Inc., 1984.

Gibran, Kahlil. *The Prophet.* New York: Alfred A Knopf, 1999.

Hammer, Reuven. *Entering Jewish Prayer: A Guide to Personal Devotion and the Worship Service.* New York: Schocken Books, 1994.

Harris, William S., Manohar Gowda, Jerry W. Kolb, et al. "A Randomized, Controlled Trial of the Effects of Remote, Intercessory Prayer on Outcomes in Patients Admitted to the Coronary Care Unit," *Archives of Internal Medicine* 159, no. 19 (Oct 25, 1999): 2273.

Harvey, Andrew. *Son of Man: The Mystical Path to Christ.* New York: Jeremy P. Tarcher/Putnam, 1998.

Heschel, Abraham J. *Man's Quest for God.* Santa Fe: Aurora Press, 1998.

Hoffman, Lawrence A. *The Way Into Jewish Prayer.* Woodstock, VT: Jewish Lights Publishing, 2000.

Hummer, R.A., R.G. Rogers, C.B. Nam, and C.G. Ellison. "Religious Involvement and US Adult Mortality," *Demography* 36 (1999): 273–285.

John Paul II. *Crossing the Threshold of Hope*. Vittorio Messori, editor. Jenny and Martha McPhee, translators. New York: Alfred A. Knopf, 1994.

Jomier, Jacques. *How to Understand Islam*. New York: Crossroad, 1989.

Katsof, Irwin. *How to Get Your Prayers Answered*. Hollywood, FL: Frederick Fell Publishers, Inc., 2000.

Keating, Thomas. *Open Mind, Open Heart: The Contemplative Dimension of the Gospel*. New York: The Continuum Publishing Company, 1992.

Khandro Rinpoche. "Compassion & Wisdom," *Shambhala Sun: Buddhism, Culture, Meditation, Life* 8, no. 6 (July 2000): 56–59.

Kit, Wong Kiew. *The Complete Book of Zen*. Boston: Element Books, Inc., 1998.

Koenig H.G., et al. "Does Religious Attendance Prolong Survival? A Six-Year Follow-Up Study of 3968 Older Adults," *Journal of Gerontology: Medical Sciences* 54A (1999): M370.

Kopciowski, Elias. *Praying With the Jewish Tradition*. Grand Rapids, MI: Wm. B. Erdmans Publishing Co., 1997.

Lavender, John Allan. *Why Prayers Are Unanswered, and What You Can Do About It*. Wheaton, IL: Tyndale House Publishers, Inc., 1980.

Leder, Drew. "What Should I Do With My Life?" In *The Power of Prayer*, Dale Salwak, editor. Novato, CA: New World Library, 1998.

Lewis, C.S. *The Problem of Pain*. New York: Simon & Schuster, Inc., 1996.

Lovasik, Lawrence G. *The Basic Book of Catholic Prayer: How to Pray and Why*. Manchester, NH: Sophia Institute Press, 1999.

Low, Albert. "The Kingdom of Heaven Lies Within." In *The Power of Prayer*, Dale Salwak, editor. Novato, CA: New World Library, 1998.

Mabey, Juliet, editor. *Rumi: A Spiritual Treasury*. Oxford, England: Oneworld Publications, 2000.

Martinson, Paul Varo, editor. *Islam: An Introduction for Christians*. Stefanie Ormsby Cox, translator. Minneapolis: Augsburg, 1994.

Mascaro, Juan, translator. *The Bhagavad Gita*. New York: Penguin Books, 1962.

McCullough, M.E., W.T. Hoyt, D.B. Larson, H.G. Koenig, and C. Thoresen. "Religious Involvement and Mortality: A Meta-Analytic Review," *Health Psychology* (2000).

Medicine Eagle, Brook. "The Power of Silence." In *The Power of Prayer*, Dale Salwak, editor. Novato, CA: New World Library, 1998.

Mermann, Alan C. "Is Anyone Listening?" In *The Power of Prayer*, Dale Salwak, editor. Novato, CA: New World Library, 1998.

Merton, Thomas. *Thoughts in Solitude*. New York: The Noonday Press, 1990.

Miller, Samuel H. "Prayer and Life." In *The Power of Prayer*, Dale Salwak, editor. Novato, CA: New World Library, 1998.

Mother Teresa of Calcutta. "On Prayer." In *The Power of Prayer*, Dale Salwak, editor. Novato, CA: New World Library, 1998.

Myers, David G. "On Assessing Prayer, Faith, and Health," *Reformed Review* 53, no. 2 (2000): 119–126.

Nanji, Azim A., editor. *The Muslim Almanac: A Reference Work on History, Faith, Culture, and Peoples of Islam.* Farmington Hills, MI: Gale Research Inc., 1996.

Norris, Kathleen. *The Cloister Walk.* New York: Riverhead Books, 1997.

Nouwen, Henri J.M. "The Paradox of Prayer." In *The Power of Prayer,* Dale Salwak, editor. Novato, CA: New World Library, 1998.

Ochs, Carol, and Kerry M. Olitzky. *Jewish Spiritual Guidance: Finding Our Way to God.* San Francisco: Jossey-Bass Publishers, 1997.

Ogilvie, Lloyd John. "Prayer Starts With God." In *The Power of Prayer,* Dale Salwak, editor. Novato, CA: New World Library, 1998.

Padwick, Constance E. *Muslim Devotions: A Study of Prayer-Manuals in Common Use.* Rockport, MA: Oneworld Publications, 1997.

Peale, Norman Vincent. *The Power of Positive Thinking.* New York: Simon & Schuster, 1987.

"Prayer: Faith and Recovery," *Country Living,* December 6, 1999.

"Prayer: The Proof," *Country Living,* December 6, 1999.

Remen, Rachel Naomi. *My Grandfather's Blessings.* New York: Riverhead, 2000.

Renard, John. *Seven Doors to Islam: Spirituality and the Religious Life of Muslims.* Berkeley, CA: University of California Press, 1996.

Robinson, George. *Essential Judaism: A Complete Guide to Beliefs, Customs,* *and Rituals.* New York: Pocket Books, 2000.

Rodwell, J.M., translator. *The Koran: Rodwell's Translation (Everyman's Library 380).* New York: E.P. Dutton & Co. Inc., 1948.

Rogers, Dale Evans. "Say Yes to God's Gift of Prayer." In *The Power of Prayer,* Dale Salwak, editor. Novato, CA: New World Library, 1998.

Russell, Jeffrey Burton. "Picture Prayer." In *The Power of Prayer,* Dale Salwak, editor. Novato, CA: New World Library, 1998.

Sakyong Mipham Rinpoche. "The Mahayana Motivation," *Shambhala Sun: Buddhism, Culture, Meditation, Life* 8, no. 6 (July 2000): 15, 17.

Salwak, Dale, editor. "Preface." In *The Power of Prayer.* Novato, CA: New World Library, 1998.

Schumann, Hans Wolfgang. *Buddhism: An Outline of Its Teachings and Schools.* Georg Feuerstein, translator. Wheaton, IL: Quest Books, 1989.

Schuon, Frithjof. "Towards the Further Shore," *Parabola: Myth, Tradition, and the Search for Meaning,* 24, no. 2 (Summer 1999): 88–89.

Sheen, Fulton J. *Lift Up Your Heart: A Guide to Spiritual Peace.* Liguori, MO: Triumph Books, 1997.

Shepard, Mark. *Gandhi Today: A Report on Mahatma Gandhi's Successors.* Arcata, CA: Simple Productions, 1987.

Silko, Leslie Marmon. *Ceremony.* New York: Penguin Publishing, 1988.

Steinsaltz, Adin. *The Essential Talmud.* Chaya Galai, translator. New York: Basic Books, Inc., 1976.

Stern, Anthony. "An Answered Prayer." In *The Power of Prayer*. Dale Salwak, editor. Novato, CA: New World Library, 1998.

Stern, Anthony. *Everything Starts From Prayer: Mother Teresa's Meditations on Spiritual Life for People of All Faiths*. Ashland, OR: White Cloud Press, 1998.

Taylor, J.A. "Koans of Silence: The Teaching Not Taught," *Parabola: Myth, Tradition, and the Search for Meaning*, 24, no. 2 (Summer 1999): 6–11.

Telushkin, Joseph. *Jewish Wisdom: Ethical, Spiritual, and Historical Lessons From the Great Works and Thinkers*. New York: William Morrow and Company, Inc., 1994.

Thera, Nyanaponika. *The Heart of Buddhist Meditation*. York Beach, ME: Samuel Weiser, Inc., 1991.

Verman, Mark. *The History and Varieties of Jewish Meditation*. Northvale, NJ: Jason Aronson Inc., 1996.

Walsch, Neale Donald. "Your Life Is Your Prayer." In *The Power of Prayer*, Dale Salwak, editor. Novato, CA: New World Library, 1998.

Willard, Dallas. "Praying the Scriptures." In *The Power of Prayer*, Dale Salwak, editor. Novato, CA: New World Library, 1998.

Wolpe, David J. *In Speech and In Silence: The Jewish Quest for God*. New York: Henry Holt & Co., 1992.

Zaleski, Philip. "The Life of Spiritual Combat: An Interview With Abbot Hugh Gilbert, OSB," *Parabola: Myth, Tradition, and the Search for Meaning*, 24, no. 2 (Summer 1999): 12–19.

WEBSITES

http://aish.com. "Explore Judaism," AISH.com.

http://aish.com/wallcam/The_Shema.asp. "Shema Yisrael," AISH.com.

http://aish.com/wallcam/Why_Pray.asp. "Why Pray?," AISH.com.

http://kabbalah-web.org/. "Bnei Baruch Home Page of the Wisdom of the Kabbalah: Kabbalah Home Page," Bnei Baruch.

http://members.ebay.com/aboutme/muslimsisters. "Muslim Sisters," The Sisters Association for Dawah in Arlington.

http://pages.hotbot.com/careers/agent1/light04.html. "Mantra of Chenrezig Buddha," Ngawang Tashi and Drepung Loseling, transcribers. From a lecture given by the Dalai Lama at Kalmuck Mongolian Buddhist Center, New Jersey.

http://skepdic.com/placebo.html. "Skeptic's Dictionary: The Placebo Effect," *Skeptic's Dictionary*.

http://www.buddhanet.net/mandalas.htm. "Buddhist Art & Architecture: Symbolism of Mandalas," BuddhaNet.

http://www.dharma-haven.org/tibetan/benefits-of-prayer-wheels.html. "Advice on the Benefits of Prayer Wheels," Lama Zopa, Ronpoche, Dharma-Haven.

http://www.dharma-haven.org/tibetan/meaning-of-om-mani-padme-hung.htm. "Exploring the Magic of OM MANI PADME HUM in Tibetan Buddhism: The Dharma-Haven 'Om' Page," Dharma-Haven.

http://www.dx.sakura.ne.jp/~kameno/zazen/401.html. "How to Practice Zen (ZAZEN)," Hermann Jordan, translator.

http://www.epub.org.br/cm/n09/mente/placebo1_i.htm. "Placebo Effect: The Power of the Sugar Pill," Julio Rocha do Amaral, MD and Renato M.E. Sabbatini, PhD, Universidade Estadual de Campinas, Brasil, July 25, 1999.

http://www.geocities.com/Capitol Hill/Parliament/3555/salat.html. "How to Pray: Learning the Basics of Muslim Prayer," Emari's Islam Page.

http://www.holisticonline.com/prayer/hol_prayer_HowToPray.htm. "How Should You Pray?," Holistic Online.

http://www.holisticonline.com/prayer/w_prayer.htm. "Prayer and the Great Religions of the World," Holistic Online.

http://www.holisticonline.com/prayer/w_prayer.htm. "Prayer, Spirituality & Healing: Introduction," Holistic Online.

http://www.holisticonline.com/prayer/w_prayer.htm. "Prayer, Spirituality & Healing: The Proof That Prayer Works," Holistic Online.

http://www.holisticonline.com/prayer/hol_prayer_whatis.htm. "Prayer, Spirituality & Healing: What Is Prayer?," Holistic Online.

http://www.Islamicnet.com/. "Islamic Net: Index," Islamic Net.

http://www.jewfaq.org/liturgy.htm. "Jewish Liturgy," JewFAQ.org.

http://www.jewfaq.org/prayer.htm/Berakhot. "Prayers and Blessings," JewFAQ.org.

http://www.kabbalah-web.org/engkab/mhtkabeng.htm. "The Essence of the Wisdom of the Kabbalah," Kabbalah-web.org.

http://www.mindbody.harvard.edu/relaxation.htm. "Mind/Body Medical Institute: Stress and the Relaxation Response," Mind/Body Medical Institute.

http://www.muslim-canada.org/salaat.html. "How to Perform Salaat, the Islamic Ritual Prayer," The Canadian Society of Muslims.

http://www.ship.edu/~cgboeree/meditation.html. "The Basics of Buddhist Meditation," Dr. C. George Boercee, Shippensburg University.

http://www.spiritualityhealth.com/spiritualityhealth/news/prayer.html. "Study: Prayer Helps Heart Patients Who Didn't Know They're Being Prayed For," *The Soul/Body Connection*, October 26, 1999.

http://www.talamasca.org/avatar/mindfulness.html. "Mindfulness Meditation," Jon Kabat-Zinn, *Mind/Body Medicine*, 1993.

http://www.viacorp.com/addiction.html. "The Benefits of Zen Meditation in Addiction and Recovery," Mary Heath, Zen Group of Western Australia, 1997.

http://www.webcom/threshld. "The Threshold Society & Mevlevi Order," The Threshold Society & Mevlevi Order.

http://www.zen-mtn.org/zmm/zazen.shtml. "Zen Meditation: The Seat of Enlightenment," Zen Mountain Monastery.

Index